DATING THE SAGAS

Dating the Sagas

REVIEWS AND REVISIONS

Edited by Else Mundal

MUSEUM TUSCULANUM PRESS
UNIVERSITY OF COPENHAGEN
2013

Dating the Sagas: Reviews and Revisions
Else Mundal (ed.)

Layout and composition: Sigríður Kristinsdóttir
Cover design: Erling Lynder
Set in Minion Pro and printed on Lessebo Smooth
Natural by Narayana Press
ISBN 978 87 635 3899 2

Cover illustrations: Courtesy of © Stofnun Árna
Magnússonar í íslenskum fræðum, Reykjavík. From:
Flateyjarbók (GKS 1005 fol.), late 14th century.
AM 162 A, fol. theta, c. 1250.
AM 476 4to, c. 1700.
AM 128 fol., 17th century.
AM 152 fol., 15th century.

This volume is published with financial support from
The Centre for Medieval Studies, University of Bergen
The Norwegian Research Council

Museum Tusculanum Press
Birketinget 6
2300 Copenhagen S
Denmark
www.mtp.dk

CONTENTS

INTRODUCTION

Else Mundal

The following collection of articles focuses on the issues and difficulties associated with the dating of the medieval texts assigned to the genre traditionally known as the "family sagas" or "sagas of Icelanders." The contributors examine questions such as the dating of individual sagas, how we might establish an age for the genre as a whole through the dating of its earliest texts, and, not least, the many problems associated with our dating methods: what exactly we are dating, the dating criteria themselves, and why is it important to date this anonymous corpus of saga literature in the first place. Additionally, the dating of individual sagas belonging to other saga genres is also discussed in a number of these articles, when relevant to the dating of the texts that are the focus of this book. Throughout the volume, we either use the term *Íslendingasǫgur* or else follow Theodore M. Andersson's lead in replacing the terms "family sagas" or "sagas of Icelanders" with "sagas about early Icelanders," which allows these sagas to be distinguished clearly from the contemporary sagas belonging to the *Sturlunga* cycle.

To a greater or lesser extent, the sagas about early Icelanders build on oral tradition, and the stories they tell may have existed, perhaps in a less artistic form, prior to being written down. We may therefore ask whether the transferral of sagas belonging to this genre from an oral to a written medium was really an important step in the development of an Icelandic literary culture and therefore important to date. To the followers of the old freeprose theory, the change from the oral to the written form was not very important, since the written saga was not regarded as being fundamentally different from the previous oral art form. To the followers of bookprose theory, however, the first written text of a saga was something quite new, and the change from the oral to the written form represented a major step in medieval Iceland's cultural development. Today, most scholars are inclined to attach importance both to the oral tradition behind the written sagas and to the process of the movement of narratives into a written medium. In addition, an interest in the individual manuscripts and the alteration of the written text during the textual transmission grew with the development of so-called New Philology. When discussing saga dating, or the dating of the original written text, it is a fact that this text does not exist. What exists as a basis for dating are later manuscripts that sometimes might be close to the original text and sometimes might have changed; how and how much they might have changed is not easy to say. In addition, it is not only a question of what originated from that "writing" author that is embedded in the later manuscripts – together with some later changes – but also motifs and narrative structures brought over by the author from the oral tradition. However, even though fluctuations within the medieval textual tradition must never be forgotten, neither should they be overestimated. In spite of the fact that the text changed from one manuscript to another, the different textual variants were recognized as being versions of the same saga.

The emergence of the sagas about early Icelanders constituted a remarkable development in the literary culture of medieval Iceland. The sagas of kings, which had emerged as a written genre before the sagas about early Icelanders, had partly been modelled on European chronicles of kings. By contrast, the sagas about early Icelanders were not modelled on a European genre, nor were the so-called contemporary sagas (the sagas of the *Sturlunga* cycle) even though they resembled the chronicle style in some respects. In all likelihood, the first sagas belonging to this genre also came into being during the first decades of the thirteenth century. The sagas of bishops was the third genre that came into existence in the same period of time. The sagas written about holy bishops belong to the European genre of legends. The other sagas of bishops were of course modelled on the legends about holy bishops, but despite their structural similarities with the stories of bishops' lives, they developed in a way more similar to the contemporary sagas about Icelandic "worldly" chieftains. All these three genres tell stories about people living in Iceland, both in the distant past and in the near past. Since we do not know the exact date for any of the sagas belonging to these genres, we do not know for sure which of these genres developed first and the nature of the relationship between them. However, in any case, all these Icelandic genres devoted to Icelandic subjects developed during a short period of time. We are in fact talking about a phenomenon that can be described as a "literary explosion" in Iceland.

This flourishing literary life must certainly be seen in connection with the cultural life and literary activity of the previous period. Early on in its history, Iceland had established centres of learning: the episcopal sees (Skálholt established in 1056 and Hólar in 1106) must be considered to be such centres. We also know that there was writing activity in some of the convents; in the last decades of the twelfth century, the convent at Þingeyrar in particular had a flourishing literary culture. Centres of another kind, particular to Iceland, also developed with some chieftains establishing schools at their farms. The first of these that we know of is the school at Haukadalr, which was established as early as the late eleventh century. In the late twelfth century, Oddi, where Snorri Sturluson grew up, had developed into an important "worldly" centre of learning, while in Snorri's own time, his farm at Reykholt became a major centre of writing. In addition to literature about kings that had been written from the early twelfth century onwards, and works about Icelandic history (*Íslendingabók* and the first *Landnámabók*), we must assume that texts were also being translated that were needed by the church, such as sermons and legends. From around the middle of the twelfth century we know that learned literature was being translated and also produced, *The First Grammatical Treatise* probably being the first Icelandic text of this type. In the period just before and around 1200 several so-called quasi-historical works were translated. In many cases, it is a matter of debate whether translations of different types were made in Norway or in Iceland, and it is most likely that they were made in both countries. In any case, the culture in Iceland at the end of the twelfth century was no doubt vital and flourishing, and a good basis for further cultural growth. The three new indigenous genres that came into being, of which the sagas about early Icelanders is the most important, nevertheless represent a very important step in the development of Icelandic written culture, and for that reason it is important to establish a date for them. To be able to construct a good picture of the development of the history of literature in Iceland in the first half of the thirteenth century, it would also be very useful to know which of the three genres was first put into writing, thereby acting as a catalyst in the process of Iceland's literary development and perhaps stimulating other saga genres to be written down.

The authors of the present anthology approach the problem of saga dating from many different angles, discussing old dating criteria and in some cases suggesting new ones. What the authors have in common is not that they share the same views on the dating of individual sagas or on how useful the different dating criteria might be, but the view that, in spite of the complexity of the subject, the debates surrounding saga dating must be taken further and the questions readdressed and reviewed in light of changes and developments in saga scholarship, which may alter our views of this literary corpus and the period during which its texts were written.

In his article, Jürg Glauser asks the important question: What is dated, and why? He examines the implicit and explicit saga dating criteria from the time of Peter Erasmus Müller early in the nineteenth century up to our own time. His article reminds us that the criteria that are used to date the sagas about early Icelanders and the questions related to this topic must be seen in connection with and in the light of the broader field of saga research in the period in question. When it comes to the dating of an individual saga, the dating of the saga corpus as a whole and the issue of more general developments within the genre, there is a close connection between what scholars of a certain period think they know about this literature and the common opinion and theories of the time. Saga dating is therefore a question that continuously has to be readdressed and reviewed in the light of the latest research in the field.

Else Mundal focuses on the dating of the oldest written sagas of the genre in particular. In the earliest periods of saga research, the origin of this genre in its written form was dated to as early as the beginning of the twelfth century, but this date was gradually shifted towards the end of the century, with some in the latest generation of scholars arguing that the earliest sagas about early Icelanders were written in the 1230s or around 1240. Mundal argues in favour of a dating of the earliest sagas of the genre to around 1200. Since two other Icelandic genres, the sagas of bishops and the contemporary sagas (sagas belonging to the *Sturlunga* cycle), originated early in the thirteenth century too – the sagas of bishops probably a little earlier than the contemporary sagas – and the writing of sagas of kings reached its zenith with the sagas attributed to Snorri Sturluson in the 1220s and around 1230, the dating of the oldest sagas about early Icelanders is crucial in order to build up a good picture of the development of literary history in this interesting period in Icelandic society and of the relationship between the different saga genres.

Fóstbrœðra saga is one of the sagas that has both been dated to very early as well as very late within the time span during which sagas about early Icelanders are thought to have been written. Theodore M. Andersson's discussion of the dating of this particular saga demonstrates the importance of always taking the previous oral tradition into account when the dating of written texts and the relationship between them is debated. In addition to the account in *Fóstbrœðra saga*, the story about the death of the saga hero Þormóðr Bersason after the Battle of Stiklarstaðir is preserved in the two sagas of kings, the *Legendary Saga* and *Heimskringla*, as well as most probably in different versions in a few lost sagas as well. If *Fóstbrœðra saga* were indeed a late saga, then the story about Þormóðr's death as it is preserved here would be the youngest version. However, it has not been easy to explain the similarities and differences between the different versions of the story and how they relate to each other. Andersson argues that the best explanation for these similarities and differences is that *Fóstbrœðra saga* and the earliest saga of kings to tell the story (probably the so-called *Oldest Saga*) draw on a common oral tradition. Andersson's conclusion is that the independence of *Fóstbrœðra saga* from other written texts indicates an early date rather than a late one.

The dating of *Gísla saga Súrssonar* has been less disputed than the dating of *Fóstbrœðra saga*. This saga, however, presents many interesting challenges connected to the problem of dating. The saga exists in three rather different versions, each of which conveys distinctive emphases and interpretations of aspects of the narrative, and there is no consensus amongst scholars as to which version is the oldest. This very interesting saga is regarded as one of the masterpieces within its genre, and it is the focus of the article written by Emily Lethbridge. She examines existing arguments for the dating of the saga and the basis upon which these arguments have been constructed, thereby highlighting a number of problematic methodological issues.

The saga at the centre of Torfi Tulinius's article is *Eyrbyggja saga*. The dating of this saga has not varied as much as the dating of *Fóstbrœðra saga*, but the forty years between 1230 and 1270, which today are regarded as the earliest possible and the latest possible time of writing, is still a long period in the development of the written culture in Iceland in the thirteenth century. Torfi Tulinius takes as his starting point Einar Ól. Sveinsson's book *Dating the Icelandic Sagas* (1958), providing a summary of this work and discussing its methodology, as well as the value the author ascribes to different types of evidence for dating. Torfi Tulinius then goes on to discuss particular attempts to date *Eyrbyggja saga*, both Einar Ól. Sveinsson's early dating to the 1230s and later datings, and he suggests that there are arguments both in favour of an early date and a later date. Even though the discussion has not brought us closer to an undisputed dating of *Eyrbyggja saga*, Torfi Tulinius emphasizes that such considerations are useful, because they make us look at the texts in a certain way. Texts are acts of communication on certain issues in certain contexts. By exploring such contexts in the search for indications of dating, we may arrive at a better understanding of what the sagas are about.

Jonna Louis-Jensen's article examines linguistic evidence for saga dating in combination with genealogical or stemmatic studies. This method, which yields some interesting results, does not enable us to date the original written saga, but perhaps it can help us to date the archetype, which may or may not be identical to the oldest written version of the saga. Louis-Jensen applies this method to two sagas about early Icelanders, *Eyrbyggja saga* and *Egils saga Skallagrímssonar.* The linguistic evidence combined with what we know about the place of the preserved redactions in the manuscript stemma of the saga indicates that *Eyrbyggja saga*, or at least its archetype, is considerably younger than *Egils saga*. The linguistic evidence for dating of *Egils saga* is partly the same as the evidence that has been used to argue that Snorri Sturluson was the author of this saga. Louis-Jensen's preliminary conclusion after having reviewed previous linguistic research on the manuscripts of *Egils saga* is that the archetype of the saga must be dated to before 1235. The time of writing fits with the idea that Snorri was its author. However, the language used in *Heimskringla* I and III – the two parts of *Heimskringla* that we can ascribe to Snorri with valid arguments – is sufficiently different that a common author with *Egils saga* is unlikely.

Slavica Ranković takes a new approach to the dating of sagas. Her method is to map the use of certain *formulae*, in this case the blue/black clothing of a killer, across the extant corpus of the sagas about early Icelanders. Using many examples and analyses of scenes where blue clothing is worn, she shows how the motif is used and varied. Some of the variations may have something to do with how a motif developed over time and how an oral formula sometimes departed from its original meaning when used in a literary context. The use of one formula is probably not much help in terms of general saga dating, but many studies of this type of mapping and studying the use of formulaic devices and motifs across the saga corpus will hopefully provide some hints as to where a saga can be placed within the development of the genre. As Ranković concludes, the regular usage of a formula is likely to be found in both early and late sagas while radical departures, misapplications, parodies and metatextual uses seem more likely to be later developments. Used in combination with other dating criteria, studies of the use of formulas may prove to be helpful.

Guðrún Nordal's approach has much in common with Ranković's, since she investigates two features of saga composition across the whole genre and considers whether these two features – the use of skaldic verse and the way the settlement is depicted – can be used as guides to the time of writing. There are great differences between various sagas about early Icelanders in terms of their use of skaldic verse, and less than half of them open with the settlement of Iceland. Guðrún Nordal connects the differences in the use of skaldic verse to changing attitudes to the importance and significance of skaldic verse in the thirteenth and fourteenth centuries, and she connects the interest in the settlement, or lack thereof, to the political conditions of the time and to the relationship between Iceland and Norway. These two features can hardly help us to date any saga accurately, and as Guðrún Nordal clearly demonstrates in her comparison of *Laxdœla saga* and *Eyrbyggja saga*, the use of skaldic verse and the picture of the settlement can be very different in two sagas that probably were written more or less in the same time period and possibly in the same cultural milieu. However, if we are able to draw up more and more lines that show a general development through the saga corpus – with some sagas fitting nicely with the larger patterns and others not – such lines of development, together with other criteria, could prove to be very useful in our attempts to date the sagas.

Through their discussions and analyses, the contributors probably pose more questions than they answer, and on the occasions when various solutions are offered to the question of when a certain saga was written, the answers are not always the same. This is, however, how it must and should be when the debate under scrutiny is as complex and ever-evolving as the question of how to date the literary corpus known as sagas about early Icelanders.

WHAT IS DATED, AND WHY?

Saga Dating in the Histories of Old Norse-Icelandic Literature

Jürg Glauser

I am not in a position to correct the dating of any particular saga; rather, I would like to discuss some more general questions, such as: when a date is given to a saga, what is it that is dated, and why? My answer to these questions will be based on a reading of histories of literature (from Finnur Jónsson to *Íslensk bókmenntasaga*) and relevant research (Gísli Sigurðsson, *The Medieval Icelandic Saga*, 2004, etc.), and will concentrate on the analytical levels and implicit and explicit criteria for saga dating in these works.

PRELIMINARY NOTES

I would like to discuss some general issues arising from the problem of saga dating and I will do this against the background of a reading of various histories of Old Norse-Icelandic literature in a more or less chronological order. I shall look primarily at the implicit and explicit criteria and levels of analysis that are taken as a basis for dating (the) sagas in the most important histories of literature. Consequently, the aim is not so much to determine the exact age of sagas, nor am I able to suggest a new dating of any specific saga. It goes without saying that this does not mean that I am in any way denying the meaning and justification of such dating. On the contrary, I have much respect for the immense amount of philological work that has been and is being invested in the dating of sagas as a whole, as well as in establishing the precise dates of individual sagas, even if in the third part of this article some aspects are taken up that actually call into question the conventional methods of dating.

As stated, the focus in the following discussion will be on some works that can be considered representative of the genre of histories of Old Norse-Icelandic literature, especially saga literature. The reason for choosing histories of Old Norse-Icelandic literature as a main source is that they convey concepts that are typical for saga scholarship at a given time, also with regard to the dating of sagas. Accordingly, what follows is to be understood as a minor contribution to the history of saga scholarship.

SAGA DATING AND HISTORIOGRAPHY OF LITERATURE

The main focus of the following discussion will be on saga research concerning the historiography of Old Norse-Icelandic literature during the twentieth century. However, it is necessary for this brief overview to go back in time and focus on at least one early representative of saga scholarship. Since the aim of this article is to examine the explicit and implicit criteria that are the basis of saga dating in some specific histories of literature, an overview can (and must) begin with Peter Erasmus Müller (1776–1834).[1] The reason for Müller's pre-eminence in this context is that his predecessors in the eighteenth century such as Hálfdan Einarsson (1732–85) still represented to a large extent the state of early modern bibliographical arrangement of texts by alphabetical criteria and consequently did not aspire to providing a coherent account of literary and historical developments (Halfdanus Einari 1777; 1786).

Compared with these works, Müller's *Sagabibliothek med Anmærkninger og indledende Afhandlinger* (1, 1817; 2, 1818; 3, 1820) and his essay "Om den islandske Historieskrivnings Oprindelse, Flor og Undergang" (*Nordisk Tidsskrift for Oldkyndighed*, 1, 1832)[2] provide the first systematic attempts to combine Icelandic prose-literature and Icelandic history in the sense of an Old Norse-Icelandic history of literature as defined by concepts of romanticism. Müller's definition of what a saga is can be found in the "Fortale"

1 For the following discussion of Müller compare particularly Andersson 1964: 22–40 (ch. 2, "The Romantic Era").

2 This paper was published in German in 1813 with the title *Ueber den Ursprung und Verfall der isländischen Historiographie*.

(Foreword) to his first volume of the *Sagabibliothek*, where he writes that it is "ethvert Sagn, enten det er sandfærdigt eller opdigtet [...] og Islænderne havde baade fortalt og nedskrevet saavel blotte Æventyr som troværdige Oldtidssagn" (every legend, whether it is credible or invented [...] and the Icelanders had both narrated and written down both mere adventures and credible old legends) (Müller 1817: X). It is exactly this latter criterion – "Troværdighed" (Müller 1817: XI), credibility, in the sense of historicity – which plays a major part in Müller's assessment of individual sagas and their age, and which became so important for the reception of this concept in later saga scholarship.

Of the various possible means of categorizing credibility – "Paalidelighed" (trustworthiness), "Omfang" (extent), "Geographie" (geography) and "Tiden" (time) – Müller chooses the last one of these, "fordi denne snarest leder hen til at sætte Grundene for hver Sagas Paalidelighed i deres rette Lys" (because this will put the basis for each saga's trustworthiness in the right light) (Müller 1817: XVII–XVIII).

With regard to the first category – trustworthiness – Müller makes an observation that continues to be voiced in works written over one hundred years later by scholars such as Jón Helgason: "de tidligst nedskrevne Sagaer ere de paalideligste [...] de sidst nedskrevne blotte Æventyr" (The sagas that were first written down are the most credible ones [...] the ones that were written down last are mere adventures) (Müller 1817: XIX). For the further career of this dichotomy (early / late, credible in the sense of historical / invented), it is important to point out that Müller is the Old Norse scholar back to whom the formula can be traced, or who at least was the first to express it with such precision.

Also in his "Inledning" (Introduction), Müller understandably focuses on the fact that in his opinion the sagas preserve historical events that had taken place in Iceland and Scandinavia. Müller's table of contents structures for the first time the entire corpus of saga literature along a diachronic axis. In the section "Almindelige Bemærkninger om Reglerne, hvorefter de islandske Sagaers Ægthed kunde bestemmes" (General comments on the rules by which the authenticity of the Icelandic sagas can be established) (Müller 1817: 15–33), Müller classifies the sagas according to their dating, established by a relative or absolute chronology based on the two criteria "authenticity" and "reliability." According to Müller, there are internal and external features for determining the authenticity of a saga; the latter include the manuscripts themselves or comparisons with other sagas, while the former is the form of a saga, including features such as language (including words, phrases and sentence structure); performance (i.e., prose or verse); and sound (in Danish "Tone," Müller 1817: 21). These are categories that come very close to Andreas Heusler's concepts, which will be addressed in later paragraphs.

From the perspective of German poetics (see Schiller), Müller's essay is interesting in that it denotes the basic attitude of the sagas as "naïve" and by this refers to the dialogical form, the artlessness of the narrative and the absence of "Betragtninger" (contemplations) (Müller 1817: 22). Here one already finds criteria concerning saga style that later become differentiated *in nuce*. As for the content of sagas as a criterion for authenticity, Müller argues above all for the importance of the narrator's insight and his close proximity or distance to the events he describes (Müller 1817: 26). If the content carries a trace of falsity in itself, this is a sign of a saga's late origin; fantastic elements or implausible stories (such as *Króka-Refs saga*) debunk sagas as recent inventions (Müller 1817: 28–32). Generally, compared with today's attempts at dating, the early age ascribed to the Icelandic sagas by Müller is striking, most of all, of course, the early dating of *Njáls saga* to the beginning of the twelfth century (Müller 1817: V: "Fra Begyndelsen af det tolvte Aarhundrede"; Müller 1817: 61: "Den er neppe yngre, end Are Frodes og Sæmunds Tider" (It [i.e. *Njáls saga*] is hardly younger than the days of Ari the Wise and Sæmundr).

Paradoxically, the magisterial history of Old Norse-Icelandic literature by Finnur Jónsson (1858–1934), *Den oldnorske og oldislandske litteraturs historie*[3] (Finnur Jónsson 1920–24), can be treated rather quickly in the present overview, because the author – in his specifically pragmatic and untheoretical way of dealing with literature and writing a history of literature – did not devote many lines to a discussion of the criteria he used as a basis for his classification of the body of texts. In the preface to the first volume of *Den oldnorske og oldislandske litteraturs historie* Finnur Jónsson states succinctly: "Den oldnordiske litteraturhistorie falder naturligst i 3 perioder" (Old Norse literature is divided most naturally into three periods) (Finnur Jónsson 1920: 6):

3 The sagas are dealt with in volumes II and III.

> Det første tidsrum går fra begyndelsen af den historiske tid, o. 800, til o. 1100, til den tid, i hvilken man begyndte at skrive og forfatte prosaværker. [...] dette tidsrum (kan) med fuld ret kaldes skjalde-tidsrummet. / Det andet tidsrum omfatter 200 år, o. 1100–1300. I den falder hele den originale, prosaiske frembringelse, saga-skrivningen, lovenes nedskrivning [...]. Dette tidsrum, navnlig dets første halvdel, er litteraturens guldalder. [...] Dette tidsrums mest betegnende navn vilde efter dens vigtigste hovedfrembringelse være sagatidsrummet. / Det tredje tidsrum går fra o. 1300 til o. 1450; så langt ned går oldtiden med rette. Dette tidsrums hovedvirksomhed er at afskrive og samle tidligere værker. [...] den mest træffende betegnelse for tidsrummet vilde være afskrivnings- og samlingstidsrum. (Finnur Jónsson 1920: 6–7)

> The first period spans from the beginning of the historical time, c. 800, up to c. 1100, when one began writing and composing prose works. [...] This period can with good reason be called the *skaldic period.* / The second period spans 200 years, ca. 1100–1300. During this period, the whole original production of prose, the writing of sagas and the writing-down of the laws, take place. [...] This period, especially its first half, is the golden age of [Icelandic] literature. [...] The most characteristic name for this period would be the *saga period*, after its most important main production. The third period covers from ca. 1300 to ca. 1450; antiquity can be said to last this long. The principal activity of this period was to copy and collect earlier works. [...] The most characteristic name for this period would be the *period of copying and collecting.*

In Finnur Jónsson's unequivocal diction comes to light the classical model of the development of literary genres, a three-period model consisting of a first period of "rise" followed by a period of "blossom" and ending after a period of "decline." Finnur Jónsson does of course date individual sagas in his history of Icelandic literature, but he never makes any substantial comments on his criteria for dating, and statements like the following are therefore quite frequent: "På grund af traditionens renhed og fremstillingens klassiske form hører sagaen [i.e. *Eyrbyggja saga*] afgjort til sagaskrivningens bedste tid, til den senere halvdel af det 12. årh. Yngre end 1200 er den ganske sikkert ikke" (Due to the pureness of the tradition and the classical form of the presentation, the saga belongs decidedly to the best period of saga-writing, to the second half of the twelfth century. It most surely is not younger than 1200) (Finnur Jónsson 1923: 432).

Jón Helgason (1899–1986) in his *Norrøn litteraturhistorie* (Jón Helgason 1934) makes a preliminary note on the specific aspect of uncertainty when it comes to dating: "De fleste værker er overleverede uden forfatternavne og uden datering. I mange tilfælde maa man gætte sig til, fra hvilket tidsrum et værk maa stamme, uden at have afgørende holdepunkter" (Most of the works are transmitted without their authors' names and without dates. In many cases one must guess from which period the work stems, for there is no decisive evidence) (Jón Helgason 1934: 14). In a similar way to Finnur Jónsson, but also to Andreas Heusler and Knut Liestøl, Jón Helgason is interested not only in the texts in their transmitted form, but also in their pre-histories. These pre-histories are divided, on the one hand, into the "erindringsstof" (memory material) of eye witnesses with only few transmitting links and basically of a historical nature, and, on the other hand, into the "traditionsstof" (traditional material) into which accretions and non-historical elements were added over several generations. During the process of "nedskrivning" (writing down) it is decided what will be retained in the written text and what will be omitted (Jón Helgason 1934: 106). Jón Helgason also adheres very clearly to the tripartite model of saga evolution; at the beginning was the tradition; after that, the saga evolved into the direction of an historical novel; the saga ended up as late invention. Jón Helgason's attempts to differentiate individual phases within "traditionens udvikling" (development of the tradition), the role of "sagamændene" (the saga men) and "den skrevne saga" (the written saga) have many parallels with Heusler's version of the "Freiprosalehre" (Jón Helgason 1934: 116–27). In this model, the relatively older or younger age of a saga determines its historicity: "Ved bedømmelsen af en sagas historiske troværdighed maa først og fremmest dens alder og dens art tages i betragtning" (For the assessment of the historical credibility of a saga, first of all its age and its nature must be taken into consideration) (Jón Helgason 1934: 129). The equation "old" = "historical" is considered to be unequivocal. Circular arguments, which may result from the uncertain dating, hardly play a role in Jón Helgason's line of argument.

The sagas of the Icelanders begin, according to Jón Helgason, "med de typiske traditionssager" (with the typical traditional sagas) such as *Heiðarvíga saga*, *Reykdœla saga*, *Vápnfirðinga saga* and *Droplaugarsona saga*. These are followed by *Ljósvetninga saga* and *Eyrbyggja saga*, and next come the "store sagaer" (grand sagas) *Egils saga*, *Laxdœla saga*, *Njáls saga* and *Grettis saga* (in that order), whereupon the development comes to a close with "helt opdigtede og temmelig virkelighedsfjerne romaner" (entirely fictitious and rather unrealistic novels) (Jón Helgason 1934: 131–32). More clearly than other authors of histories of Old Norse-Icelandic literature, Jón Helgason identifies the process of saga development (a movement from oral tradition to writing-down), dating and historicity, and brings these elements into the formula "credibility" versus "invention / fantasy," which again is reflected in the precise pattern of "early – high – late."

Although Andreas Heusler (1865–1940) did not conceptualize *Die altgermanische Dichtung*[4] (Heusler 1967) primarily as a history of literature, he does deal with dating issues in connection with the Icelandic sagas. It must be pointed out, however, that in his definition of "Altgermanisch" (Old Germanic) in the sense of "pre-Roman" and "pre-chivalrous" (Heusler 1967: 202), Heusler talks of a basically timeless or rather a-chronical / super-chronical entity, which finds its expression mainly in the so-called "Formstreben" (strive for form) and "Stilwillen" (stylistic will). The primary concern in such an approach is not chronology and even less the exact dating of specific texts, as such operations could potentially be an obstacle. "Old Germanic" is therefore not a chronological, but rather an intellectual, mental, or cultural category. That Heusler's "Altisland" (Ancient Iceland) (Heusler 1967: 210) is not a completely timeless space is shown by his overview over the time limits of saga development – "Pflege der buchlosen Saga" (tradition of the bookless saga) (Heusler 1967: 211) – that begins with the saga time (930–1030/1050) and continues with the time of saga writing in the second half of the twelfth century, after which the early period of the written sagas of Icelanders follows, beginning with Snorri's *Egils saga* (around 1210) and continuing until 1230. This period reaches its zenith between 1230 and 1264, before the "Nachblüte" (aftermath) begins with "einzelne[n] hochstehende[n] Gestaltungen" (individual high-standing productions) (Heusler 1967: 212) and brings the production, but not the copying and collecting, to an end in the "frühvierzehnte[n] Jahrhundert" (early fourteenth century). As a small annex to the great building of the Ice-

4 The first edition of *Die altgermanische Dichtung* appeared in 1923, the second edition in 1941, although the titles of the reprints give the date as "1943."

landic saga comes the "Isländerfabel" (Icelandic fable) (Heusler 1967: 231), the "erfabelte, romanhafte Isländergeschichte" (the fictitious, novel-like story of Icelanders) (Heusler 1967: 202).

For Heusler, the object of saga dating is both the oral and the written saga. With regard to the general problem of saga dating, Heusler's following observations are crucial. He states: "die Niederschrift zog sich durch 3–4 Menschenalter" (the writing-down took three to four generations), and "der Begriff 'die ursprüngliche Saga' hat [...] etwas Schattenhaftes. Was meint man damit? Die erste Niederschrift? … oder das, was sich zufrühest aus der Denkwürdigkeit zum Vortragsstück ballte?" (the term "the original saga" is somewhat shadowy. What does one mean by it? The first writing-down? … or what was formed from the memorabilia to the performance piece?) (Heusler 1967: 215). Heusler's scheme of development – as always very differentiated and operating with (too?) many unknown entities – presupposes the following course: first, so-called house-chronicles ("Hauschroniken") emerged from an event ("Ereignis"), which developed into a performance piece ("Vortragsstück"), from which an oral saga ("mündliche Saga") arose, which again became the source saga ("Quellensaga"), which ultimately led to the writing-down ("Niederschrift") (Heusler 1967: 216–17). Like Liestøl, Heusler accentuates the gradual nature of this process ("Gradmäßige"), as well as emphasizing what might concern the saga writer ("Sagaschreiber"), whom he conceived of as a recorder, collector, reviewer and creatively rewriting author. As mentioned before, Heusler was particularly interested in the style: "Wichtiger als Jahreszahlen ist uns die Erkenntnis, was eine Saga altertümlich aussehen macht" (To us, more important than the dating by years is an awareness of what makes a saga look ancient) (Heusler 1967: 217). Inequalities "im Seelischen und Handwerklichen" (in the emotion and handycraft) – that is to say the categories of taste and ability – define individual time steps, but do not allow for precise dating. According to Heusler, differences in style cannot always be equated with differences in age (Heusler 1967: 218). A list of elements that in Heusler's view suggest a young age of sagas contains such elements as disorder in genealogies and topographies, exaggerations, inclinations to fabulous and fairy-tale-like elements, chivalrous and Christian aspects, an increase in loan words etc. (Heusler 1967: 217–18).

Compared to the histories of Old Norse-Icelandic literature mentioned so far, Jan de Vries's (1890–1964) *Altnordische Literaturgeschichte* (de Vries

1999) is remarkable because he was probably the first literary historian to make an attempt at dissociating himself from the diachronic perspective. The task he sets for himself is defined as follows:

> Eine altnordische Literaturgeschichte hat zur Aufgabe, die literarischen Erscheinungsformen, die sich während eines bestimmten Zeitabschnitts der vor- und frühhistorischen Perioden im skandinavischen Norden gebildet und weiterentwickelt haben, zu beschreiben und zu erklären. (de Vries 1999: 1)

> The task of a history of Old Norse-Icelandic literature is to describe and to interpret the literary manifestations, which have been established and refined during a certain period of time in the pre-historical and early historical periods in the Scandinavian North.

Jan de Vries discusses in detail the issue of dating when he writes:

> Eine Literatur, die für einen beträchtlichen Teil aus Werken besteht, von denen weder der Name des Verfassers noch die Entstehungszeit überliefert sind, bietet mehrere Schwierigkeiten, wenn man sie in einer Übersicht zusammenfassen will. Die chronologische Festlegung solcher anonymen Werke bleibt immer fraglich; die Meinungen können sogar weit auseinander gehen. Wenn sichere Entscheidungen fehlen, ist es gefährlich, die überlieferten Literaturwerke nach chronologischen Gesichtspunkten einzuteilen; man unterscheidet in einem solchen Fall lieber die Dichtarten als die einzelnen Werke. […] Es ist daher leicht begreiflich, daß man in den Handbüchern immer diese Literaturen (Eddalied – Skaldik – Saga) gesondert und nacheinander behandelt findet; man erspart sich dadurch die Mühe, anonym überlieferte Werke einer bestimmten Periode einzuordnen, und es ist leichter, hier ein typologisches Verfahren anzuwenden. (de Vries 1999: 2)

> A literature, which consists to a considerable extent of works from which neither the name of the author nor the time of its origin are transmitted, offers several difficulties, if one wants to summarize it in an overview. The chronological fixation of such anonymous works always remains doubtful; even the positions (of scholars) can diverge greatly. When secure decisions are missing, it is dangerous to classify the transmitted literary works according to the chronological cate gories; in such cases it is preferable to distinguish between poetic modes rather

> than single works. […] It is therefore easy to understand that in handbooks one always finds this literature (Eddic poetry – Skaldic poetry – Saga) handled separately and successively; this way, one avoids the trouble of attempting to classify anonymously transmitted works from a specific period, and it is easier to apply a typological procedure here.

In this shift from diachrony to synchrony, de Vries also sees the main merit of his own history of literature. Thus, he continues:

> Literatur ist eine historisch bedingte Kunstform. Jedes Geschlecht spricht darin sein eigenstes Wesen aus, und dieses Wesen offenbart sich auch dort, wo altüberlieferte Formen das persönliche Erleben überdeckt haben. Das Eigenleben der literarischen Ausdrucksformen ist sicherlich einer besonderen Untersuchung wert, aber noch wichtiger scheint es mir, den Geist der Künstler und den Geist der Zeit kennenzulernen. Nur eine synchronische Behandlung der Literatur wird ihren geistesgeschichtlichen Charakter deutlich hervortreten lassen. […] Wenn wir uns dazu entschlossen haben, die bis jetzt befolgte diachronische Betrachtungsweise aufzugeben und die altnordische Literatur in ihrer historischen Bezogenheit darzustellen. (de Vries 1999: 3)

> Literature is a historically determined form of art. Through it, each generation expresses its own essence, and this essence reveals itself also where forms transmitted from ancient times have covered personal experience. The separate life of the literary expression is certainly worth examining in its own right, but it seems to me even more important to get to know the spirit of the artists and the spirit of the time. Only a synchronic study of literature will reveal the historical character of its ideas. […] Thus we have decided to break with the diachronic point of view adhered to until now and to present Old Norse-Icelandic literature in its historical dimension.

> Das Bild der vorangehenden Periode ist nicht vollständig, falls wir nicht auch diese mündliche Tradierung […] würdigen; aber wie werden wir diese behandeln können, wenn hier die Quellen gänzlich schweigen? Dann ist es freilich leichter, die Saga als eine einheitliche Kunstgattung zu behandeln und uns über den Anteil der aufeinander folgenden Perioden den Kopf nicht zu zerbrechen. […] Ich bin […] der Überzeugung, daß man endlich den Versuch zu einer synchronischen Behandlung machen soll. (de Vries 1999: 4–5)

> The picture of the previous period is not complete if we do not appreciate this oral tradition as well […], but how can we treat it if the sources are completely silent? Then it is of course easier to treat the saga as a homogeneous genre and not to rack one's brain considering the periods that follow one after the other. […] I am […] of the opinion that we should finally make an attempt at a synchronic study.

However, characteristically, de Vries can only partly convert his project. Already on page six, he establishes the following distinction of periods: 1. the pre-historic period (until the end of the ninth century); 2. the pagan period (until 1000); 3. the time after the conversion (until the middle of the twelfth century); 4. the Icelandic renaissance (until the thirteenth century); and 5. the transition period until the Christian Middle Ages. Of the latter part of this process he states: "Auf dem Höhepunkt ihrer Blüte bricht die altnordische Literatur jäh ab. Die Kräfte der Vorzeit sind verbraucht; das Alte hat keine Anziehungskraft mehr" (At the height of its blossoming, Old Norse-Icelandic literature stops abruptly. The strength of the olden times is consumed; the old has no longer any attraction) (de Vries 1999: 8). As becomes very clear, in de Vries's as well as in Heusler's view, Old Norse-Icelandic literature is therefore literature that has not come in contact with "medieval" (that is, continental Christian) poetry. Accordingly, de Vries's patterns of interpretation are characterized by blasting disrespect and misunderstanding, especially in his treatment of late medieval saga literature. The sober conclusion must be that de Vries's remarkable and thought-provoking considerations failed, not least because of his outdated presuppositions and because of his dichotomic, black-and-white thinking.

Sigurður Nordal's (1886–1974) compressed overview of the saga literature (Sigurður Nordal 1953) has the following aim: "at give en *oversigt over sagaskrivningen efter tidsfølgen, med hovedvægten paa fortidssagaerne*" (to provide an overview of saga writing according to a chronological sequence, with the main focus on the sagas of antiquity) (Sigurður Nordal 1953: 183). He describes the importance of dating in the context of a historiography of literature as follows: "Kronologi er nerven i alle historiske videnskaber, ogsaa litteraturhistorien. Skønt man ikke uden videre kan gaa ud fra, at *post hoc* er det samme som *propter hoc*, at et yngre arbejde er afhængigt eller paavirket af et ældre, ved man ialfald, at det modsatte ikke kan være tilfældet" (Chronology is the nerve of all historical sciences including literary history. Although one cannot assume that *post hoc* is the same as *propter hoc*, that a younger work is dependent on or influenced by an older one, we know in any case that the opposite may not be the case) (Sigurður Nordal 1953: 183). In reaction to this positivist view of history, as Sigurður Nordal expresses it here, poststructuralist theory has responded, as is well known, with models such as intertextuality. In a similar way to scholars such as Einar Ólafur Sveinsson, Sigurður Nordal's aim was to study the sagas in their existing, written forms, although his goal was in no way to deny the value of tradition: "Skrevne sagaer eksisterer. Den mundtlige tradition er tabt, selv den, som vi har de sikreste vidnesbyrd om, d.v.s. vi kan kun slutte os til den ved at studere de skrevne sagaer, ved at gaa fra det mere til det mindre kendte" (Written sagas exist. The oral tradition is lost, even the one about which we have the firmest evidence, i.e. we can only make conjectures by studying the written sagas, by going from the more known to less known) (Sigurður Nordal 1953: 184).

Sigurður Nordal also designed a beautifully symmetrical course of saga development:

> Bortset fra muligheden af enkelte historiske optegnelser før 1100 og fra de sidste udløbere af annaler og opdigtede sagaer efter 1400, strækker sagalitteraturen (i videste forstand) sig over tre aarhundreder, 1100–1400. Den er en afgrænset litteraturart, der trods alle nydannelser og yderliggaaende modsætninger mellem værker og grupper udgør et organisk hele, har en begyndelse og afslutning, sin ubrudte sammenhæng [...]. (Sigurður Nordal 1953: 270)

> Apart from the possibility of individual historical notes before 1100 and apart from the last offshoots of annals and invented sagas after 1400, saga literature (in its widest sense) spans three centuries, 1100–1400. It is a well-defined kind of literature, which in spite of all neologisms and extreme contrasts between works and groups forms an organic whole, has a beginning and an end, an unbroken continuity [...].

Sigurður Nordal's arguments here fall completely within the framework of the metaphor of the organic and of the three phases.

As is well known, Einar Ólafur Sveinsson (1899–1984) argues from the same kind of bookprose-stance as Sigurður Nordal, in his numerous and influential works about saga literature and questions of dating methods. Thus he writes in his essay *Ritunartími Íslendingasagna* (Einar Ól. Sveinsson 1965): "En hvað var, áður en þetta væri?" (But what was before it was?) (Einar Ól. Sveinsson 1965: 147).[5] Even more directly in relation to the question of oral or written sources he states:

> Einkennilegt kann að þykja, að stundum er engu líkara en mönnum sjáist yfir það, að sögurnar í vorri merkingu, hin rituðu verk, *eru til í raun og veru*, en þær munnlegu heimildir, sem menn ætla, að farið sé eftir, *eru ekki til* – og ekki ber þess að dyljast, að vel má vera, að þegar vér teljum víst, að það eða það atriði sé úr munnlegum frásögnum, þá sé það ekki annað en missýning, þetta atriði hafi aldrei verið til í munnlegum frásögum af þessari hetju. Þennan mun þess, sem til er, og hins, sem ekki er til, hins vissa og hins óvissa, skyldi vísindamaður aldrei láta sér úr huga líða. (Einar Ól. Sveinsson 1965: 14)

This passage corresponds closely to the English version:

> It may seem strange, but sometimes it appears as though people overlook the fact that sagas, as we designate them, the written works, really exist, while the oral sources, upon which they are supposed to be based, do not exist. We must not close our eyes to the danger when we feel certain that one incident or another is derived from an oral tradition, that this may be only an illusion; this incident may never have existed in oral tradition about the same hero. Scholars should never lose sight of the difference between that which exists and that which does not – the certain and the uncertain. (Einar Ól. Sveinsson 1958: 7)

Also in Einar Ólafur Sveinsson's book, which, it must be stressed, is not a history of literature, one finds the traditional tripartite division of the sagas, i.e. "fornlegar sögur" (archaic sagas), "klassiskar sögur" (classical sagas) and "unglegar sögur" (youngish sagas).

In his history of Icelandic literature, Jónas Kristjánsson devotes a separate section to the question, "When were the sagas written?" (Jónas Krist-

5 I quote from the Icelandic version from 1965, since it has a substantially fuller text than the original English edition from 1958 (Einar Ól. Sveinsson 1958).

jánsson 1988: 217–23). For him, too, the dating of the sagas constitutes a central key in literary history:

> A critic may turn to sagas in search of information about the history of the tenth and eleventh century, or for evidence of the ideas and values of the writers' own time, or he may be primarily interested in them as works of literary art freely created by their authors. Whatever his attitude, it is clearly of the utmost importance for him to discover when they were written – and that has proved a hard puzzle to solve. (Jónas Kristjánsson 1988: 217)

Given the traditional preference for the ancient, Jónas Kristjánsson points out the remarkable fact that the late stages of saga literature in particular have received little attention, and not least when it comes to the matter of dating:

> It is usually assumed that the last (sagas) were written about the middle of the fourteenth century, so that the genre as a whole spans about a century and a half. In fact, little serious work has been done on dating the youngest sagas, and it may be that in future their chronology will be revised and the whole period extended. There is also some doubt as to which sagas among later productions should be counted as Íslendinga sögur: they are texts which have been neglected and need further study. (Jónas Kristjánsson 1988: 217)

With regard to the influence of the translated chivalric poetry on the development of Icelandic saga literature, Jónas Kristjánsson completely adheres to the traditional patterns of interpretations, which see the supposed decline of the Icelandic literature around 1300 as a direct result of the political developments, that is, the loss of national independence in 1262/64. As part of his treatment of the art of the sagas, Jónas Kristjánsson speaks of the various changes that had taken place:

> The greatest changes were caused by the influence of the imported "sagas of chivalry" (*riddara sögur*), first translated in Norway, and the indigenous "sagas of ancient times" (*fornaldarsögur*) that came in their wake. *Riddara sögur* were translated at the instigation of King Hákon the Old, the first king to gain sovereignty over Iceland, so it is not purely accidental that the influence of such sagas on Íslendinga sögur more or less coincides with the end of the Icelandic

> commonwealth. [...] In light of all this we can see that influence from translated *riddara sögur* could conceivably have been exerted as early as c. 1230, but it more probably belongs to a slightly later period, about 1250 and later. It seems safe to assume that Íslendinga sögur that appear deeply influenced by *riddara sögur* or *fornaldarsögur* were not composed until after the middle of the thirteenth century. (Jónas Kristjánsson 1988: 219)

In general, Jónas Kristjánsson pleads for caution with regard to the dating on the basis of artistic features:

> [I]t is only with the greatest caution that we should give a verdict on the age of a saga based on some generalised opinion of the level of its artistry. The primitive and the decadent are not always easy to tell apart: and what is archaic to some scholars is bright novelty to others. (Jónas Kristjánsson 1988: 222)

The methodological difference between this approach and, among others, the one taken by Andreas Heusler becomes very clear in Jónas Kristjánsson's plea for caution concerning the possibilities of dating sagas on stylistic grounds. In the same context, Jónas Kristjánsson also outlines the different methods of evaluating shorter versions of sagas as being older than longer versions of sagas, in which their relative length is a criterion for their age (Jónas Kristjánsson 1988: 223).

Vésteinn Ólason devotes some attention to the question of dating in the latest extensive history of Old Norse-Icelandic literature (Vésteinn Ólason 1993). For his categorization of the sagas, Vésteinn adheres in part to the traditional chronological pattern and speaks of "fornlegar deilusögur" (oldish feud sagas), "sígildar deilusögur" (classical feud sagas), "harmsögur" (tragic sagas) and "unglegar Íslendingasögur" (youngish sagas of Icelanders) (Vésteinn Ólason 1993: 80–82, 143). For him, too, the dating of the texts is a main function of the historiography of literature:

> [E]nda ekki ótítt að skoðunum sem lengi hafa verið teknar góðar og gildar sé bylt við. Mestar líkur eru til að mark sé takandi á áhrifum frá ungum lögbókum og stundum á sambandi við Landnámu. En aldursgreiningin er svo mikilvæg fyrir skilning á þróun sagnalistarinnar að menn munu halda áfram að reyna fyrir sér. (Vésteinn Ólason 1993: 42)

> It is not unusual that opinions that have been accepted for some time are changed. It is most likely that influences from young law books and sometimes connections with *Landnámabók* are most convincing. But dating is so important for the understanding of the development of saga art that scholars will continue to give it a try.

For Vésteinn Ólason it is certain that one has to draw a line between two periods ("tímamót," Vésteinn Ólason 1993: 43) in the development of the written saga around or shortly after 1300. He also posits that the later sagas of the fourteenth century are characterized by "ýkjur" (exaggerations), "áhrif frá fornaldarsögum og mikið af kynjum og ævintýraminnum" (influences from sagas of ancient times and a lot of fantastical elements and adventure-motifs) (Vésteinn Ólason 1993: 43; see also Vésteinn Ólason 2007). These late sagas are posited against the ancient sagas, which however do not necessarily have to be older than the classic ones, in which a developed saga art ("þroskuð sagnalist," Vésteinn Ólason 1993: 43) dominates. The established trichotomy, which was common in earlier literary historiography, is clearly reflected in Vésteinn Ólason's essay too, although he highlights the overlaps and provides the dating issue with many question marks. For the first time in a history of Old Norse-Icelandic literature, Vésteinn Ólason pays attention to the temporal space between the first dating of a saga as postulated by scholars and the first dating of the extant manuscript which actually transmits the saga (see Vésteinn Ólason 1993: 42).

The fundamental question, that is, what actually is being dated when one dates sagas, can only be answered selectively after this very brief reading of some of the histories of Old Norse-Icelandic literature. One older line of scholarship, which is mainly represented in the works of Peter Erasmus Müller, Finnur Jónsson, Andreas Heusler and partly even Jón Helgason and Jan de Vries, was mostly interested in dating the subject matter, that is, the *contents* of the sagas. In contrast, scholars such as Sigurður Nordal, Einar Ólafur Sveinsson and Jónas Kristjánsson attempted mainly to make the traditional *forms* of the sagas the subject of dating. Whereas the first group primarily aimed to take into account the no-longer-extant pre-forms for the dating of the stories, the second group excluded these same phenomena completely from the issue of dating.

A certain paradox emerges from this reading of the histories of literature. Although the question of dating, with the exception of Finnur Jónsson, is declared in each literary history to be a crucial one, scholars agree that the reliable instruments necessary for conducting such dating attempts are still missing. Nevertheless, with varying degrees of caution, dating – which is for the most part held to be unachievable due to the specific textuality of medieval sagas – is made the actual basis of the procedure of writing the history of Old Norse-Icelandic literature.

Another remarkable point deserves to be pointed out here. There is of course a close correlation between the dating of a particular saga and a general understanding of how the saga as a genre emerged and developed. In short, the concept of literature defines its dating. In the context of this review of research, it is interesting to see how the dating of the sagas of Icelanders today is still considerably determined by Müller's concepts of the emergence ("Oprindelse"), the blossoming ("Flor") and the decline ("Undergang") of a literary genre. For Finnur Jónsson, Old Norse-Icelandic literature divides itself altogether "naturally" into three parts, but there is, since the time of Müller, hardly one history of Old Norse-Icelandic literature that is not attracted by the fascination of the scheme that poses a movement from a "pre-classical period" through a "classical period" to a "post-classical period." This tripartite model is especially used when it comes to separate the "post-classical" sagas from the "genuine" sagas, and here the dichotomies mainly depend on the opposition of the "realistic" versus the "fictitious" (see Heusler's list, but also other histories of literature up to Vésteinn Ólason). This division, which seems rather absurd from the point of view of modern literary theory, still serves an important role in the dating of the sagas and thereby also for the writing of histories of the Old Norse-Icelandic literature.

OUTLOOK

In order to construct a brief summary of my selective chronological passage through a number of representative histories of Old Norse-Icelandic literature, I would like to formulate the following generalizations:

1. With a few exceptions (e.g. Vésteinn Ólason), the manuscript tradition of the sagas as a criterion for dating plays hardly any or at least no considerable role in histories of Old Norse-Icelandic literature. Only a few histories seem to see a problem in the fact that there usually is a great span of time between the postulated age of a certain saga and the oldest extant manuscripts. In other words, as a rule, historiographers of Old Norse-Icelandic literature are dating something that is mere conjecture. What actually is extant and can still be studied (in the form of manuscripts from a much later period) is only used to a very small extent in the dating of sagas and thereby for tracing the development of saga literature. This far-reaching neglect of the handwritten basis of the sagas as a criterion for the dating and interpretation of sagas exists independently of the respective position that a given history of literature takes. Both histories of literature that are informed by freeprose-theory (such as those by Heusler, Jón Helgason and de Vries) and those that lean towards the principles of bookprose theory (including those by Sigurður Nordal and Jónas Kristjánsson), as well as a more recent work that connects the two theoretical positions (Vésteinn Ólason), all take as their points of departure the alleged age of a saga, and do not usually address the significance of the actual manuscripts preserving the texts.

Already in an essay from 1990, Örnólfur Thorsson pointed out the discrepancy between the "aldur sögu samkvæmt flestum fræðimönnum" (age of a saga according to most scholars) and the "elstu handrit eða brot" (oldest manuscripts or fragments) and presented this information in the form of a table, a sort of forerunner to the one Vésteinn Ólason gives in his literary history (Örnólfur Thorsson 1990: 47). The conclusions we can draw from the article by Örnólfur Thorsson for the dating as a basis of a historiography of literature are massive and complex. At this point it may suffice to say that it would be essential to take seriously the relatively late age of the manuscript tradition of the Icelandic saga literature and to focus not only on the *creation* of a saga, but also on its creative reception and other changes in the course of its history of literature, that is, its *transmission*.

2. Traditional approaches to saga dating have recently been fundamentally challenged by Gísli Sigurðsson in his work *The Medieval Icelandic Saga and Oral Tradition: A Discourse on Method* (2004). Taking his stance from more recent trends of oral theory, Gísli argues about the issue of dating inter alia as follows:

> If we take the view that the sagas were grounded in an oral tradition, we have to assume that their audiences already possessed a certain amount of knowledge about the people who turn up in them. Each saga then becomes a link in the unrecorded, "immanent" tradition as a whole, something we can now approach only at several removes by reading the sagas, *Landnámabók*, the myths, and other ancient writings whose material was plundered from the tradition as it existed at the time when these works were written. If, on the other hand, we imagine the sagas to be creative fictions produced by individual authors, we have to assume that all the material that is of any relevance to a saga and its characterization is available from the text itself; such an approach also brings with it the need to arrange the sagas into chronological order and entails the supposition that no knowledge was available until it had been written down and then came little by little into wider circulation.
> […]
> One of the most striking implications of a theory of oral origins for our overall view of the sagas and how they should be studied concerns their dating: if they were written against a living background of oral tales, the age of the written sagas becomes considerably less significant. These implications also extend to the methodology used in dating the sagas. The received methods are based largely on comparing supposedly literary relations (*rittengsl*) – correspondences of diction or material taken as evidence of borrowing between written sources. But such relations are seldom verifiable, and so, if information can also be transmitted through an oral tradition, it is only in rare instances that we will be able to say with any confidence that one written work took its material from another, and thus must have been written after it. (Gísli Sigurðsson 2004: 330–31)

There are some clear parallels between Gísli Sigurðsson's line of argument and Andreas Heusler's position on the pre-history and chronology of the sagas.

3. Additionally, from the perspective of general literary studies, one has to ask whether the search for the original – which is, as we have seen, inherent to the problem of dating – is really adequate, given the specific nature of the semi-oral, manuscript-transmitted saga literature. Quite apart from the question of the oral or written modes in which sagas originated, the aim of "new philology" or "material philology," influenced by recent literary and cultural studies, is to break with the teleological perspective of the conven-

tional historiography of literature. As scholars such as Gísli Sigurðsson[6] and Vésteinn Ólason emphasize, the coexistence of different phases and media is in fact constitutive for the literature of medieval Iceland, and this is of course important for the different chronological layers of a saga and consequently for its dating. The constantly changing dates given for individual sagas that are considered important for the genre point to the fundamental problem of fixing a text that is per se unstable in time – quite apart from all the implications that arise from the aversion to all presumed lateness in literature, as the historiography of Old Norse-Icelandic literature still shows very clearly.

If the previously frequent image of blossoming and withering, that is, of the rise, the classical phase and the decline of a genre, is replaced by the now more familiar metaphor of the text as a fluid continuum, then dating – if it is at all philologically possible – can only refer to and define a selected – that is, isolated – stage in this process of textual changes and instabilities (regardless of whether the text happens to be in an oral, written or other medial form). Thus, the dating of a saga, on whatever basis it is made, can never represent more than a small section of the text's development. It is – to use an image from modern media history – a photographical recording, or perhaps rather a still of a film, which otherwise is largely lost.

Bibliography

Andersson, Theodore M. 1964. *The Problem of Icelandic Saga Origins: A Historical Survey*. New Haven, London: Yale University Press.

Einar Ól. Sveinsson 1958. *Dating the Icelandic Sagas: An Essay in Method.* Viking Society for Northern Research. Text Series III. London: Viking Society for Northern Research.

——— 1965. *Ritunartími Íslendingasagna. Rök og rannsóknaraðferð.* Reykjavík: Hið íslenzka bókmenntafélag.

6 For example, as Gísli Sigurðsson states: "the stories it [a saga] contained existed before the time of writing and continued to exist after it" (Gísli Sigurðsson 2004: 332). If this is true, then what should be dated, and how?

Finnur Jónsson [1894–1902] 1920–24. *Den oldnorske og oldislandske litteraturs historie* I–III. Copenhagen: Gad.

Gísli Sigurðsson 2004. *The Medieval Icelandic Saga and Oral Tradition: A Discourse on Method.* Translated by Nicholas Jones. Publications of the Milman Parry Collection of Oral Literature 2. Cambridge, MA: The Milman Parry Collection of Oral Literature, Harvard University. English translation of Gísli Sigurðsson. 2002. *Túlkun Íslendingasagna í ljósi munnlegrar hefðar. Tilgáta um aðferð.* Stofnun Árna Magnússonar á Íslandi. Rit 56. Reykjavík: Stofnun Árna Magnússonar á Íslandi.

Halfdanus Einari 1777. *Sciagraphia Historiæ Literariæ Islandicæ* […]. Havniæ: Sander et Schröder.

——— 1786. *Historia Literaria Islandiæ* […]. Editio Nova. Havniæ: Gyldendalius; Lipsiæ: Proftius.

Heusler, Andreas [1923] 1967. *Die altgermanische Dichtung.* Unveränderter Nachdruck der zweiten neubearbeiteten und vermehrten Ausgabe (1943). Darmstadt: Wissenschaftliche Buchgesellschaft.

Jón Helgason 1934. *Norrøn litteraturhistorie.* Copenhagen: Levin & Munksgaard.

Jónas Kristjánsson 1988. *Eddas and Sagas: Iceland's Medieval Literature.* Translated by Peter Foote. Reykjavík: Hið íslenska bókmenntafélag.

Müller, Peter Erasmus 1813. *Ueber den Ursprung und Verfall der isländischen Historiographie, nebst einem Anhange über die Nationalität der altnordischen Gedichte.* Aus dem Dänischen übersetzt von L. C. Sander. Copenhagen: Johann Friederich Schultz.

——— 1817–20. *Sagabibliothek med Anmærkninger og indledende Afhandlinger* I–III. Copenhagen: J. F. Schultz.

——— 1832. "Om den islandske Historieskrivnings Oprindelse, Flor og Undergang." *Nordisk Tidsskrift for Oldkyndighed* 1: 1–54.

Örnólfur Thorsson 1990. "'Leitin að landinu fagra.' Hugleiðing um rannsóknir á íslenskum fornbókmenntum." *Skáldskaparmál. Tímarit um íslenskar bókmenntir fyrri alda* 1: 28–53.

Sigurður Nordal 1953. "Sagalitteraturen." In *Litteraturhistorie. B. Norge og Island,* edited by Sigurður Nordal (Nordisk Kultur VIII:B). Stockholm: Albert Bonniers förlag; Oslo: H. Aschehoug & Co.s Forlag; Copenhagen: J. H. Schultz Forlag, pp. 180–273.

Vésteinn Ólason 1993. "Íslendingasögur og þættir." In *Íslensk bókmenntasaga* II, 23–164. Reykjavík: Mál og menning.

Vésteinn Ólason 2007. "The Icelandic Saga as a Kind of Literature with Special Reference to its Representation of Reality." In Judy Quinn, Kate Heslop and Tarrin Wills (eds.), *Learning and Understanding in the Old Norse World: Essays in Honour of Margaret Clunies Ross*. Turnhout: Brepols, pp. 27–47.

Vries, Jan de [1941–42] 1999. *Altnordische Literaturgeschichte*. 3. unveränderte Auflage in einem Band. Mit einem Vorwort von Stefanie Würth. Grundriss der Germanischen Philologie 15–16. Berlin, New York: de Gruyter.

THE DATING OF THE OLDEST SAGAS ABOUT EARLY ICELANDERS

Else Mundal

In the medieval literary corpus known as the sagas about early Icelanders, the texts are all anonymous and so their exact time of writing is not known. The sagas about early Icelanders are, however, regarded as the zenith of Icelandic medieval literature. Consequently, it is important to obtain as clear a picture as possible of their development during this most interesting of periods in Icelandic history and their place in the history of literature. As far as establishing their position in the literary culture of medieval Iceland is concerned, the dating of both the genre as a whole as well as of individual sagas is essential.

The dating problem is very complicated for many reasons. We do not have the original manuscripts of any sagas, and since the copying of manuscripts in the Middle Ages involved changes – sometimes only minor, but at other times major changes both concerning style and content – the manuscripts we have preserved do not always provide a firm basis for drawing conclusions about the original written texts. The changes made to a certain saga in later manuscripts may be a good indication of literary tastes in the time period in which the new version of the saga was created, but at the same time such reworked versions of sagas are complicated sources for the period in which they were originally written, even though some distinctive marks of the original saga and the time in which it was created will always be embedded in the reworked text. (For more on this, see Jürg Glauser's article in the present volume.)

The dating of both the sagas about early Icelanders as a genre and of individual sagas within this literary corpus are topics which are, of course, closely related. The productive period of the genre is limited by the earliest sagas at one end and by the latest texts at the other, and the development of the genre can be explained only by the extent to which we can correctly approximate the date of the majority of individual sagas. This sounds simple in principle, but in reality there is no agreement among scholars about which sagas are the oldest or when the sagas about early Icelanders began to be written. Consequently, the dates of most of these sagas are often disputed. Only one thing seems to be agreed upon by most scholars: which of the sagas about early Icelanders are among the youngest.

In this article I will concentrate on the dating problem of the genre, and consider at what time the first sagas about early Icelanders were most likely committed to writing. Additionally, I will discuss a few of the dating criteria that are used both to argue that a particular saga is among the oldest in the genre, and also to redate some of the sagas that were previously regarded as very old, but have now been assigned a much later date by some scholars.

Opinions on when the sagas about early Icelanders began to be written have varied over time. In the nineteenth century it was a common – but not unchallenged – opinion that the majority of the sagas about early Icelanders were written in the last half of the twelfth century. The reason for this dating of the genre was the so-called *Sturlunga* prologue, which is not actually a prologue but a short text that combines *Sturlu saga* and *Prestsaga Guðmundar ins góða* in the compilation *Sturlunga saga*. In one of the manuscripts of *Sturlunga saga*, Króksfjarðarbók, there is a well known passage that reads:

> Flestar allar sǫgur, þær er hér hafa gerzk á Íslandi, váru ritaðar, áðr biskup Brandr Sæmundarson andaðisk, en þær sǫgur, er síðan hafa gerzk, váru lítt ritaðar, áðr Sturla skáld Þórðarson sagði fyrir Íslendinga sǫgur.

> Most of the sagas about events that have taken place here on Iceland were written before Bishop Brandr Sæmundarson died, but only a few sagas about events that took place later were written before the poet Sturla Þórðarson dictated Íslendinga sǫgur.

Up to 1865 this was the only known text of the *Sturlunga* prologue, and the text says clearly that most histories about events that had taken place in Iceland had been written before the death of Bishop Brandr, in 1201. The only matter of discussion seemed to be whether *sǫgur* meant only sagas of the type in the *Sturlunga* compilation or whether the definition also included the sagas about early Icelanders. The scholars were divided in their views.

The discovery of a copy of the other medieval manuscript of *Sturlunga saga*, Reykjarfjarðarbók, revealed another variant of the passage quoted above:

> Flestar allar sǫgur, þær er gerzk hǫfðu á Íslandi, áðr Brandr biskup Sæmundarson andaðist, váru ritaðar, en þær sǫgur, er síðan hafa gerzk, váru lítt ritaðar, áðr Sturla skáld Þórðarson sagði fyrir Íslendinga sǫgur.[1]

> Most of the sagas about events that have taken place on Iceland before Bishop Brandr Sæmundarson died were written, but only a few of the sagas about events that took place later were written before the poet Sturla Þórðarson dictated Íslendingasǫgur.

After this text had been discovered, it soon became clear that it gave the correct reading, and the *Sturlunga* prologue could no longer be used as an argument to date the majority of the sagas about early Icelanders to the period before 1200. Only Finnur Jónsson stuck to his previous view, and continued to argue – partly based on the *Sturlunga* prologue – that many sagas about early Icelanders had been written in the twelfth century.[2]

In the 1920s a new theory was developed that sought to explain how and when the sagas about early Icelanders began to be written. The Danish historian of literature Paul V. Rubow suggested that the first sagas were modelled on the translated *riddarasǫgur*, which would make the genre younger than 1226.[3] Rubow did not find much support for his theory, but since then

1 Both the variants of the text are quoted from Meulengracht Sørensen (1992). He bases his text on Reykjarfjarðarbók, adding variants mentioned in Kr. Kålund's edition of *Sturlunga saga*.

2 An overview of the scholarly discussion about the *Sturlunga* prologue can be found in Meulengracht Sørensen 1992.

3 In the prologue of the Norwegian translation of *Tristrams saga ok Ísondar* it is mentioned that the saga was translated on the request of King Hákon Hákonarson by a Brother Robert in the year 1226. Most scholars assume that this is the first translation of courtly romances into Old Norse.

very different views of when the first sagas about early Icelanders began to be written have existed side by side.

From 1933 onwards the sagas about early Icelanders have been edited in the series Íslenzk fornrit – with *Egils saga Skallagrímssonar*, edited by Sigurður Nordal, as the first to be published. The dating of the sagas in question is always one of the issues that is discussed in the introductions of this series. In the first decades after the series started, the editors of Íslenzk fornrit were the most prominent members of the so-called Icelandic school of saga research, and the introductions to the sagas express the views of this school. Works from scholars belonging to the Icelandic school from around this period that focus on the dating problem include Sigurður Nordal's *Sagalitteraturen* (Nordisk Kultur VIII: B) (1953) and Einar Ól. Sveinsson's *Dating the Icelandic Sagas* (1958), which was later revised and published in Icelandic with the title *Ritunartími Íslendingasagna. Rök og rannsóknaraðferð* (1965). None of the sagas about early Icelanders are dated before 1200 in the introductions to their Íslenzk fornrit editions. In his *Literaturhistorie* Sigurður Nordal divides the sagas about early Icelanders into five groups. His first group consists of five sagas written in the three first decades of the thirteenth century. He dates one saga (*Heiðarvíga saga*) to around 1200 and another (*Fóstbrœðra saga*) to the first decade of that century, sketching a slow and gradual beginning for the genre before writing began in earnest around 1230.

In the first half of the twentieth century and into the 1960s there was opposition between the adherents of bookprose theory, to which the scholars of the Icelandic school belonged, and the adherents of freeprose theory. The two schools had different views on many subjects concerning the sagas about early Icelanders, but they did not disagree very much on the question of when the first sagas were put into writing. Even so there was still a tendency for the adherents of freeprose theory to date the oldest sagas of the genre to a decade or so earlier than the adherents of bookprose theory. In his important book *Upphavet til den islendske ættesaga* (1929), Knut Liestøl, the last big defender of freeprose theory, assumed that the sagas about early Icelanders were put into writing from the beginning of the thirteenth century or a little earlier (Liestøl 1929: 29). In fact, the question of when the first written sagas came into existence was a less important question for the adherents of freeprose theory than for the adherents of bookprose theory since they saw the transition into writing as less fundamental a change. Jón

Helgason, who was not a typical supporter of any of the schools, followed the freeprose school in their slightly earlier dating of the genre. He thought it possible that the oldest sagas were written before 1200 (Jón Helgason 1934: 108).

In recent decades there has been a tendency – especially among Icelandic scholars – to make both individual sagas and the genre as young as possible. Jónas Kristjánsson has, for instance, suggested that *Egils saga* may have been the first saga about early Icelanders to be written, without making the saga older than was previously thought, namely from the 1230s (Jónas Kristjánsson 1990).[4] Torfi Tulinius later suggested that *Egils saga* may have been written as late as around 1240 (Torfi Tulinius 2004: 208–10), while simultaneously supporting Jónas Kristjánsson's theory about *Egils saga* being the first in its genre (Torfi Tulinius 2004: 229–33).

Even after the dating of the genre based on the *Sturlunga* prologue was proved to be fallacious, the first sagas about early Icelanders are dated by different scholars anywhere between c. 1200 and c. 1240. That is an enormously long period of time in literary history, especially if we take into consideration the fact that the thirteenth century in Iceland was a period when many new literary genres came into being and that this was a time of fast development in the history of literature.

If the first sagas about early Icelanders were written around 1200, then another saga corpus, the sagas of kings, would already have been a well-established genre. Similarly, the legends of the Church would have been well known by this time, and the oldest sagas of bishops might have seen the light of day around the same time as the first sagas about early Icelanders. Conversely, the traditions that were later used by the authors of the *fornaldarsǫgur* only existed in oral form at this time, and chivalric sagas were not yet translated. If, on the other hand, the first sagas about early Icelanders were written as late as around 1240, the writing of sagas of kings would have already reached its zenith, although people did not yet know that. The sagas of bishops would have been a well-established genre, probably some of the contemporary sagas already existed, a number of chivalric sagas had been translated in Norway and were probably also well known in Iceland,

4 In his history of literature, *Eddas and Sagas* (1988), Jónas Kristjánsson expressed the more common view that the earliest sagas about early Icelanders were written about 1200 or at the beginning of the thirteenth century (Jónas Kristjánsson 1988: 217).

and the oldest written *fornaldarsǫgur* would have been just around the corner. Consequently, the cultural and literary background for the first written sagas about early Icelanders would have been very different in around 1240 compared to the period around 1200.

Literary works that are possible to date with some degree of accuracy may be beneficial in dating the sagas about early Icelanders. Sturlubók, Sturla Þórðarson's (d. 1284) version of *Landnámabók*, probably written late in his life, makes use of many sagas about early Icelanders, and may thus help us to date these sagas before the period of time when Sturlubók was written. One complicating factor here is that Sturla used Styrmir's (d. 1245) version of *Landnámabók*, Styrmisbók, as a source, and since Styrmisbók is lost it is impossible – or at least very difficult – to know whether Sturla quotes from a written saga about early Icelanders directly or whether he quotes Styrmisbók's quotations from the same saga. In any case, the versions of *Landnámabók* cannot help us in dating the oldest written sagas of the genre.

When writing his sagas of kings, Snorri Sturluson built on a lot of older written works. Snorri wrote his sagas in the late 1220s and around 1230, and at least *The Separate Saga of Óláfr inn helgi* must have been written in the 1220s.[5] The fact that we are able to date Snorri's sagas with some degree of accuracy makes these texts a fixed point in history that can help us to date some works to before the 1220s, or to the early 1220s at the latest. I am not going to discuss the possible use of any saga of Icelanders by Snorri Sturluson (on this subject, see Theodore M. Andersson in the present volume). I will, however, argue that one of the sagas that we know with certainty was used as a source for *The Separate Saga of Óláfr inn helgi* and *Heimskringla*, namely *Færeyinga saga*, may indicate that the sagas about early Icelanders were established as a written genre before *Færeyinga saga* was written.

Færeyinga saga is quoted both in *The Separate Saga of Óláfr ins helgi* and in *Óláfs saga ins helga* in *Heimskringla*. Ólafur Halldórsson, who has edited

5 Whether Snorri Sturluson is the author of the work known as *Heimskringla*, or the author of all parts of this work, is a matter which will not be discussed here. On this problem, see Louis-Jensen 1997.

Færeyinga saga, suggests that Styrmir Kárason inn fróði knew and used *Færeyinga saga* when he wrote his version of the saga about King Óláfr *inn helgi* (Ólafur Halldórsson 1987: ccxxxii–ccxxxiii). Styrmisbók is normally dated to around 1215. It has also been suggested that Gunnlaugr Leifsson *munkr* (d. 1218) used *Færeyinga saga* as a source for his saga about Óláfr Tryggvason.[6] Gunnlaugr Leifsson probably wrote his saga not much later than 1200, and because of this Finnur Jónsson dated *Færeyinga saga* to around 1200 – which is not a very early dating on his part. It is, however, impossible to say for certain whether Styrmir and Gunnlaugr knew and used *Færeyinga saga* or not. *Færeyinga saga* has, however, been dated to around 1200 by other scholars who have not based their dating of the text on the possibilty of *Færeyinga saga* being used as a source shortly after 1200 (Foote 1993: 222; Jónas Kristjánsson 1988: 164–66).

In his edition of *Færeyinga saga*, Ólafur Halldórsson discusses the relationship between *Færeyinga saga* and *Orkneyinga saga*, and he draws the conclusion that the author of *Færeyinga saga* knew and used *Orkneyinga saga* (Ólafur Halldórsson 1987: clxvi–clxx). In addition to Ólafur Halldórsson's arguments I will draw attention to one little detail in *Færeyinga saga* which, in my opinion, points in the same direction. In *Orkneyinga saga* the author carefully reports who is master over the islands – all the islands or half the islands – at any given time. This pertains directly to *Orkneyinga saga* since the islands were an earldom and power was divided most of the time among two branches of the princely family. When the author of *Færeyinga saga* does the same and reports who is the master over all the islands or over half the islands every time there is a change in the power balance among the chieftains in the islands, it sounds more strange since none of these chieftains could be compared with the earls even though they may have executed some power on the king's behalf. Thus, it is very tempting to see *Orkneyinga saga* as the model used by the author of *Færeyinga saga* as far as this little detail is concerned. *Orkneyinga saga* could, of course, have functioned as a model long after it had been written. However, I consider it most likely that this brief remark would have been copied only if *Færeyinga saga* was written so early that the author had very few models besides *Orkneyinga saga* for how to write a saga like *Færeyinga saga*.

6 This was suggested by Finnur Jónsson in the introduction to his edition of the saga (Finnur Jónsson (ed.) 1927: ix).

Orkneyinga saga exists only in a reworked version, probably from around 1230 or some time in the 1230s. The original saga has been dated by most scholars to the early thirteenth century, but it has also been dated slightly earlier, to around 1200 (Ólafur Halldórsson 1987: ccxxxiii; Sigurður Nordal 1913–16: ii–v; Jónas Kristjánsson 1988: 164). In his introduction to *Orkneyinga saga*, Finnbogi Guðmundsson suggests that the saga should be dated to before 1189, because the man he found most likely to be the author died in this year (Finnbogi Guðmundsson 1965: xc–cvi).

I think there is one minor item in the text which may support a very early dating of *Orkneyinga saga*. In chapter 84, Bishop Bjarni Kolbeinsson is mentioned as *Bjarni skáld*. If Bjarni Kolbeinsson, who was appointed bishop in the year 1188, had already been appointed bishop when chapter 84 was written, I think that, in all likelihood, he would have been mentioned as Bishop Bjarni. *Orkneyinga saga* states in chapter 103 that Bishop Bjarni – and here he is called *Bjarni biskup* – had Rǫgnvaldr's bones exhumed and enshrined. According to Icelandic annals this happened in 1192. We do not know for sure whether the notice about Bishop Bjarni transferring Rǫgnvaldr's bones was part of the original saga, but if it was, I think we are approaching the most likely time of writing. The author must have started writing and have written most of the saga before Bjarni was appointed bishop, and since it is not reasonable to assume that it took many years to complete the saga, it was probably finished shortly after 1192. If the passage about Bishop Bjarni transferring Rǫgnvaldr's bones derives from the reworked version of *Orkneyinga saga*, the saga was most likely written while Bjarni was known as Bjarni *skáld*. There is one problem connected to a dating before 1188, or shortly after 1192, namely that it has been suggested that the author of *Orkneyinga saga* used the Norwegian chronicle *Ágrip*, which is dated to around the same time.[7] The author of *Orkneyinga saga* could, however, have used *Ágrip* shortly after it was written. The fact that in the saga Bishop Bjarni is spoken of as *Bjarni skáld* is one of those small details which can be very helpful in the puzzle of dating of sagas.

If *Orkneyinga saga* – or most of *Orkneyinga saga* – was written at a time when Bjarni Kolbeinsson was still only *Bjarni skáld* and not *Bjarni biskup*, *Færeyinga saga* could have used *Orkneyinga saga* as a model and still have been written as early as around 1200 or shortly after. This makes *Færeyinga*

7 See Finnbogi Guðmundsson 1965: civ.

saga a very interesting text in connection with the question of when to date the first sagas about early Icelanders – if strong arguments can be put forward in favour of the view that the author must have used sagas about early Icelanders in addition to *Orkneyinga saga* as models for his work.

While *Orkneyinga saga* has much in common with the chronicles or the sagas of kings, *Færeyinga saga* is very close to the sagas about early Icelanders. The only reason why it is not counted among these sagas is probably that it tells of events that took place in the Faroe Islands, not in Iceland. It is commonly believed that *Færeyinga saga* was written in Iceland – though certainly built on Faroese tradition – which poses the fundamental question of whether an Icelandic author would have had the idea to write about conflicts between Faroese families without the existence of written sagas in which the main theme was conflict between Icelandic families. In my opinion it would be strange if a saga about Faroese families were the first saga about early Icelanders.

There is another small detail in the composition of *Færeyinga saga* that may indicate that the author looked for a model for how to begin his saga and found that model in one or more written sagas about early Icelanders: many sagas about early Icelanders begin the story by mentioning the forefathers who emigrated from Norway and settled in Iceland. The author of *Færeyinga saga* begins his story by mentioning the first settler in the Faroe Islands, Grímr kamban.[8] He is, however, not the forefather of any of the saga characters. As in many sagas about early Icelanders, the author here also mentions that a lot of people fled from Norway during the reign of Haraldr hárfagri. Furthermore, he states that the family of Þrándr í Gǫtu descended from Ólof, the daughter of Þorsteinn rauðr who belonged to one of those families who fled, but he does not say how Þrándr í Gǫtu and Ólof were related. It is obvious that the author has tried to put together elements that he felt were necessary components of the beginning of a saga, but in *Færeyinga saga* these elements are totally disconnected. The best explanation for this simultaneously "traditional" and disconnected beginning of the saga is that the author found his model in some already written sagas about early Icelanders. The oral tradition behind the sagas would be a less

8 It has been argued that the mention of Grímr kamban was not part of the original saga. The textual problems connected to the beginning of the saga have been investigated by Ólafur Halldórsson who arrived at the conclusion that the first chaper of the saga is original (Ólafur Halldórsson 1987: c–ci).

obvious model since it is not likely that a story about a certain hero had to start with his forefathers in Norway every time it was told. In the written sagas, however, this beginning is not compulsory but very common.

It is impossible to say which sagas about early Icelanders the author of *Færeyinga saga* knew and used as his model. It must, however, have been sagas with the opening that detailed the forefathers who fled from the Norwegian king and settled in Iceland.

The criteria used for dating the earliest sagas have, of course, varied over time, from one school of saga research to another. To which dating criteria they attached the most importance may also have differed from one scholar to another.

The adherents of freeprose theory – at least at an early stage – were inclined to say that the oldest sagas were the best; these were put into writing at the time when the art of oral storytelling had reached its zenith. Later, the oral art form declined as a result of the written culture. Conversely, adherents of bookprose theory would say that the first authors of sagas about early Icelanders must have had some initial difficulties because of the lack of models for the new written genre. Characteristics of the oldest sagas would then be a clumsy and helpless composition. These two views were not so contrary to each other as it may seem since the adherents of freeprose theory attached importance to well-told episodes when judging the quality of the texts, while the adherents of bookprose theory gave importance to the overall composition. Therefore they would in fact agree on the early dating of some sagas, for example *Heiðarvíga saga*.

Sigurður Nordal saw the sagas about early Icelanders as a genre that grew out of the sagas of kings, with the *þættir* as a connecting link between the two genres (Sigurður Nordal 1953: 244, 251). He listed the sagas *Heiðarvíga saga*, *Fóstbræðra saga*, *Hallfreðar saga*, *Kormáks* saga, *Bjarnar saga* and *Egils saga* (in that chronological order) as older than Snorri's sagas of kings (Sigurður Nordal 1953: 236). The connection to the sagas of kings would, however, be only an indication of early composition since the relationship between the king and a hero of a saga about early Icelanders could also be a theme in later sagas.

Sigurður Nordal also outlined a development in the writing of the sagas about early Icelanders from sagas that built on tradition – especially skaldic stanzas – written in the first three decades of the thirteenth century, through those that were less dependent on tradition, written between 1230 and 1280, to those written at the end of the century, which were more or less fictional with only a limited use of oral tradition such as *Njáls saga* and *Hrafnkels saga* (Sigurður Nordal 1953: 235–61). The adherents of freeprose theory also believed in a somewhat similar development, from a very close relationship between the oral and the written saga to a stage where the contribution of the writer could be considerable. However, according to freeprose theory this was a development that was found only in the long sagas.[9] In his *Norrøn litteraturhistorie* Jón Helgason expresses a view that, in this case, is closest to the principles of freeprose theory:

> Islændingesagaerne begynder med de typiske tradisjonssagaer, f. eks. *Heiðarvíga saga, Reykdœla saga, Vápnfirðinga saga, Droplaugarsona saga.* ... Til de ældste slutter sig *Ljósvetninga saga* og *Eyrbyggja saga*, som også først og fremmest gengiver tradition, skønt de er for lange og episodiske til at kunne føres tilbage til en enkelt mundtlig saga. (Jón Helgason 1934: 131)

> The sagas of Icelanders started with the typical tradition-based sagas, for example, *Heiðarvíga saga, Reykdœla saga, Vápnfirðinga saga, Droplaugarsona saga.* ... *Ljósvetninga saga* and *Eyrbyggja saga* join the oldest. They, too, primarily retell tradition, even though they are too long and episodic to be based on one single oral saga.

In his book *Dating the Icelandic Sagas* from 1958, and in the Icelandic reworked version from 1965, Einar Ól. Sveinsson discusses the different dating criteria used to date the sagas about early Icelanders. I will not go into his different dating criteria in detail (see Torfi Tulinius's discussion of his methods in the present volume). However, some of the criteria he discusses at length that have been used in the dating – and redating – of sagas have provoked discussions in the later decades. I will comment on the use of three of these dating criteria in particular: 1) The literary relationship – or in Icelandic *rittengsl* – between different sagas, which can at least help us devise a relative chronology; 2) The method of dating a saga by looking for events or conditions in the authors' own time that may be reflected in the sagas; and 3) The artistic quality of the text.

9 See Mundal 1977: 141–57, especially p. 155.

Attempting to map out the relationship or *rittengsl* between different sagas is a method that has been used quite frequently. We have *rittengsl* when it is obvious that one text has used the other, and this helps us to place two sagas in a relative chronology, which in some cases may be nearly as helpful as knowing the absolute chronology. The oldest sagas should be the ones that do not use other sagas about early Icelanders in this way.

A good point of departure for a discussion of this problem is Bjarni Guðnason's book about *Heiðarvíga saga* (1993). He argues that this saga is not one of the oldest, but considerably younger than previously believed. In the introduction to the saga in Íslenzk fornrit 3 (1938), Sigurður Nordal stated that the author built on oral tradition, and he was not able to point to any written text that this author had used. The author of *Heiðarvíga saga* used a saying, which is also found in three sagas of kings, the so-called *Oldest Saga*, *Ágrip* and *Sverris saga*. However, sayings are not good examples of *rittengsl*, and in any case the *Oldest Saga* and *Ágrip* must be older than *Heiðarvíga saga* (Sigurður Nordal 1938: cxv and cxxxix–cxl).

Bjarni Guðnason, on the other hand, found *rittengsl* between *Heiðarvíga saga* and many other sagas, and according to him *Heiðarvíga saga* had not only been used by later authors, but the author of *Heiðarvíga saga* also knew and used older sagas. He was convinced that *Heiðarvíga saga* borrowed from, for example, *Laxdœla saga*, which most scholars agree was written around the middle of the thirteenth century. Another saga that has also been regarded as one of the oldest, *Bjarnar saga*, has, according to Bjarni Guðnason, borrowed from *Heiðarvíga saga* and is therefore even younger.

The problem is deciding whether this really is the case. Sometimes it is very difficult to know which of the sagas is the borrower and which has been borrowed from. This is, of course, a complicating factor of this important dating criterion. In saga genres that are less artistically composed than the sagas about early Icelanders, such as in some *fornaldarsǫgur* and young Icelandic romances, motifs that are borrowed will sometimes include elements that have no function in the new text and become so-called blind motifs. In such cases it is relatively easy to identify borrowings and to see which text is the elder and the younger. In the well-crafted sagas about early Icelanders there are not many borrowings of this type, and in cases where common motifs fit equally well in two sagas we lack the methods to decide which way the borrowing goes.

Another very important question is what kinds of similarities and how many of them must be found in two texts before we can talk about *rittengsl* at all. Common motifs, themes and so on could, of course, be examples of *rittengsl*, meaning that one author has used an older written saga as his source, but this is a very complicated matter in relation to the sagas about early Icelanders. What makes this so complicated is that there is – more or less – oral tradition behind the written sagas. Even though most scholars admit that the written sagas were based on oral tradition – at least to some extent – there is often, in my opinion, a tendency to forget this fact when drawing conclusions about the relationships between written sagas. If the sagas about early Icelanders had been the works of authors who made up the whole story themselves with no basis in oral tradition, similarities in themes, use of the same motifs and so on could indicate *rittengsl*, especially if the similarities were close and numerous. If we take the oral tradition on which the written sagas were built into account, it is no longer obvious that similarities in themes and motifs indicate connections between two written texts. It is equally possible that a story about one hero at the oral stage influenced another story about a different hero. From later folklore we know that such "borrowings" at the oral stage were very common. This means, in my opinion, that undisputed examples of *rittengsl* between sagas demand much closer similarities than *rittengsl* when used in the context of modern literature. I would in fact be reluctant to accept anything other than striking verbal resemblances of some length as reliable examples of *rittengsl*, and even in such cases there would be the possibility of a common source.

Of course, similarities in themes and motifs could indicate *rittengsl*. As argued above, I think that there are reasons to believe that the author of *Færeyinga saga* knew both *Orkneyinga saga* and one or more of the written sagas about early Icelanders. However, the weight of evidence of similarities of a kind other than striking verbal resemblances of some length must be judged individually, and how convincing they are will depend on how unique they are. The reason to believe that the author of *Færeyinga saga* had picked up the little detail from *Orkneyinga saga* – namely that he repeatedly reports who ruled over half the islands or all the islands – is that this detail is very unique and could not have been borrowed from any other saga than *Orkneyinga saga*. The direction of the borrowing is revealed by the fact that the information about rulership is much more relevant in a saga about Orcadian earls than in a saga about Faroese chieftains. The possibility of borrowing at the oral stage is not very likely, partly because the oral traditions behind *Orkneyinga saga* and *Færeyinga saga* in all likelihood did not intermingle very much but were transmitted on separate islands, and partly because this sort of information was not a central part of oral storytelling. It is more likely a detail that was added by the author of *Orkneyinga saga*. In a case such as this, the borrowing author did not necessarily have the text he borrowed from in front of him. He could remember something he had read previously or something that had been read to him. The similarities between the beginning of *Færeyinga saga* and the sagas about early Icelanders can be explained in the same way. There is, however, a gradual transition from a *rittengsl* of the type that shows close verbal resemblances of some length through to verbal resemblances that are less convincing (such as parallel motifs, themes or common details in two sagas that for some reason or other are likely to be the result of a *rittengsl*), to common motifs that could be the result of influence at the oral stage as well as at the written, or are too frequent and too common to show anything at all. In many cases it is extremely difficult to determine in which cases we have a *rittengsl* and in which cases a *rittengsl* is only a possibility, and as a dating criterion it is a difficult criterion to use.

An even more important dating criterion for Bjarni Guðnason than *rittengsl* when dating *Heiðarvíga saga* to the last half of the thirteenth century was that it was the period of time in which the ideas that the saga expressed fit. He read the saga as a *friðarsaga*. The author is critical of the old custom of blood vengeance, and the saga is seen in connection with the Norwegian king's attempt to abolish blood vengeance from the middle of the thirteenth century onwards.

If this was the only possible reading of the saga, the ideology of the saga might be a good dating criterion – although in the middle of the thirteenth century the Church had, at least in principle, been critical of blood vengeance for a long time. Therefore the middle of the thirteenth century is not the earliest possible time for the writing of a saga that expresses a negative attitude towards blood vengeance. Moreover, to read *Heiðarvíga saga* as a saga which speaks against blood vengeance is only one interpretation, and I do not think it is the only possible one, and therefore not convincing as a dating criterion.

I agree, however, with Bjarni Guðnason that reflections of ideas of the times in some cases can provide interesting arguments for dating. In a previous work I have suggested a dating of *Eyrbyggja saga* to the period after the union with Norway in 1262–64, partly based on an interpretation of the ideology of the saga (Mundal 2000a). Contrary to other sagas about early Icelanders, *Eyrbyggja saga* reveals that the first settlers did not flee from Norway for idealistic reasons. Some of them were negative elements in society who fled from the king's law and order. The saga draws up a picture of settlers who never managed to create a stable society: everyone was fighting everyone. The critical attitude towards the idealized picture of the past in the rest of the genre – especially in the first chapter – may be seen as being in dialogue with *Laxdœla saga*, which shows a close parallel in the first chapter.[10] The cynical Snorri goði, who is the strong chieftain in *Eyrbyggja saga*, is modelled on the chieftains of the Sturlunga period. From the beginning, the society these people created was condemned to submit to the Norwegian king from whom they had initially fled. The non-idealized picture of the Icelandic society is, according to this analysis, written by an analytical author who was disappointed with the fall of the Icelandic Commonwealth.

Ideas and ideologies are, however, very seldom expressed clearly in the sagas about early Icelanders, and since different scholars will very often see different ideas and ideologies reflected, this is a criterion that should be supported by other dating criteria. Additionally, reflections of ideas from the author's time will only in a very few cases – if in any at all – provide us with an exact dating criterion, but may perhaps help us to distinguish very early sagas from very late ones – if scholars agree on what ideas are being expressed.

Reflections in the sagas of events in the author's own time may be more specific than reflections of conditions and ideas, but there will always be the question of whether an episode in a saga is a reflection of a certain historical event, whether it is a reflection of another event that we might not know of, or whether it is not a reflection of a historical event in the author's own time at all but simply a story the author knew from oral traditions, or one he had made up himself.

The time in which the author lived is no doubt reflected in the written sagas through events, conditions and ideas. It may, however, be a matter of debate whether such reflections from the author's own time are to be seen as good dating criteria. How this is judged is probably also dependent on

10 There is also a reference to *Laxdœla saga* at the end of *Eyrbyggja saga*.

the individual scholar's view of the sagas. A scholar who holds the opinion that the saga authors first and foremost wanted to tell stories about the past might be less inclined to see the author's own era reflected in the sagas than a scholar who reads the sagas first and foremost as literary works that express the author's views and ideas. Many scholars have argued that the oldest sagas were *tradisjonssagaer*. If that is correct, then reflections from the author's own time period are perhaps a less obvious dating criterion concerning the oldest sagas than the sagas written at a later date.

The artistic quality of a saga is one of the dating criteria that Einar Ol. Sveinsson discusses in some detail (Einar Ól. Sveinsson 1965: 143–60). His judgement of *Heiðarvíga saga* is:

> Öll er frásögn hennar ójöfn og hvergi fáguð, og má vænta slíkra einkenna á æskuárum bókmenntategundar, en þau hverfa nokkuð eftir því sem íþrótt vex við æfingu. (Einar Ól. Sveinsson 1965: 148)

> All its narrative is uneven and never elaborate, and one should expect such characteristics in the youth of the genre, but they disappear to some extent as the exercise improves with practice.

Just as it seems logical that the authors of the earliest sagas were more dependent on oral tradition than later authors – as many scholars have argued – it also seems logical that authors who wrote without having older sagas as models had a more difficult task than authors who wrote at a time when the written genre was well established. In the individual cases these dating criteria are, however, very uncertain criteria even if they generally happen to be correct. Authors who wrote at the beginning of the thirteenth century were dependent on the oral tradition because oral stories were the only sources available to them, except for an early version of *Landnámabók*, but authors who wrote later may have *chosen* to build primarily on oral tradition. The establishment of the written genre, of course, gave later authors patterns to follow, but the quality of a written saga was not only dependent on good patterns and models. The authors' artistic skill and individual talent must have been more decisive for the final result. Therefore we should not expect all early sagas to fit the description given by Einar Ól. Sveinsson above, and not all authors of late sagas were able to write artistic masterpieces.

Another complicating factor is that it is very hard to determine whether authors and audiences in the thirteenth century would have agreed with saga scholars of today on the characteristics of literary quality. Moreover, it is a matter of discussion whether we can be sure that characteristics which normally have been taken as hallmarks of an early saga, such as loose composition and uneven style, really are hallmarks of an early saga, or whether they are the result of an author who has intentionally chosen this way of writing, not because he is helpless or unskilled. Again, *Eyrbyggja saga* offers a good example of characteristics that most scholars have held to be hallmarks of an old saga, but which I think also could be something else.

In his introduction to *Eyrbyggja saga* in Íslenzk fornrit 4 (1935) Einar Ól. Sveinsson sums up his characteristics of the saga by stating that, to a large extent, it builds on oral tradition and that it is difficult to find anything that the author definitely made up himself. Further hallmarks that he pointed out were:

> að efnið hefði ekki runnið saman í eina heild, og vísindi og sagnaskemmtun væri ekki eins samgróið og hjá Snorra Sturlusyni. Mælir þetta allt með allmiklum aldri. (Einar Ól. Sveinsson 1935: li)

> that the subject matters have not been blended to become a whole, and that learning and amusement were not so interwoven as with Snorri Sturluson. All this indicates a considerable age.

Einar Ól. Sveinsson in fact gave a positive evaluation of *Eyrbyggja saga*. What he intended by his critical remarks was that the causal relation between different parts of the saga was sometimes too weak, and particularly that the style of some chapters was very different from the style of other chapters. The factual and sober style of the story that dealt with Snorri goði and most of the other chieftains of the region contrasted with the romantic story about Þuríðr and Bjǫrn Breiðvíkingakappi, which again stood in sharp contrast to the ghost stories about Þórólfr bægifótr and the so-called *Fróðáundr*. Einar Ól. Sveinsson saw this uneven style as the result of the author's inability to make an artistic whole out of his material, and in this respect he saw his failure as an indication of an old saga.

The question is, however, whether this mixing of writing modes could signify anything other than an early saga written at a time when the "rules" of the genre were not fully developed. If we take a closer look at the saga, literary patterns seem to emerge that are different from those found in other sagas about early Icelanders. *Eyrbyggja saga* does not actually have a principal character, but Snorri goði is the most central figure in the saga. The stories of his youth, his manhood and his old age are divided from each other by the two big ghost scenes: the story about Þórólfr bægifótr (chapters 30–34) and the story about the *Fróðáundr* following Þorgunna's death (chapters 50–55) that function as a sort of division between the three main parts of Snorri's story. In addition, the story about Þórólfr bægifótr binds the loosely composed saga together. The author ends the story about Þórólfr bægifótr in chapter 34 in a way that signals that his ghost will turn up again later, and until that has happened the saga cannot be ended. The romantic story about Þuríðr and Bjǫrn Breidvíkingakappi serves the same end. The story is divided into several episodes, and small pieces of the story are told with intervals up to chapter 47 when Bjǫrn had to leave Iceland for the second time. However, as in the case of Þórólfr bægifótr, the author ends the story so as to indicate that we will hear somthing more about Bjǫrn, and *Eyrbyggja saga* cannot end until we have got the final part of the story. Snorri goði's story is brought to an end in the last chapter of the saga, the story about Þuríðr and Bjǫrn Breiðvíkingakappi ends in the penultimate chapter, and the story about Þórólfr bægifótr in the previous chapter. Both the story of Þórólfr bægifótr and the story about Þuríðr and Bjǫrn function as very visible tacking threads – in different colours – that serve to bind a loosely composed saga together.[11]

There is somthing about the composition of *Eyrbyggja saga* that seems to be so consciously arranged that there is reason to ask whether the very unique construction of *Eyrbyggja saga* could be the result of an author's experiments with the established conventions of saga composition and modes of writing rather than the result of "starting problems." If that should be the case, then what seems to be loose composition and uneven style are more likely to be the hallmarks of a late saga rather than of an early saga.

11 A fuller analysis of the saga is found in Mundal 2002a.

We do not know which of the sagas about early Icelanders were written first. We have, however, a very early saga that closely resembles the sagas about early Icelanders, namely *Færeyinga saga*. As I have argued, the author of this saga tried to find models for how to write it. This can be regarded as a sort of "starting problem" of the same kind as the clumsy and helpless composition that the adherents of bookprose theory saw as indications of early composition. I have argued in a previous work that *Bjarnar saga*, which most scholars have regarded to be among the oldest sagas but has been redated by Bjarni Guðnason, is modelled on the genre of the sagas or legends of bishops as far as the composition is concerned (Mundal 2000b). That could indicate that the saga was written at a time when the sagas of bishops was a well known genre, but only very few, if any, sagas about early Icelanders existed. This type of reasoning is similar to Sigurður Nordal's argument that the first sagas about early Icelanders grew out of the sagas of kings, which in fact existed prior to the oldest sagas about early Icelanders. There is, however, one important difference: in many cases a thematic overlapping exists between the sagas of kings and the sagas about early Icelanders, since the heroes of the sagas about early Icelanders spent time at the Norwegian court. The relationship between the Norwegian king – or earl – and the Icelandic hero may be a subject in late sagas as well as in early sagas, and the relation to sagas of kings is therefore not a good dating criterion even if the existence of written sagas of kings may be one of the factors that explains the origin of the genre of sagas about early Icelanders. The thematic overlapping between sagas or legends of bishops and sagas about early Icelanders is far less extensive. It is therefore reasonable to believe that if an author of one of the sagas about early Icelanders used the sagas of bishops, he was in need of a model for writing. Such a need would have been considerably greater at the beginning than at the end of the thirteenth century.

One characteristic of *Færeyinga saga* mentioned by Ólafur Halldórsson in his introduction to the saga is that this very early saga shares some motifs with much younger sagas, even *fornaldarsǫgur* and fairy tales (Ólafur Halldórsson 1987: clxvi–cxciv). Here I think we may have a characteristic of early sagas that has been overlooked: as in the very young sagas, they are more modally mixed than the sagas written later when the genre was well established. I have suggested earlier that the oral tradition was less divided into genre types and consequently more modally mixed than the later written sagas (Mundal 2005). One example of this is *Bjarnar saga*. The hero of this saga kills a *flugdreki*, a flying dragon, which is a typical *fornaldarsaga* motif, and the characteristic that they are modally mixed probably fits with some of the other sagas that we assume to be old. It may, however, be very difficult to see the difference between the modal mixing derived from the modally mixed tradition upon which the first authors of the sagas about early Icelanders had to build, and the modal mixing derived from authors of late sagas about early Icelanders who were influenced by written *fornaldarsǫgur* at a much later date.

There are strong indications that the first sagas about early Icelanders were written before *Færeyinga saga*. This would place the origin of the written genre to the period around 1200, which is earlier than is considered to be the case by most scholars today. The period around 1200 is, however, a date that, in my opinion, fits very well with the development of a written culture in Iceland. If the first sagas about early Icelanders were written around 1200, the literary development from the last decades of the twelfth century onwards would be a steady and in many ways expected one. In the last decades of the twelfth century, sagas of kings were written in Iceland. Both the two sagas about Óláfr Tryggvason written by the monks Oddr Snorrason and Gunnlaugr Leifsson in Þingeyrar belong to this period, as well as probably the so-called *Oldest saga* about Óláfr the saint. *Grýla,* the first part of *Sverris saga,* was written in this period, but in Norway. It is difficult to say whether Karl Jónsson finished *Sverris saga* after he had returned to Iceland as abbot of the convent in Þingeyrar in 1188 or whether it was completed by someone else and somewhere else. However, it seems that the writing of literature about kings, which started very slowly with the works of Sæmundr fróði (in Latin) and Ari fróði (*Konunga ævi*) early in the twelfth century, had become a popular genre by the later decades of the century. The translation of legends must have begun in the very early stages of the development of centres of writing, since these texts were important to the Church. However, in the last decades of the twelfth century a new type of literature started to be translated, pseudo-historical works such as *Romverja saga* and *Bretta sǫgur*. At this time, literature was also being produced in Iceland that can be characterized as learned literature, starting with the so-called *First Grammatical Treatise* written around 1150. Centres of learning and writing existed that were connected to convents (for example Þingeyrar), to the episcopal sees (Bishop Jón Ǫgmundarson founded a school in Hólar) and to the residences of chieftains (for example Oddi where Snorri Sturluson was raised). The literary milieu in Iceland around 1200 was such that we might expect that the first decades of the thirteenth century would be a continuation of the flourishing literary life that had developed in the previous decades. However, if the first sagas about early Icelanders were written as late as the 1230s or around 1240, the first sagas about Icelandic bishops would have been written somtime before then but after the beginning of the century, although they were few in number for good reasons. A few sagas about kings were written in the period between Gunnlaugr Leifsson's saga about Óláfr Tryggvason (around 1200) and Snorri's sagas of kings. *Morkinskinna* was written in Iceland in this period, as was Styrmir's saga about Óláfr the saint, which was a rewriting of the so-called *Oldest saga*. If Karl Jónsson completed *Sverris saga* himself, then this must have been done in the convent of Þingeyrar after the death of King Sverrir in 1202 and before Karl Jónsson died in 1213, but the saga may also have been completed by someone else than Karl. It is a common opinion that the short version of *Bǫglunga sǫgur*, which covers the period from King Sverrir's death up to 1208, was written by an Icelander. Whether it was written in Iceland is more uncertain, and even less certain is the provenience of the longer version of the saga, which covers the period up to 1217 and must have been written after that time. As Knut Helle argued (Helle 1958: 93–111), this version may have been written in Norway (Niðarós), and it is most likely that *Fagrskinna* was also written there. This means that the number of sagas of kings written in Iceland in the thirteenth century before the writings of Snorri was not very high.

The so-called *Sturlunga* prologue in Reykjarfjarðarbók indicates that the majority of contemporary sagas were written late in the thirteenth century, and it is commonly believed that the first *fornaldarsǫgur* were put into writing around 1250. If the first sagas about early Icelanders were written in the 1230s or around 1240, then the middle of the thirteenth century must have been an extremely productive period, while by contrast, not very much was produced during the first decades of the century. On the other hand, if the writing of sagas about early Icelanders started around 1200, the development from a very solid literary and cultural basis laid in the late twelfth century would be more steady and logical.

From the discussions of the dating criteria – *rittengsl*, the author's use of contemporary historical events as models, and the artistic quality of the text – we can conclude that none of these criteria are by themselves sufficient as a foundation upon which to base firm conclusions. However, if several criteria point in the same direction, they might together create a more solid basis for dating a saga. Fitting certain sagas into more general patterns of development – for example their relationship to the sagas of kings, their relationship to oral tradition or their use of certain formulas (see the article of Slavica Ranković in the present volume) – places an individual saga within the history of the genre. However, this cannot be used as an exact dating criterion, but taken together with other criteria, a saga's relationship to the general developments of a genre may give us some interesting hints.

A saga's structural or stylistic dependence on a genre other than the sagas about early Icelanders is in my opinion an indication of an early date, as I have argued in the case of *Bjarnar saga Hítdœlakappa.* Following the same reasoning, sagas using motifs which are typical of the *fornaldarsǫgur* should be ascribed a relatively young age and considered to be influenced by that genre. However, motifs can be borrowed from oral tradition as well, and if the tradition behind the saga genres – including the sagas about early Icelanders – was more modally mixed than with the written genres, all examples of such modal mixing must be judged individually.

The most interesting dating criteria are perhaps small and very exact details recorded in the texts, such as when the bishop Bjarni Kolbeinsson is called Bjarni *skáld* in *Orkneyinga saga*. However, details that can date the writing of a certain saga in relation to people of the author's own time are not often found in sagas about the past. References to other sagas, such as the mention of *Laxdœla saga* and *Heiðarvíga saga* in the last chapter of *Eyrbyggja saga*, are small details of a similar type that can be very useful for a relative dating – provided that we can take it for granted that the sagas mentioned are written sagas. The problem with small details such as the name of a person or a saga and the title or occupation of a person is that names might easily have been added and titles changed in later manuscripts. However, such small details should not be overlooked in the discussion of saga dating.

Bibliography

Bjarni Guðnason 1993. *Túlkun Heiðarvígasögu* (Studia Islandica 50). Reykjavík: Bókmenntafræðistofnun Háskóla Íslands.

Einar Ól. Sveinsson and Matthías Þórðarson (eds.) 1935. *Eyrbyggja saga* (Íslenzk fornrit 4). Reykjavík; Hið íslenska fornritafélag (Einar Ól. Sveinsson is the author of the introduction to *Eyrbyggja saga*).

——— 1958. *Dating the Icelandic Sagas: An Essay in Method.* London: Viking Society for Northern Research.

——— 1965. *Ritunartími Íslendingasagna. Rök og rannsóknaraðferð.* Reykjavík: Hið Íslenska bókmenntafélag.

Finnbogi Guðmundsson (ed.) 1965. *Orkneyinga saga* (Íslenzk fornrit 34). Reykjavík: Hið Íslenska fornritafélag.

Foote, Peter 1993. "Færeyinga saga." In Phillip Pulsiano (ed.), *Medieval Scandinavia: An Encyclopedia.* New York and London: Garland Publishing.

Finnur Jónsson (ed.) 1927. *Færeyingasaga.* Copenhagen: Det kongelige Nordiske Oldskriftsselskab.

Jónas Kristjánsson 1988. *Eddas and Sagas.* Reykjavík: Hið íslenska bókmenntafélag.

——— 1990. "Var Snorri Sturluson upphafsmaður Íslendingasagna?" *Andvari*, n.s., XXXII: 85–105.

Jón Helgason 1934. *Norrøn litteraturhistorie.* Copenhagen: Levin & Munksgaard.

Liestøl, Knut 1929. *Upphavet til den islendske ættesaga.* Oslo: Aschehoug.

Meulengracht Sørensen, Preben 1992. "Næsten alle sagaer var skrevet." In Finn Hødnebø et al. (eds.), *Eyvindarbók. Festskrift til Eyvind Fjeld Halvorsen 4. Mai 1992.* Oslo: Institutt for nordistikk og litteraturvitenskap.

Mundal, Else 1977. *Sagadebatt.* Oslo, Bergen and Tromsø: Universitetsforlaget.

——— 2000a. "Introducción [to *Saga de los Habitantes de Eyr*]." In Ma Pilar Fernández Álvaez and Teodoro Manrique Antón (eds.), *Saga de los Habitantes de Eyr.* Valencia: Publicationes De La Residencia De Estudiantes.

——— 2000b. "*Bjarnar saga Hítdœlakappa.* Svak soge med interessante sider." *Nordica Bergernsia* 23 [Bergen]: Nordisk intitutt, Universitet i Bergen, pp. 187–202.

——— 2005. "Færeyinga saga – A Fine Piece of Literature in Pieces." In Andras Mortensen and Símun V. Arge (eds.), *Viking and Norse in the North Atlantic: Select Papers from the Proceedings of the Fourteenth Viking Congress, Tórshavn, 19–30 July 2001*. Tórshavn: Føroya Fróðskaparfelag, pp. 43–51.

Ólafur Halldórsson (ed.) 1987. *Færeyinga saga*. Reykjavík: Stofnun Árna Magnússonar á Íslandi.

Rubow, Paul V. 1928. "Den islandske Familieroman." *Tilskueren* 45. Copenhagen.

Sigurður Nordal 1953. "Sagalitteraturen" (*Nordisk Kultur* VIIIB). Stockholm, Oslo and Copenhagen: Bonniers förlag, H. Aschehoug & CO.s forlag, J.H. Schults forlag.

Sigurður Nordal (ed.) 1913–1916. *Orkneyinga saga*. Copenhagen: Samfund til Udgivelse af Gammel Nordisk Litteratur.

Sturlunga saga. 1906–11. Edited by Kr. Kålund. Copenhagen: Det kongelige Nordiske Oldskriftselskab.

Torfi Tulinius 2004. *Skáldið í skriftinni – Snorri Sturluson og Egils saga*. Reykjavík: Hið Íslenska bókmenntafélag.

REDATING *FÓSTBRŒÐRA SAGA*

Theodore M. Andersson

The general proposition I would like to offer here is that the sagas could be dated somewhat earlier than is now commonly the case, and, by extension, that saga writing is largely concentrated in the first half of the thirteenth century. We may begin by reviewing what we can deduce about saga-writing activity in the period ca. 1200 to 1250. An important hinge is *Heimskringla*, which is almost always dated to fit within Snorri Sturluson's life span and is accordingly assigned to the period 1225–1235. But it cannot be proved absolutely that Snorri was the author of *Heimskringla*, and his dates are therefore not a perfectly secure index.[1] Nonetheless, if the Kringla version is from the middle of the century, and furthermore represents a reworking of the original redaction of *Óláfs saga helga*, it is perhaps safe to say that the original cannot date from much later than 1240 and may serve as a key to what saga texts already existed at that time.[2]

Óláfs saga helga alone presupposes and subsumes a number of earlier sagas, notably the *Oldest Saga of Saint Olaf*, the *Legendary Saga*, and the largely lost version by Styrmir Kárason. Exactly how far back this tradition reaches is not clear, but 1210 to 1220 might be a reasonable guess for the first full-fledged sagas. *Heimskringla* as a whole also presupposes the existence of the other king's saga compendia, *Morkinskinna* and *Fagrskinna*. Internal criteria in *Morkinskinna* suggest a date around 1220, with *Fagrskin-*

1 See most recently Jon Gunnar Jørgensen 2007: 2. In what follows I am indebted to Torfi Tulinius for several bibliographical references.

2 On the dating issues Jørgensen 2007: 80–86. On the chronology of composition Jørgensen 2007: 90–91.

na a little later. Returning to *Óláfs saga helga*, we can observe that it also presupposes other large-scale sagas, some version of *Orkneyinga saga* and *Færeyinga saga*. Ólafur Halldórsson has dated *Færeyinga saga* around 1215, and *Orkneyinga saga* must be at least that old, though it has also been dated much earlier.[3]

In the first part of *Heimskringla* it is also clear that the author made use of Oddr Snorrason's *Óláfs saga Tryggvasonar* and a version of *Jómsvíkinga saga*. There is no hard evidence on when Oddr's saga was translated from the original Latin into Icelandic, but since the original of *Óláfs saga Tryggvasonar* dates from the period 1180–1200, and since there was so much activity in Icelandic after 1200, it seems likely that Oddr's saga had been turned into Icelandic, along with Gunnlaugr Leifsson's version, before the author of *Heimskringla* made use of it.[4]

The relationship of *Heimskringla* to *Egils saga* is not transparent, but they are thematically related. *Egils saga* centers on the relationship of Icelandic chieftains and Norwegian kings, and this is an important subtheme in *Óláfs saga helga*. The two sagas are therefore political companion pieces and might plausibly belong to the same period.[5] The sagas tabulated here are tantamount to a list of *Heimskringla*'s sources, and the list is an imposing one. It includes a number of sagas about Óláfr Haraldsson and Óláfr Tryggvason, the large-scale compendia *Morkinskinna* and *Fagrskinna*, the island sagas *Orkneyinga saga* and *Færeyinga saga*, together with *Jómsvíkinga saga*, and perhaps the classical family saga *Egils saga*. This is not just a considerable library of saga texts but a list of full-length and distinguished texts. *Egils saga*, *Færeyinga saga*, and *Morkinskinna* stand out in particular. If saga writing was so extensive and of such high quality in the first half of the thirteenth century, why is it that the bulk of sagas is so frequently dated in the middle or even late in that century? It is particularly mysterious that sagas of distinctly inferior quality are dated so long after the great surge

3 See Ólafur Halldórsson in Íslenzk fornrit (ÍF) 25: LXXI–LXXVII. In this volume Else Mundal offers seductive reasons for dating *Orkneyinga saga* before the turn of the century and *Færeyinga saga* to ca. 1200, with the added suggestion that the composition of *Færeyinga saga* presupposes the existence of some sagas about early Icelanders.

4 Neither Ólafur Halldórsson (footnote 3) nor Bjarni Aðalbjarnarson (1937: 75) pinpoints a date for the translation of *Oddr's saga*.

5 Jonna Louis-Jensen presents a reasoned case in this volume for believing that *Egils saga* is older than *Heimskringla* I and III.

in the early decades of the century; I have in mind such texts as *Reykdœla saga*, *Víga-Glúms saga*, *Droplaugarsona saga*, or *Vatnsdœla saga*. It appears that the default option in the last sixty years or so has been to date sagas late when there is no completely compelling evidence, such as an early manuscript, to show that they are early.

I have consequently found myself arguing rather persistently for earlier dates. It has seemed to me that *Ljósvetninga saga*, *Reykdœla saga*, and *Víga-Glúms saga* belong together with *Morkinskinna* in a burst of literary activity in Eyjafjǫrðr in the 1220s or before.[6] I see no reason to believe that northern Iceland lagged behind western Iceland in literary development. There was constant interaction between the two regions and every reason to believe that they would have kept pace with each other. *Ljósvetninga saga* refers to a certain Þorvarðr Þorgeirsson as a recent figure; he died in 1207 and would hardly have been referred to in this way in the middle of the century. I have also tried to show that the author of *Reykdœla saga* made use of *Víga-Glúms saga*, not vice versa.[7] *Reykdœla saga* is such a poorly composed saga that it can hardly date from the same stage of saga writing as *Egils saga* and *Laxdœla saga* and is more likely to have been written around 1220. If the author made use of *Víga-Glúms saga*, the latter must be still earlier and date from before 1220.

At the risk of foolhardiness, I have also made the case that *Gunnlaugs saga* is not from the end of the thirteenth century as most scholars have believed in the wake of Björn M. Ólsen's study from 1911, but that there are indications that it influenced *Egils saga* and must have been written at the beginning of the century along with other skald sagas.[8] Thus I have been inclined to move four sagas from the middle or end of the thirteenth century back to the time around 1220.

The most conspicuous countercase is *Fóstbrœðra saga,* which was once dated as early as ca. 1200 by Sigurður Nordal but was then pushed down to the end of the century by Jónas Kristjánsson.[9] I believe there are rea-

6 Andersson 1994: esp. 28; Andersson and Miller 1989: 82–84.

7 Andersson 2006: *passim.*

8 Andersson 2008.

9 See Nordal's contribution to Vestfirðinga sǫgur (ÍF 6: LXXII); Jónas Kristjánsson 1972: 310. Preben Meulengracht Sørensen was at first inclined to accept Jónas's late date (2001: 237–39), but he later came to harbor doubts (2001: 274–75). Erik Sønderholm's detailed review of stylistic infelicities (1961) might point to an early date. On the other hand,

sons, having to do with Þormóðr Bersason's last hours in several overlapping texts, to return to the earlier dating. Þormóðr's death at the Battle of Stiklarstaðir is described primarily in the *Legendary Saga*, *Fóstbrœðra saga*, and *Heimskringla*. In this group it is reasonable to assume that the *Legendary Saga* (a redaction close to the *Oldest Saga*) is older than *Heimskringla* because, if *Heimskringla* had been available as a source and model, the *Legendary Saga* would not have been so poorly composed. *Heimskringla* is clearly an improved version. The relative dating of the *Legendary Saga* and *Fóstbrœðra saga* is more difficult to assess. They tell recognizably the same story of Þormóðr's last stand but with substantial differences in content, sequence, and phrasing. Jónas Kristjánsson tacitly acknowledges the difference in wording by reprinting the parallel passages (pp. 201–8) without the conventional use of italics to signal verbal correspondences. Such correspondences are almost completely absent.

In one passage of the matching narrative, Jónas Kristjánsson (p. 214) takes note of the surprise expressed by Sigurður Nordal (p. 150) about the lack of verbal correspondences. Nordal had undertaken to explain the textual dissimilarity by supposing that the redactor of the "Middle Saga" had made changes in the text of *Fóstbrœðra saga* in order to avoid obvious echoes of the *Oldest Saga*. In addition he considered that the text of the *Legendary Saga* was plainly abbreviated and disturbed ("forvansket"), but the "Middle Saga" is sufficiently problematical that at least half that argument seems insecure. If so, there remains only the possibility that the *Legendary Saga* made radical changes in the passage in question, but since we do not have the equivalent text in the *Oldest Saga*, it is impossible to assess the extent of the changes.

Jónas Kristjánsson (pp. 214–15) saw the difficulties involved in deriving the *Legendary Saga* from *Fóstbrœðra saga* and tried a different approach. He supposed that there were two differing accounts of the episode, a fuller and clearer account in the *Oldest Saga* and a shorter and more confused account in the *Legendary Saga*. The deviations in the text of *Fóstbrœðra saga* are then to be explained by the author's attempt to combine these two differing versions. One difficulty in this explanation is that a comparison of the *Legendary Saga* with the six extant fragments of the *Oldest Saga* suggests that

Helga Kress's Bakhtinian reading (1987) might suggest a late date, though she does not draw that conclusion herself.

the differences between these two texts were not great.[10] A second difficulty is, once again, that the argument is based on special suppositions about a text in the *Oldest Saga* that we do not have. The validity of the supposition can therefore not be tested. A third difficulty is that Jónas must assume that the author of *Fóstbrœðra saga* made use of quite outdated versions of *Óláfs saga helga* instead of making the more obvious choice of using the superior narrative in *Heimskringla*, which, if Jónas's late dating is correct, he could easily have done. Furthermore, the problem remains that the texts in hand are assumed to have been copied from each other without leaving telltale correspondences.

We should now take a somewhat closer look at the similarities and dissimilarities between the two accounts of Þormóðr's last stand. I have indicated that there is not much in the way of a verbal match, but there are two possible exceptions to this rule. The first involves a stanza in which, in response to a request for advice from the king, Þormóðr recommends that they burn down the houses in Veradalr. In both cases the king rejects the advice with the righteous objection that he does not want to burn his own lands:

> "Ia," sægir konongrenn, "trua ma þer til þess, Þormoðr," sægir konongrenn, "þu sægir þat, sem þer byr i brioste. Annur rað munu ver nu værða taka hælldr en brænna lond sialfra vara." (*Legendary Saga*, p. 186)

> "Yes," said the king, "you can be trusted, Þormóðr, to say what you have in mind. But we will have to choose a different option rather than burning our own lands."

> Óláfr konunge mælti: "Vera má, at þat hlýddi, at væri gǫrt sem þú mælir; en annat ráð munu vér taka en brenna land várt sjálfra, en þó grunum vér ekki þik um, at þú myndir svá gera sem þú mælir." (*Fóstbrœðra saga*, p. 261)

> King Olaf said: "It may be that it would be effective if it were done as you say, but we will adopt a plan other than to burn our own land, although we are in no

10 The reader can easily make the comparison by placing side by side Guðni Jónsson's editon of the fragments and Anne Heinrichs's edition of the *Legendary Saga* as follows: OS 403–4 = LS 136–38, OS 404–5 = LS 108, OS 405–7 = LS 108–10, OS 407–11 = LS 126–30, OS 412–14 = LS 132–34 and 140, OS 414–16 = LS 144–48, OS 416–18 = LS 148–52, and OS 418–20 = LS 158/166.

> doubt that you would do what you say."

The verbal echo lies in the words:

> Annur rað munu ver nu værða taka hælldr en brænna lond sialfra vara.

> En annat ráð munu vér taka en brenna land várt sjálfra.

That is indeed the closest verbal echo to be found anywhere in these two texts. Does it suggest that one is copying the other? The first difficulty is that the episode is quite differently located in the two sagas. In the *Legendary Saga* it is assigned to the last minutes after Þormóðr recites *Bjarkamál* and before the battle is engaged. In *Fóstbrœðra saga* it is attached to the story of how Þormóðr came from Iceland, at first found no favour with the king, but later was firmly attached to him to the extent of sharing his exile and returning with him to Þrándheimr. The episode precedes the recital of *Bjarkamál*. The placement in the sequence of these narratives is thus entirely different. The king's rejection of Þormóðr's advice is analogous, but his comments on Þormóðr are different. In the *Legendary Saga* he comments that Þormóðr can be counted on to speak his mind, but in *Fóstbrœðra saga* he is confident that Þormóðr would do what he says. The match between the two passages is therefore less than complete.

How then do we account for the exact echo in the rejection of Þormóðr's advice to burn the settlements? Does it derive from a further stanza not recorded in either text? To some extent each author made an independent selection from the available stanzas; the author of the *Legendary Saga* used eleven stanzas but the author of *Fóstbrœðra saga* only eight. As we will see below, the narratives into which the stanzas are inserted are quite different, to the extent that they hardly suggest a common written source. On the other hand, the stanzas are closely aligned. Both texts begin with "Brennum ǫll fyr innan" (*Legendary Saga* 52; *Fóstbrœðra saga* 31). The author of *Fóstbrœðra saga* then omits the stanzas numbered 53–55 in the *Legendary Saga*. The order of the remaining seven stanzas, 56–62 in the *Legendary Saga* and 34–40 in *Fóstbrœðra saga*, is identical. We may well ask how the narratives can be so different while the order of the stanzas is the same. If the stanzas were simply plucked out of the living tradition, it seems statistically unlikely that they would be recorded in the same order.[11] The alternative might be that they existed as a separate written list and that both authors used the order in which they were listed, filling in the narrative as best they knew the story.

I have queried whether the phrasing "ǫnnur ráð taka" and so forth might come from a lost stanza, but the quite precise match in the order of recorded stanzas, suggesting a written source, makes it unlikely that both writers would have elected independently to omit the stanza with "ǫnnur ráð taka." The alternative is to suppose that the story was sufficiently well formed and stable that it maintained the phrasing in question, so that the words were likely to recur in any retelling of the story. There is one other recurrence that deserves a closer look. It comes at the moment of Þormóðr's death. In the *Legendary Saga* (p. 204) he pulls the arrow from his wound, leans forward against a wattled fence, and dies ("læggr bringuna a vandbolkenn oc andaðezk þa"). The text in *Fóstbrœðra saga* (p. 276) is reminiscent but not identical. Þormóðr recites his final stanza (completed by Haraldr Sigurðarson) and dies: "Ok er hann hafði þetta mælt, þá dó hann standandi við bálkinn ok fell til jarðar dauðr." The echo is limited to the word "vandbǫlkr" or "bǫlkr," and that in itself may not be enough to suggest that one writer is copying another. It is perhaps sufficient to suppose that everyone who knew the story also knew that Þormóðr succumbed by a fence.[12]

This exhausts the verbal echoes in the two texts, but there are also thematic echoes. The idea that Þormóðr does not want to survive his king recurs in several iterations. In the *Legendary Saga* (198: 10–12) he leaps over a fence and voices the fear that he will not succumb with his king, but when he is struck by an arrow (198: 13–14), he is relieved at the thought that he will not be separated from his king. In *Fóstbrœðra saga* (p. 263) King Óláfr sees that Þormóðr is depressed and asks the reason. Þormóðr replies that he is afraid that they will not share the same quarters that night, and Óláfr

11 My statistician colleagues Bradley Efron and Ewart Thomas inform me that if two persons are asked to place eight items in random order, there is one chance in 40,320 that they will come up with the same order. In the case of stanzas adopted for a story line, the unlikelihood is probably not quite so great because there might be common deductions about the order of the story, but the figure gives some idea of how unlikely the identical order is. Bjarne Fidjestøl (1982: 45–60) made a general case for the written transmission of skaldic stanzas. See also Úlfar Bragason 2003: 141.

12 Sønderholm 1961: 100 surmises that there were live oral transmissions about the Battle of Stiklarstaðir in both Norway and Iceland.

consoles him by promising to do his best to ensure that they do share the same quarters. Again, when Þormóðr finds that he has been wounded (pp. 268–69), he fears that he will not share the king's quarters, but when he is struck by an arrow, he cheers up at the thought that he will die after all. There are no verbal echoes in these passages, but it seems clear that Þormóðr's reluctance to be separated from his king was part of the story.

Both stories make the point that Þormóðr is not seriously wounded. The *Legendary Saga* states (198: 8–9): "Þormóðr lec laus við i bardaganom oc fecc æigi stor sar, sem hann undraðe sialfr, oc þikcizt æigi hava lift ser" (Þormóðr had free rein in the battle and did not suffer great wounds and was himself surprised because he thought he had not done much to protect himself). *Fóstbrœðra saga* casts the same idea quite differently (p. 268): "Svá er sagt, þá er lokit var bardaganum, at Þormóðr væri ekki sárr. Hann harmaði þat mjǫk . . ." (We are told that when the battle was over, Þormóðr was not wounded. That grieved him greatly . . .). Here too the motif seems to be part of the underlying narrative, but there is no sign of copying.

After Þormóðr has after all been wounded, the *Legendary Saga* tells us (198: 28–29) that he is approached by a woman with a water container. This is a strangely abridged motif because we hear no more about her, but she must be identical with the woman who is heating water to wash wounds in *Fóstbrœðra saga* (p. 269). A woman attending with water could hardly have been invented twice independently; she too must belong to an antecedent form of the story.

In both texts there is some discussion about who distinguished himself in battle, but in the *Legendary Saga* (198: 32) the discussion is very brief: "Nu var rœtt, hværir bæzt gengo fram, oc urðu menn æigi asatter" (Now there was talk about who had distinguished himself most, and people did not agree). In *Fóstbrœðra saga* (p. 271) the discussion is slightly more extended and includes two stanzas. The author of the *Legendary Saga* may also be interpreting these stanzas, but the procedure is less explicit. It is equally possible that the oral story interpreted the stanzas in this way and that this interpretation became part of a narrative that was equally available to the writers of both texts.

We may surely reckon with a very considerable role for the stanzas in the formation of the story. The fully developed idea that Þormóðr wishes to live or die with his king shows no matching phraseology in the two texts but can be retraced to a stanza in *Fóstbrœðra saga* (p. 265) that contains Þormóðr's apostrophe to the king with the words "vilk með þér . . . lifa ok deyja" (I wish to live and die with you). These words are missing in the equivalent stanza in the *Legendary Saga* (p. 194), but the theme is present (198: 13–14) and may ultimately derive from the stanza as it is transmitted in *Fóstbrœðra saga*, even though the two texts tell the story quite differently.

I believe we may conclude from this survey that the similarities are better explained from a written list of stanzas and a common oral narrative than from the hypothesis that one text copied some version of the other. This supposition is only reinforced if we focus on the many and striking dissimilarities between the two narratives. I list fifteen such cases:

1. Þormóðr disparages Sigvatr in a stanza in *Fóstbrœðra saga* (p. 265), but Óláfr defends him. The *Legendary Saga* (p. 194) cites the first half of the same stanza, but there is no mention of Sigvatr.

2. King Óláfr refers to *Bjarkamál* as *Húskarlahvǫt* in *Fóstbrœðra saga* (p. 262) but not in the *Legendary Saga*.

3. In the *Legendary Saga* (184: 2) Óláfr asks Þormóðr how many men he has killed, and he responds by fixing the number at six. Neither the question nor the answer is found in *Fóstbrœðra saga*.

4. In the *Legendary Saga* (188: 12–13) the king posts Þormóðr in "the other wing," a position documented in the following stanza. There is no such posting in *Fóstbrœðra saga*, and the stanza is not cited.

5. *Fóstbrœðra saga* (p. 267) tells us that Þormóðr fights without shield or byrnie. The *Legendary Saga* does not have this phrase but includes an episode in which Þormóðr gives away his shield to another warrior (198: 9–10).

6. According to *Fóstbrœðra saga* (pp. 267–68), Þormóðr breaks through the enemy ranks with a two-handed ax attack. The *Legendary Saga* records no such attack.

7. In a curiously unmotivated moment in the *Legendary Saga* (198: 10–11), Þormóðr jumps over a fence before being struck by an arrow. *Fóstbrœðra saga* mentions no such fence.

8. The *Legendary Saga* (198: 12–13) states that the arrow strikes Þormóðr under the left arm and penetrates the ribs. In *Fóstbrœðra saga* (p. 269) the arrow strikes him in the chest.

9. In the *Legendary Saga* (198: 15–27) Þormóðr overhears a conversation between two dying warriors (father and son). There is no trace of this conversation in *Fóstbrœðra saga.*

10. The *Legendary Saga* mentions an older man with a poor reputation who is assigned to bandage wounds. His name is Kimbi (198: 29). The author of *Fóstbrœðra saga* (p. 271) assigns the bandaging to a woman and does not know the name Kimbi.

11. According to the *Legendary Saga* (200: 32–202: 3) Kimbi eyes Þormóðr's golden arm ring, and Þormóðr offers it to him, but when Kimbi reaches out for it, Þormóðr cuts off his hand. In *Fóstbrœðra saga* (p. 273) the golden arm ring is missing, and Þormóðr wounds a nameless man for scoffing at the wounded men in the barn.

12. In the *Legendary Saga* (200: 31–32) there is an oblique and unclear reference to the groaning of the wounded men, but the motif is fully developed in *Fóstbrœðra saga* (pp. 272–73).

13. In the *Legendary Saga* (202: 7–9) Þormóðr and a nameless man question each other about which side they fought on; each claims to have fought on the better side. The conversation is not connected with the stanza in which Þormóðr states that he fought with Óláfr (200: 12). In *Fóstbrœðra saga* (p. 270) a woman asks Þormóðr which side he fought on, and his reply is in the form of this stanza.

14. In *Fóstbrœðra saga* (pp. 274–75) the woman heating water asks Þormóðr why he is as pale as a corpse. In the *Legendary Saga* (202: 14–15), a woman carrying wood sees Þormóðr and drops the wood in horror at his pallor.

15. In the *Legendary Saga* (204: 5–9), Þormóðr extracts the arrow with tongs and comments on the good condition of his heart roots. *Fóstbrœðra saga* omits this motif altogether.

It is clear that the dissimilarities between the *Legendary Saga* and *Fóstbrœðra saga* greatly outweigh the similarities. The dissimilarities are not only numerous but seemingly random; they do not seem explicable from particular principles of recomposition. Jónas Kristjánsson's explanation of the differences is to the effect that both texts derive from the *Oldest Saga*, but that the *Oldest Saga* had a rather fuller version than the *Legendary Saga*.

Thus, when the author of *Fóstbrœðra saga* made use of both the *Oldest Saga* and the *Legendary Saga*, he produced a text that was not recognizably the same as what we find in the *Legendary Saga*.[13] In the "Summary" (p. 319) he suggests, in addition, that the author of *Fóstbrœðra saga* may also have used Styrmir's version of the text, thus distancing his text even further from his forerunners. One problem lies in the dimensions implied in Jónas's supposition that the *Oldest Saga* was "rather fuller." It is generally agreed that the *Legendary Saga* is a slightly abbreviated version of the *Oldest Saga*, but a slight abbreviation cannot begin to explain the radical differences between the *Legendary Saga* and *Fóstbrœðra saga*. What we need is a wholly different explanation. The explanation offered here is that what the two authors of the *Legendary Saga* and *Fóstbrœðra saga* had in common was not a written text but only an oral story with a list of written stanzas.

If the two authors worked from a common story, we must ask ourselves what that story might have included. At some point in the sequence Þormóðr advises burning down the dwellings of the rebels and Óláfr declines to set fire to his own land (stanza 52 in the *Legendary Saga* and 31 in *Fóstbrœðra saga*). Þormóðr does little to protect himself in battle, but he escapes serious wounds until he is struck by an arrow. He welcomes the idea of not being separated from the fate of his king (stanza 35 in *Fóstbrœðra saga* and 57 in the *Legendary Saga* diverge). He withdraws and encounters a woman with a container of water. He engages in conversation about who distinguished himself in battle (*Legendary Saga* stanzas 59–60; *Fóstbrœðra saga* stanzas 37–38). There is also a conversation about whose side he was on during the battle (*Legendary Saga* stanza 58; *Fóstbrœðra saga* stanza 36). A man (perhaps Kimbi) scoffs at the wounded men and Þormóðr inflicts a wound to test the man's mettle. A woman inquires into his pallor (*Legendary Saga* stanzas 61–62; *Fóstbrœðra saga* stanzas 39–40). He dies by a wall.

Five of the points in this common outline are supported by Þormóðr's stanzas, four are not: his failure to protect himself in battle, the woman with water, the scoffing at wounded men, and the wall by which Þormóðr dies. Each reader will have to decide whether these correspondences derive from a shared written source or a well-known oral story.[14] I prefer the second

13 Jónas Kristjánsson 1972: 210, 215.

14 Neither Sigurður Nordal (1914: 146–47) nor Jónas Kristjánsson (1972: 210) entertained any doubt about a written connection. On the greater latitude that is currently allowed for oral versions see Slavica Ranković's contribution to this volume.

supposition and imagine that two authors, neither familiar with the written version of the other, elaborated the same story based on a narrative skeleton and a written record of stanzas.

It is not very often that we are able to deduce the probable lineaments of an oral story, but this episode may well be such an exception. It is not surprising that oral storytelling would have included battle action, in this case notes on armaments and wounds, discussions of warrior distinction, and details of the hero's allegiance and death. More interesting is the evidence of extended dialogue, for example between the hero and a female attendant or an enemy. Still more interesting are the moral and psychological moments, the king's unwillingness to burn his own land, the hero's eagerness to accompany his king in death, his thought processes, and his moralizing revenge against a slanderous opponent. The story was apparently not just an action narrative but a recreation with highlights on sentiment and psyche.

There is a third piece in this puzzle, the version of the story told in *Heimskringla*. Jónas Kristjánsson reviewed the similarities and inclined to the view that the version in *Fóstbrœðra saga* is based on Styrmir's largely lost saga of Saint Óláfr, which was also the source of the episode in *Heimskringla*.[15] I will review the parallels once more.

1. In *Heimskringla* (pp. 361–62) Þormóðr recites *Bjarkamál*, of which the first two stanzas are recorded. The men thank Þormóðr and refer to the poem as *Húskarlahvǫt*. In general this corresponds to the *Legendary Saga* (182: 29–35) and *Fóstbrœðra saga* (pp. 261–62), but only *Fóstbrœðra saga* uses the title *Húskarlahvǫt*.

2. In *Heimskringla* (p. 362) Þormóðr refers briefly to Sigvatr's absence. There is also a brief reference to his absence in the *Legendary Saga* (182: 30–31), but the motif is more fully developed in *Fóstbrœðra saga* (p. 266).

3. In *Heimskringla* (p. 389) Þormóðr is struck on his left side by an arrow. That corresponds to the *Legendary Saga* (198: 12), whereas the Hauksbók text of *Fóstbrœðra saga* (p. 269) relates that he was struck in the chest. The Flateyjarbók text reverts to the left side, presumably under the influence of *Heimskringla*.

15 Jónas Kristjánsson 1972: 220–21.

4. In *Heimskringla* (p. 389) Þormóðr breaks off the shaft of the arrow, as in the *Legendary Saga* (198:14). This gesture is not found in the texts of *Fóstbrœðra saga*.

5. In *Heimskringla* (p. 389) Þormóðr is approached by a man who disparages the moaning and groaning of the wounded men. This motif is referred to cryptically in the *Legendary Saga* (200: 31–32) and fully in *Fóstbrœðra saga* (pp. 272–73).

6. The man is named Kimbi in *Heimskringla* (p. 389) and in the *Legendary Saga* (200: 31), but he is not named in *Fóstbrœðra saga* (p. 272). He appears in one incarnation in *Heimskringla* and *Fóstbrœðra saga* but in two incarnations in the *Legendary Saga*.

7. In *Heimskringla* (p. 389) Þormóðr asks the man if he has been in the battle. That matches a question put to the second incarnation in the *Legendary Saga* (202: 7) but is not found in the Hauksbók text of *Fóstbrœðra saga* (p. 273), only in the Flateyjarbók text (p. 273), where it is presumably inspired by *Heimskringla*.

8. In both *Heimskringla* (p. 390) and the *Legendary Saga* (202: 9) Þormóðr claims to have been on the better side. There is no such claim in *Fóstbrœðra saga*.

9. In *Heimskringla* (p. 390) and the *Legendary Saga* (200: 32–202: 2) Kimbi covets Þormóðr's gold arm ring. In *Fóstbrœðra saga* there is no gold ring.

10. In *Heimskringla* (p. 390) Kimbi reaches for the ring and Þormóðr slices off his hand. This matches the *Legendary Saga* (202: 3). In *Fóstbrœðra saga*, Þormóðr inflicts an unspecified wound (p. 273).

11. In *Heimskringla* (p. 390), the *Legendary Saga* (198: 32), and *Fóstbrœðra saga* (p. 271) there is a discussion about who distinguished himself most in battle.

12. In *Heimskringla* (p. 391), the *Legendary Saga* (202: 6–7), and *Fóstbrœðra saga* (p. 269) Þormóðr goes to a building where there are many wounded men.

13. In *Heimskringla* (p. 391) and *Fóstbrœðra saga* (pp. 269–71) there is a woman bandaging wounds. In the *Legendary Saga* (198: 29–30) the task of bandaging wounds is attributed to Kimbi.

14. In *Heimskringla* (p. 391) a man asks Þormóðr why he is so pale. This is also the gist of the *Legendary Saga* (202: 14–26), but it is a woman who asks the question. In *Fóstbrœðra saga* (pp. 274–75) the wording is similar.

15. In *Heimskringla* (pp. 391–92) Þormóðr brings in an armful of wood

and drops it on the floor. In the *Legendary Saga* (202: 14–15) he encounters a woman carrying a load of wood, which she drops at the sight of his pallor. It looks as though the author of *Heimskringla* has altered the motif in order to enhance Þormóðr's dying heroics. There is nothing equivalent in *Fóstbrœðra saga*.

16. In *Heimskringla* (p. 392) and the *Legendary Saga* (204: 5–6) a woman healer inspects Þormóðr's wound. She does not appear in the Hauksbók text of *Fóstbrœðra saga*, but the Flateyjarbók text follows *Heimskringla*.

17. In *Heimskringla* (p. 392) Þormóðr advises the physician to cut into the wound so that the arrow tip can be extracted with tongs. The wording in the *Legendary Saga* (204: 5–8) is closely related, but nothing equivalent is found in the Hauksbók text of *Fóstbrœðra saga*; again the Flateyjarbók version follows *Heimskringla*.

18. In *Heimskringla* (p. 393) Þormóðr extracts the arrow and admires the fat "heart roots" betokening the king's solicitude. The *Legendary Saga* (204: 8–9) has a briefer version of the same motif, but it does not appear in the Hauksbók text of *Fóstbrœðra saga*, only in the contaminated version of Flateyjarbók.

The question that now confronts us is: how closely does *Heimskringla* resemble either or both of the other texts? In seven cases (1–2, 5, 11–14) *Heimskringla* has similarities with both. Number 10 is a borderline case. All three texts indicate that Þormóðr wounds his antagonist, but only *Heimskringla* and the *Legendary Saga* specify that the antagonist is Kimbi and that Þormóðr slices off his hand. In number 1 (on the recitation of *Bjarkamál*), *Heimskringla* is clearly closer to *Fóstbrœðra saga* than to the *Legendary Saga*, for example, in the use of the designation *Húskarlahvǫt*. In number 2 as well (on the absence of Sigvatr) *Heimskringla* is clearly closer to *Fóstbrœðra saga* than to the *Legendary Saga*. In number 5 (on the disparagement of the groaning men), *Heimskringla* is again closer to *Fóstbrœðra saga*. In numbers 11–14 the differences are not great, although the bandaging of wounds is attributed to a woman in one case and a man in the other.

If we change the perspective and look for cases in which *Heimskringla* seems to echo only the *Legendary Saga* and not *Fóstbrœðra saga*, the result is quite interesting. There are eleven such cases (3–4, 6–10, 15–18). But there are also the cases noted above in which *Heimskringla* echoes only, or is at least closer to, *Fóstbrœðra saga* (1–2, 5). From a purely quantitative standpoint it is clear that *Heimskringla* is considerably more in line with the *Legendary Saga* than with *Fóstbrœðra saga*.

The next question is whether the similarities between the *Legendary Saga* and *Heimskringla* are so great that we must assume a textual connection. Previous scholars believed that there was such a connection, but that it did not involve the direct use of the *Legendary Saga* by the author of *Heimskringla*. Indeed, there is general agreement that *Heimskringla* made no direct use of the *Legendary Saga*. This view should perhaps be revisited. The *Legendary Saga* is a poor narrative, and it is easy to believe that the skilled author of *Heimskringla* rejected it for that reason and elected to make a fresh start. On the other hand, Þormóðr's last stand is one of the better sections of the *Legendary Saga*, and the author of *Heimskringla* may have made an exception and decided to consult it just this once.

Jónas Kristjánsson was more focused on the relationship between *Fóstbrœðra saga* and *Heimskringla*. He attributed the similarities between the *Legendary Saga* and *Fóstbrœðra saga* to a shared use of Styrmir's version. At the same time, he was definite in dismissing the idea that either made use of *Heimskringla*, and that seems persuasive. On the other hand, the assumption that both the *Legendary Saga* and *Fóstbrœðra saga* are, despite substantial differences throughout, both based on a combination of the *Oldest Saga* and Styrmir's saga seems unduly complicated. Simpler is the hypothesis that the *Legendary Saga* is a slight reworking of the *Oldest Saga* and that *Fóstbrœðra saga*'s rendering is an independent recording of the tradition.

There are also complications in Jónas's theory on the dating of the texts. If, as he believes, *Fóstbrœðra saga* is from the end of the thirteenth century, why would the author have used the outdated *Oldest Saga* or the equally outdated saga by Styrmir instead of using *Heimskringla*? To place *Fóstbrœðra saga* in the context of the *Oldest Saga* and Styrmir's saga is tantamount to making it an early saga.

We must return to the problem of *Heimskringla*. Jónas Kristjánsson analyzes the special correspondences with *Fóstbrœðra saga* and singles out ten cases in which these two texts run counter to the *Legendary Saga*.[16] Some

16 Ibid., pp. 218–19.

of the cases are more compelling than others. Most significant are a few similarities in phrasing.

Fóst. s.	*Heimskringla*
"Sighvati skáldi þykkist þú nú sneiða, ok þarftu þess eigi, . . ."	"Ekki þarf Sighvati at sneiða, þótt hann sé eigi hér."
You are trying to put down the poet Sigvatr, and there is no need for that . . .	There is no need to put down Sigvatr even though he is not here.
"Vera má at svá sé, en þat hygg ek at þunnskipat væri þá um merkistǫngina í dag, ef þann veg hefði margir farit."	"Vera má þat, konungr, at þér sé nú bæna mest þǫrf, en þunnt myndi vera um merkistǫngina, ef allir hirðmenn þínir væri nú á Rúmavegi."
It may be so, but I think there would be thin manpower around the standard today if everybody had followed that path.	It may be, lord, that you are mostly in need of prayers, but mostly in need of prayers, but there would be thin manpower around the standard if all your followers were on the road to Rome.
Kona ein vermði vatn í katli til þess at þvá sár manna.	Eldr var á gólfinu, ok vermði hon vatn í katli til at fægja sárin.
A woman was heating water in a kettle to wash the men's wounds.	There was fire on the hearth and she was heating water in a kettle to wash the wounds.

The question is whether these verbal echoes, together with the general correspondences under 1, 2, and 5 above, are sufficient to demonstrate a textual relationship between *Fóstbrœðra saga* and *Heimskringla*. Nordal believed that the story of Þormóðr in his "Middle Saga" derived from *Fóstbrœðra saga* and the *Oldest Saga*, and in turn served as the basis for the *Legendary*

Saga.[17] The version in *Heimskringla* was then derived from Styrmir's text. The use of the "Middle Saga" in this construction may, however, be subject to doubt.[18]

Jónas Kristjánsson rightly makes the point that *Fóstbrœðra saga* cannot have made use of *Heimskringla* because, if such had been the case, the author would have made greater use of it.[19] He is therefore obliged to seek the explanation of the correspondences in other, lost versions. If, however, we reverse the order and posit that *Heimskringla* made use of *Fóstbrœðra saga*, the difficulties dissolve. Our hypothesis would then be that the author of *Heimskringla* largely followed the *Legendary Saga* (or a related version) – he was after all writing a biography of Óláfr Haraldsson – and added a couple of small improvements from *Fóstbrœðra saga*, a lateral source not centrally focused on Óláfr Haraldsson.

We may now review the proposals that have been advanced so far. Nordal suggested that the versions of the story in *Fóstbrœðra saga* and the *Oldest Saga* converged in the hypothetical "Middle Saga," which in turn provided the basis for the *Legendary Saga* and Styrmir's version. Styrmir's text then became the source for *Heimskringla*. The weaknesses in this scheme are the following:

1. It does not explain the supposed correspondences between the *Oldest Saga* and *Fóstbrœðra saga*, correspondences that can be stipulated on the basis of the similarities between the *Oldest Saga* and the *Legendary Saga*.
2. It depends on three largely hypothetical entities: the *Oldest Saga*, the "Middle Saga," and Styrmir's version.

Jónas Kristjánsson's dating of *Fóstbrœðra saga* led him to a quite different result. He supposed that the *Oldest Saga* provided the foundation for the *Legendary Saga* and Styrmir's text. The author of *Fóstbrœðra saga* then made use of all three of these texts, while the author of *Heimskringla* relied only on Styrmir. One difficulty is the supposition that the author drew on three separate texts for what, in the context of his saga, is only an inciden-

17 Nordal 1914: 153–54.

18 Jonna Louis-Jensen 1970: 51–56 operates with the "Middle Saga," but Jónas Kristjánsson 1972: 221, 223 is inclined to believe that the use of Styrmir's redaction is an adequate assumption.

19 Jónas Kristjánsson 1972: 220.

tal episode. That seems to be a rather extravagant philological exertion for an author who seems otherwise not to be reliant on textual sources, apart from the stanzas.[20] A further difficulty is that Jónas makes the author of *Fóstbrœðra saga* dependent on three outdated versions of Óláfr's biography from ca. 1200 to 1220, at a time at the end of the thirteenth century when *Heimskringla* had become the standard version.

My own hypothesis explains the correspondences between the *Oldest Saga* (assuming that it was not very different from the *Legendary Saga*) and *Fóstbrœðra saga* from a common oral tradition and leaves open the question of which redaction or redactions the author of *Heimskringla* modeled himself on, while at the same time using *Fóstbrœðra saga* as a lateral source. The implication of this view is that *Fóstbrœðra saga* is not the last text in the narrative history of Þormóðr's last stand but one of the first texts, presumably not much later than 1200. It should, however, be emphasized that Jónas Kristjánsson's construction of the textual relationships was not his only argument for assigning a late date to *Fóstbrœðra saga*. He also argued loans from (or stylistic associations with) late texts, the use of "den florissante stil," and the use of *einn – ein – eitt* as an indefinite article. These arguments have not been touched on here and remain to be evaluated more closely. But with respect to the narrow question of how *Fóstbrœðra saga* fits into the complex of related texts, it seems to me that the hypothesis of a late date may be open to question.

20 Jónas Kristjánsson 1972: 224–35 argues a number of influences from the sagas about early Icelanders, but not all are persuasive and the direction of borrowing, if such there was, is not clear.

Appendix

(Nordal 1914: 154)

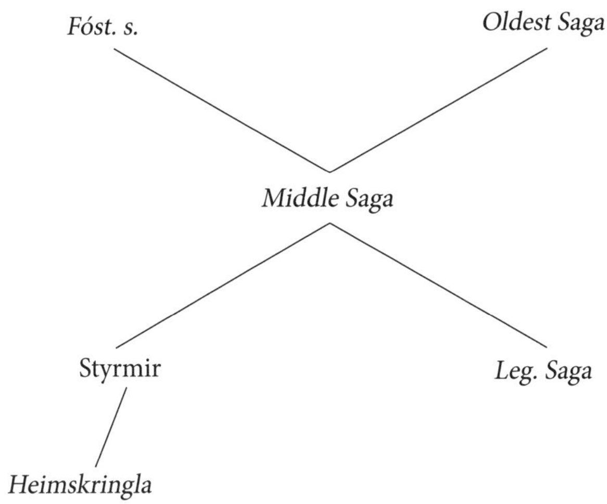

(Jónas Kristjánsson 1972: 215, 221, 319)

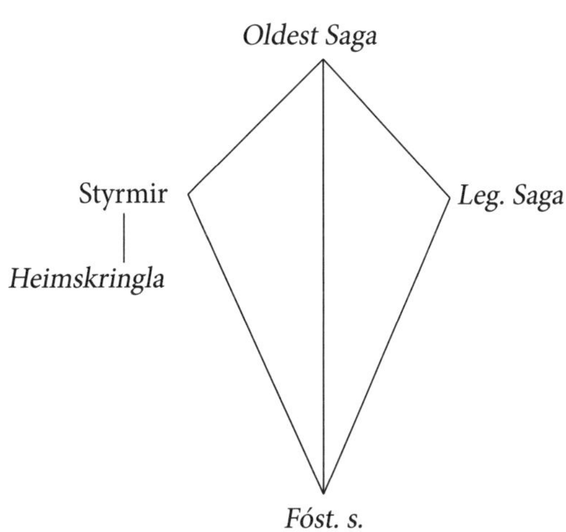

(Andersson 2013)

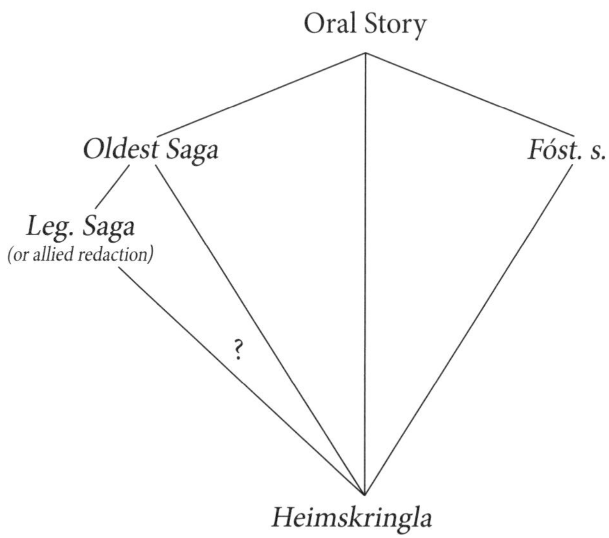

Bibliography

Andersson, Theodore M. 1994. "The Literary Prehistory of Eyjafjörður." In *Níunda alþjóðlega fornsagnaþingið: Samtíðarsögur. Forprent.* 2 vols. Akureyri, vol. 1, pp. 16–30.

——— 2006. "Víga-Glúms saga and the Birth of Saga-Writing." *Scripta Islandica* 57: 5–39.

——— 2008. "The Native Romance of Gunnlaugr and Helga the Fair." In Kirsten Wolf and Johanna Denzin (eds.), *Romance and Love in Late Medieval and Early Modern Iceland: Essays in Honor of Marianne Kalinke* (Islandica 54). Ithaca: Cornell University Library, pp. 33–63.

Andersson, Theodore M. and William Ian Miller 1989. *Law and Literature in Medieval Iceland: Ljósvetninga saga and Valla-Ljóts saga.* Stanford, CA: Stanford University Press.

Bjarni Aðalbjarnarson 1937. *Om de norske kongers sagaer* (Skrifter utgitt av Det Norske Videnskaps-Akademi i Oslo II. Hist.-Filos. Klasse. No. 4). Oslo: Jacob Dybwad.

Fidjestøl, Bjarne 1982. *Det norrøne fyrstediktet*. Øvre Ervik: Alvheim & Eide.

Færeyinga saga; Óláfs saga Tryggvasonar eptir Odd munk Snorrason 2006. Edited by Ólafur Halldórsson (Íslenzk fornrit 25). Reykjavík: Hið íslenzka fornritafélag.

Guðni Jónsson 1957. "Brot úr elztu sögu Óláfs helga." In *Konunga sögur*, vol. 1. Reykjavík: Íslendingasagnaútgáfan, pp. 403–26.

Jónas Kristjánsson 1972. *Um Fóstbræðrasögu*. Reykjavík: Stofnun Árna Magnússonar á Íslandi.

——— 1976. "The Legendary Saga." In *Minjar og menntir. Afmælisrit helgað Kristjáni Eldjárn 6. desember 1976*. Reykjavík: Bókaútgáfa menningarsjóðs, pp. 281–93.

Jørgensen, Jon Gunnar 2007. *The Lost Vellum Kringla* (Bibliotheca Arnamagnæana 45). Copenhagen: Reitzel.

Kress, Helga 1987. "Bróklindi Falgeirs. Fóstbræðrasaga og hláturmenning miðalda." *Skírnir* 161: 271–86.

Louis-Jensen, Jonna 1970. "Syvende og ottende brudstykke. Fragmentet AM 325 IVα 4to." In *Opuscula* 4 (Bibliotheca Arnamagnæana 30). Copenhagen: Munksgaard, pp. 31–60.

Meulengracht Sørensen, Preben 2001. "On Humour, Heroes, Morality, and Anatomy in *Fóstbrœðra saga*"; "Mundtlig tradition i *Fóstbrœðra saga*."; "Modernitet og traditionalisme. Et bidrag til islændingesagaernes litteraturhistorie. Med en diskussion af *Fóstbrœðra sagas* alder." In *At fortælle historien; Telling History. Studier i den gamle nordiske litteratur*, edited in collaboration with Sofie Meulengracht Sørensen. Trieste: Edizioni Parnaso, pp. 207–39; 263–75.

Nordal, Sigurður 1914. *Om Olaf den helliges saga*. Copenhagen: Gad.

Olafs saga hins helga. Die "Legendarische Saga" über Olaf den Heiligen (Hs. Delagard. Saml. Nr. 8^II) 1982. Edited and translated by Anne Heinrichs, Doris Janshen, and Elke Radicke. Hartmut Röhn. Heidelberg: Winter.

See, Klaus von 1976. "Die Überlieferung der Fóstbrœðra saga." *Skandinavistik* 6: 1–18. Reprinted in his *Edda, Saga, Skaldendichtung. Aufsätze zur skandinavischen Literatur des Mittelalters*. Heidelberg: Winter, pp. 443–60.

Snorri Sturluson 1945. *Heimskringla* II. Edited by Bjarni Aðalbjarnarson (Íslenzk fornrit 27). Reykjavík: Hið íslenzka fornritafélag.

Sønderholm, Erik 1961. "Samtíningur um Fóstbræðrasögu." *Skírnir* 135: 99–109.

Úlfar Bragason 2003. "Fóstbræðra saga og munnleg geymd." *Ársrit Sögufélags Ísfirðinga*. 43: 137–45.

Vestfirðingasǫgur 1943. Edited by Björn K. Þórólfsson and Guðni Jónsson (Íslenzk fornrit 6). Reykjavík: Hið íslenzka fornritafélag.

DATING THE SAGAS AND *GÍSLA SAGA SÚRSSONAR*

Emily Lethbridge

INTRODUCTION

Finnur Jónsson, in the introduction to his 1903 edition of *Gísla saga Súrssonar*, writes confidently that "[es] kann kein zweifel darüber bestehen, wann die saga geschrieben ist" (1903: xvii) (there can be no doubt regarding when the saga was written). Sixty years later, in a wide-ranging and instructive essay on *Gísla saga* and its medieval Icelandic background, Peter Foote introduced his reflections on the composition of the saga with the statement: "The saga of Gisli is a work of art written centuries ago and in a civilization different from our own. We shall never penetrate the essential mystery of its creation" (1963: 112). Understandably, the force that essential mysteries of creation tend to exert on scholars is a compelling one; accordingly, one dominant thematic strand in nineteenth- and twentieth-century *Gísla saga* scholarship has comprised attempts to dispel the shadows that occlude the circumstances surrounding the saga's composition, i.e. its date and place of production, and the identity of the individual responsible for the first written text of the saga. A second, related strand has been concerned with establishing how the extant – and significantly diverging – manuscript texts of *Gísla saga* relate to each other, and the stages by which these texts may have derived from the posited first written articulation of the saga.

Conclusions about the dating of *Gísla saga* have not been subjected to such radical reassessment as have those regarding the ages of certain other *Íslendingasögur*, such as *Heiðarvíga saga* (on which see, e.g., Bjarni Guðnason 1993, and responses by Fries 1995 and Finlay 2003). But the range of dates for *Gísla saga* suggested by scholars over the course of the nineteenth and twentieth centuries suggests that the question is not quite as clear-cut as Finnur asserted. It is not my intention to defend any single date that has been proposed for *Gísla saga*, nor to advance any new theories about the saga's age. Rather, through examining existing arguments and the bases on which these arguments have been constructed, I hope to highlight a number of problematic methodological issues, and to note the implications for the wider debate on "dating the sagas" – the subject of the two stimulating meetings organized and hosted by Else Mundal in Norway in May 2007 and May 2008.

To begin, in order to contextualize the ensuing discussion about dating *Gísla saga*, it may prove useful to review the few facts that seem to be relatively secure. Irrespective of the extent to which the events narrated in *Gísla saga* have any basis in historical reality, at one end of the diachronic "timeline" it seems that the eponymous Gísli Súrsson (whose historical existence is confirmed by sources other than that of his saga, such as the Icelandic annals[1]) died at some point in the last years of the 970s or circa 977–79.[2] At another point further along this rudimentary timeline, we have the earliest extant texts of the saga, as preserved in two medieval manuscripts, and then post-medieval paper copies of a third, now-lost, medieval manuscript. The oldest surviving text of *Gísla saga* is found in the fragmentary manuscript AM 445 c I 4to which has been dated to c. 1390–1425 (see McKinnell 1970: 311–13, 335–36); the second extant medieval manuscript is AM 556 a 4to ("Eggertsbók"), dated to c. 1475–1500 (see Hast 1960: 82–86); it is thought that the third medieval parchment known to have contained a text of *Gísla saga*, the so-called "Membrana Regia Deperdita," was produced no later than the mid-fourteeth century (see Loth 1960: lxxxvi–lxxxvii).

It is a commonplace that no *Íslendingasögur* survive as "original" autograph texts: all extant manuscript texts of the sagas are demonstrably copies of copies, often at indefinite removes from a posited archetype or hypothetical "original" text (see Örnólfur Thorsson 1990: 35 for a diagram that

1 Events in the saga that are mentioned in the annals are the arrival of Þorbjǫrn súrr in Iceland (952), the birth of Þorgrímr goði (938), Þorgrímr's death (963), and Snorri goði's birth (963). See Storm 1888.

2 For a summary of the correspondences between the saga's inner chronology and presumed historical fact, see Björn K. Þórólfsson and Guðni Jónsson 1943: xli–xliii, and Guðbrandur Vigfússon 1856: 362–64.

illustrates the gap between the posited dates of individual sagas' composition and the earliest surviving manuscript evidence for each respective saga). *Gísla saga* is no exception and, since it is clear that none of the three medieval texts of the saga we know of can be directly identified as the "original" text of the saga, we are forced to confront a gap of approximately 350 to 400 years between the only two more-or-less fixed chronological poles we have for the medieval composition and transmission of *Gísla saga* (i.e. that of Gísli's presumed lifetime, and the dates of the production of the earliest extant manuscripts). It is necessary, therefore, to contemplate what the stages in the composition and transmission of *Gísla saga* as an oral and/or written narrative might have been, over the course of these three or four centuries. From the outset, however, it is important to recognize that inevitably attempts to reconstruct the compositional and transmissional phases of any one saga will – to some degree – be influenced both by the general spirit of the time and trends in scholarship, and by the specific views that an individual critic may hold on the question of saga origins. The tendency amongst most scholars in recent years has been to take a moderate position between the two extreme bookprose and freeprose positions acknowledging the importance of oral traditions and the likely existence of some coherent oral narratives about "söguöld" characters or events on the one hand, but, on the other hand, emphasizing the extent to which these traditions were transformed during the process of the writing down of individual saga narratives, as a result of their being mingled with, or subjected to, new influences, both foreign and native.

It is more likely than not that *Gísla saga*, in approximately the written form that we know, was not created *ex nihilo*. It seems reasonable to assume that, firstly, orally-circulated traditions or anecdotes about Gísli Súrsson – perhaps associated with specific places that feature in the narrative which is, for the most part, anchored firmly in the landscape of the Vestfirðir – must have grown up by the end of the tenth century following Gísli's death, if not during his lifetime. At one or a number of points, this material may have been conjoined with genealogies and/or the verses in the saga that are attributed to Gísli, and consciously organized into some kind of coherent narrative or narratives. At a still later point, if this (or these) relatively stable oral prosimetric forerunner(s) to the saga as we know it existed, one person – to begin with, at least – must have been responsible for crystallizing it into written prose/prosimetrum form. In the process of so doing, this individual presumably made certain calculated, creative decisions about the structural and thematic organization of the narrative, resulting in the narrative being cast in essentially the form familiar to us. On the other hand, as Tommy Danielsson concedes in his evaluation of possible oral strata in the written saga, "perhaps there was no saga before it was written down, and perhaps the underlying traditions were just scattered and broken fragments assembled by scribes or authors or writers and put into position in the framework and context of a written genre" (2007: 40).

Assuming this latter scenario was not the case, we may well then ask when, exactly, each of the posited stages outlined above – especially the final stage, that of the writing down of the saga for the first time – might have occurred? Establishing precisely when individual sagas may have been first written down is obviously crucial for refining our critical understanding of the origins and development of saga writing in medieval Iceland. But arriving at a specific date for the written composition of any one saga narrative, and thence constructing a relative chronology of other extant written sagas, is an exercise that is notoriously fraught with difficulties. The first obstacle here is, as already mentioned, thrown up by the nature of the extant manuscript evidence for the sagas. Because this manuscript evidence is not contemporaneous with assumed original acts of written composition, arguments for dating individual saga narratives (and for postulating the date of the inception of saga writing as a widespread activity in medieval Iceland) are necessarily based on the cumulative weight of various other pieces of evidence, both internal and external to the texts in question, that might suggest a *terminus post* or *ante quem*. Thus, scholars have evaluated the stylistic or artistic expression of individual saga narratives; have attempted to detect linguistic strata in extant texts; have speculated over the poetic and prose sources on which a saga narrative might be founded, or the influences that may have shaped the written articulation of a narrative; have inferred instances of direct literary borrowing between texts; and finally, have pointed to historical events that, if contemporary to the time of writing, might have informed the written expression of any one saga narrative.

Given how equivocal and subjective these categories of evidence for dating individual sagas can be, the certainty with which many past scholars have arrived at sometimes very precise dates for individual sagas gives pause for thought. In early saga scholarship, the evaluation of a saga's artistic style was a widespread means of determining the relative age of individual saga narratives. The equation of age with superior artistic quality, along with the notion that terseness of expression is an indication of artistic quality, and therefore greater age, is, however, one of the most subjective and deep-rooted paradigms underlying traditional pre-classical/classical/post-classical models of stylistic development in saga literature: as Jónas Kristjánsson has warned, "the primitive and the decadent are not always easy to tell apart: and what is archaic to some scholars is bright novelty to others. It is no less important to remember that some authors are more adroit than others. ... Artistic advance is not a smooth and straight progression" (1988: 222; see also Einar Ól. Sveinsson 1958: 39–40). The much-admired structural cohesion and artistic expression of *Gísla saga* has led many critics to consider it to be one of the best *Íslendingasögur*, and, accordingly, one of the oldest. *Gísla saga* has thus, more often than not, been assigned to the relatively early or middle period of saga production in general chronological surveys of the *Íslendingasögur*, and grouped with other sagas perceived to represent the "classical" saga ideal rather than the "post-classical" narratives (see, for example, Sigurður Nordal 1952: 244, 248; Schier 1970 (following Sigurður Nordal): 52; Vésteinn Ólason 1993: especially 42; 2005: 114–15). It does seem plausible that relatively speaking, and compared with *Njáls saga* for example, *Gísla saga* in the form with which we are familiar is an older rather than younger composition; no scholars have put forward arguments for *Gísla saga* being a late saga as far as I am aware. Nevertheless, many of the arguments that critics have used to reach a date for the saga are somewhat flawed: in what follows, I will first survey the different dates that critics have assigned to the saga, and then consider certain lines of reasoning adopted by some of these critics in greater detail.

As discussed by Jürg Glauser in the present volume, many nineteenth- and twentieth-century saga critics were inclined to date the emergence of the *Íslendingasögur* genre (and accordingly, those sagas thought to be early or "classical" manifestations of the genre) earlier than has been customary over the past sixty years or so, primarily on the basis of the well-known statement about saga writing in the AM 122 a fol. prologue to *Sturlunga saga* (see further discussion in Meulengracht Sørensen 2001a). Early *Gísla saga* scholars thus postulated a late twelfth-century or c. 1200 date for the saga's written composition: Finnur Jónsson, for example, asserted in his history of Icelandic literature that "fremstillingen og sagaens hele karakter forbyder at sætte dens tilblivelsestid senere end c. 1200" (1920–24: II, 458) (the presentation and the saga's whole character rules out placing the time of composition later than c. 1200), and in the introduction to his 1903 edition of the saga, he claimed that *Gísla saga* "gehört zu der ältesten und besten gruppe isländischer familien-geschichten" (1903: xvii) (belongs to the oldest and best group of Icelandic family sagas). Finnur's remarks are typical (see also Müller 1817–20: I, 175; Rafn and Finnur Magnússon 1838–45: 576; Guðbrandur Vigfússon 1858: 168). An even earlier date is hinted at by Guðbrandur Vigfússon and F. York Powell in their discussion of *Gísla saga*'s age in *Origines Islandicæ* (1905: II, 189) where, in the context of interpreting a variant reading, they make a reference to images on French seals which date to 1138–40, this being "presumably the time that the first draught [*sic*] of our Saga was put on vellum."

Few scholars would now challenge the assumption that the thirteenth century was the period when the most highly-regarded *Íslendingasögur*, traditionally described as "classical," were set down in writing – although Jesse Byock notes that this late twentieth-century consensus is "more a matter of faith than of fact" and a conclusion framed by bookprose precepts (1984: 169, note 2). Furthermore, Byock points to Hallvard Magerøy's shrewd observation that one corollary of assigning the written production of the *Íslendingasögur* to the thirteenth century is that the genre can thereby be seen as a natural branch of European literature in the high Middle Ages (Byock 1984: 168–69, note 2, citing Magerøy 1978: 167). It has been argued that this notion fundamentally informed the ideological stance of the so-called "Icelandic school" of saga criticism, and underpinned the conclusions regarding the dates of individual *Íslendingasögur* found in the introductions to the Íslenzk fornrit series editions (see Lie 1939 and Örnólfur Thorsson 1990 for critiques of the Íslenzk fornrit editions; on the Icelandic School, see Andersson 1964: 82–119 and Clover 2005: 241–45). As the Íslenzk fornrit editions are widely used by scholars, Byock's scepticism regarding the methodological bases for ascertaining dates for the *Íslendingasögur* is a useful corrective to commonly-held assumptions. At the same time, however, there is good evidence to suggest that some *Íslendingasögur* (if not most of those typically categorized as the "classical" *Íslendingasögur*), at least, were written down in the thirteenth century: the oldest extant manuscript evidence for the *Íslendingasögur* includes fragments of *Egils saga* (AM 162 a θ fol.) and *Laxdœla saga* (AM 162 D 2 fol.) which have been dated to c. 1250, and c. 1250–1300, respectively. Moreover, certain features in the texts of sagas preserved in fourteenth-century manuscripts such as Möðruvallabók are taken by scholars as evidence for their scribes having worked from earlier exemplars (see van Weenen 2000: especially at 3).

Accordingly, the majority of twentieth-century editors and critics of *Gísla saga* situate the date of the saga's written composition firmly in the thirteenth century, albeit with varying degrees of exactitude. Björn K. Þórólfsson, in the introduction to his Íslenzk fornrit edition, advocates a date "rétt fyrir en eftir 1250" (1943: xli) (just before rather than just after 1250); this date is acknowledged or tacitly accepted by many scholars. Theodore M. Andersson, in his *BONIS* survey and review of perennial *Gísla saga* issues, observes that the "fifty-year span 1220–1270 would surely satisfy everyone and the twenty-five year span 1225–1250 would do nearly as well" (1968: 11). In a review published some years later, Andersson narrows this margin down to the 1220s (1985: 1018), which is the decade Björn M Ólsen suggests (1937–39: 130); Franz Seewald, too, advocates an early thirteenth-century date (1934: 112). Peter Foote suggests a date soon after 1225 as most likely (1963: 131); Gabriel Turville-Petre, in his *Origins of Icelandic Literature*, believes *Gísla saga* to have been written "at a comparatively early date, or at any rate not later than the middle of the thirteenth century" (1953: 244). Turville-Petre develops this stance further in his article on Gísli Súrsson and his poetry, arguing that the saga author most likely belonged to Óláfr hvítaskáld's generation (b. 1210) rather than to Snorri Sturluson's (b. 1178) (1944: 391); in the postscript appended to the reprint of the article, Turville-Petre notes that the author "probably worked towards the middle of the thirteenth century" (1972: 148).

While these statements might seem straightforward, in many cases, we are immediately confronted with one fundamental difficulty. Carol Clover has commented that "when the main events of a given saga took place is in most cases clear; but when the saga took its final form is notoriously difficult to pin down" (2005: 247): the question of what, exactly, constitutes a saga's "final form" and how this might relate to the extant manuscript texts of that saga is rarely taken up directly by critics. In addition to the often ambiguous nature of the various types of investigation to which critics customarily make recourse (i.e. stylistic and linguistic analysis, identification of literary relations with other texts, etc.), this constitutes a major obstacle when surveying critical attempts to date individual *Íslendingasögur* – and is a serious caveat of many of the arguments advanced for the dating of *Gísla saga*. The phrase "final form" is meaningful within a traditional text-critical framework but is not necessarily compatible with the evidence for Old Norse saga narratives where multiple, diverging textual manifestations of a single saga, such as *Gísla saga*, exist. Arguably, because of the conditions and impulses that shaped the composition and transmission of individual saga narratives, those concerned with their composition and transmission never conceived of them in such terms as having a "final form" (see further Lethbridge 2010).

The extant texts of *Gísla saga* as found in AM 445 c I 4to, AM 556 a 4to, and in the paper copies of the lost Membrana Regia Deperdita, are witnesses to three quite distinct redactions or versions of the saga narrative. Guðbrandur Vigfússon and F. York Powell are unusual in explicitly distinguishing between the first written text of *Gísla saga* on the one hand (purportedly from the twelfth century in their opinion, as noted above), and what they identify as a thirteenth-century reworking of the narrative, on the other, from which the extant manuscript texts of the saga supposedly derive (see also Guðbrandur Vigfússon 1878: I, lii on the notion of a thirteenth-century "editor" of *Gísla saga*). Overwhelmingly in the nineteenth and twentieth centuries, the text of *Gísla saga* as found in AM 556 a 4to has been judged to be superior to the others, principally on the basis of its artistic expression which was perceived to be closer to idealized notions of "classical saga style." This text, therefore, was thought to stand closer to the presumed archetype of the extant texts, and sometimes, by extension, to the hypothetical original text of the saga. When *Gísla saga* critics discuss or propose a date for the saga, it has to be tacitly inferred that it is the shorter version as represented in AM 556 a 4to that is equated with the first written articulation of the saga, rather than texts of the fragmentary or longer versions; when later dates for the manifestation of the longer version texts are given, this oversight is revealed (see, for example, Finnur Jónsson 1920–24: II, 458, and 1929, viii).

LINGUISTIC CRITERIA AS EVIDENCE FOR DATING *GÍSLA SAGA*

The uncertainties surrounding the precise textual relationships between the extant texts of *Gísla saga*, and to a posited archetype and/or original text of the saga, are highlighted when attempts to identify linguistic strata or features are made in order to establish the saga's age. Ulrike Sprenger, for example, includes *Gísla saga* in her investigation into the alternation of the historical present and preterite tenses in saga prose (1951). Her fundamental premise is that the use of the historical present in written saga texts declines as saga writing develops over the course of the thirteenth century, so that its presence or absence in saga texts may be considered to indicate early or late composition, and the extent to which sagas might be regarded as "free-prose" or "bookprose" compositions. Sprenger takes *Heiðarvíga saga* as an example of an early saga, *Gísla saga* and *Hœnsa-Þóris saga* as examples of mid-thirteenth-century sagas, and then *Egils saga*, *Eyrbyggja saga*, *Laxdœla saga*, *Njáls saga*, *Grettis saga*, and *Heimskringla* as examples of later sagas. Beyond the simplistic premise of Sprenger's basic thesis itself (see Jakob Benediktsson 1951 and Hollander 1954 for critical reviews), the underlying limitation here is that her statistical findings do not take account of the variation, which is sometimes extensive, between individual manuscript copies of the same saga.[3] Sprenger's figures for *Gísla saga* in fact are quite unreliable, since she uses Finnur Jónsson's 1903 edition of the saga – which does not include a variant apparatus indicating where the text has been emended – as the basis for her calculations.

The distribution patterns of the synonymous verbs *hitta*(*sk*) and *finna*(*sk*), together with other idioms and linguistic features or formulas, have been examined by Peter Hallberg (1965; 1968) in his work on the related question of the authorship of Old Norse saga texts.[4] In compiling statistics for *Gísla saga*, Hallberg does distinguish between the shorter and longer versions of the saga, counting twenty-five instances of *hitta* to one instance of *finna* for the former, and thirty-two instances of *hitta* to nine instances of *finna* for the latter. Hallberg accordingly calculates that in the shorter version, the verb *hitta* is used 96.2 per cent of the time, as opposed to in the longer version, where it is used only 78.2 per cent of the time (1965: 178; 1968: 172–73). In conjunction with this, Hallberg counts 404 instances of normal subject/predicate word order and seventy-three instances of inverted word order (i.e. 15.3 per cent) in the shorter version of *Gísla saga*; in

3 This is the case also for studies that attempt to approach the question of the relative dating of sagas by examining the varying proportions of direct speech to indirect speech (e.g. Jeffrey 1934; Ludwig 1934; and Hallberg 1994).

4 See also Peter Foote's (1955) examination of the use of the prepositions *of* (earlier) and *um* (later) in Old Icelandic and Old Norwegian prose. For a review and critique of Hallberg's methodology, see Roe 1970: 76–80.

the longer version, he counts 449 instances to 148 instances (i.e. 24.8 per cent) (1965: 175). These two sets of statistics were nicely congruent with the premises on which they were based – that *finna* was used with increasing frequency in the place of *hitta* over the course of the thirteenth century, and that the occurrence of inverted subject/predicate word order became more common over the same period – as long as it was accepted that the shorter version text of *Gísla saga* as preserved primarily in AM 556 a 4to was older and closer to the posited archetype or original text of the saga than the longer version texts derived from the Membrana Regia Deperdita. However, the reverse conclusions about the priority of the *Gísla saga* versions advanced by Jónas Kristjánsson and Guðni Kolbeinsson in their 1979 article – that the longer version of *Gísla saga* was older and closer to the posited original *Gísla saga* text than the shorter version – directly challenged the validity of Hallberg's conclusions (see Clover 2005: 248).

Moreover, a major limitation of basing conclusions on data of this kind resides in the fact that linguistic strata in individual texts can easily be obscured as a result of scribes altering the orthography and phrasing of the texts that lay in exemplars before them, so as to make their copies more in accordance with prevailing, contemporary "norms," or, occasionally, from a wish to archaize their texts. What is more, as with Sprenger, Hallberg's statistics are compiled from edited texts of sagas and he does not make allowances for the extent to which the use of *hitta* or *finna*, for example, or normal or inverted subject-predicate word order, may vary across different manuscript texts of the same saga where more than one manuscript witness survives. While the NKS 1181 fol. manuscript of the longer version (the copy of the Membrana Regia Deperdita made by Jón Jónsson in c. 1780) has thirty-two instances of *hitta*, for example, the AM 149 fol. (the copy of the Membrana Regia Deperdita made by Ásgeir Jónsson in c. 1700) has thirty-three instances of *hitta*. Similarly, while Hallberg notes there are nine occurrences of *finna* in the longer version, this is true of NKS 1181 fol. and AM 149 fol., but in AM 482 4to (also by Ásgeir Jónsson, thought to have been copied from AM 149 fol.), there is one fewer instance of *finna*.

A further limitation is that Hallberg does not make any reference to the evidence of the *Gísla saga* text preserved in AM 445 c I 4to which, while fragmentary, is nonetheless quite different as far as it survives throughout in its wording to the shorter version text as preserved in AM 556 a 4to, and the longer version texts copied from the Membrana Regia Deperdita. In what is extant and legible of the AM 445 c I 4to *Gísla saga* text (which corresponds approximately to the narrative found in chapters 12–27 in Björn K. Þórólfsson's edition of the shorter version/AM 556 a 4to text of the saga, and chapters 17–24 of Agnete Loth's edition of the longer version/AM 149 fol. text), there are no attestations of *finna* but fifteen instances of *hitta*, four of which occur in contexts without an exact (i.e. a corresponding *hitta*) or synonymous parallel (i.e. a corresponding *finna*) in either the longer or the shorter version texts, as preserved in the paper copies of the Membrana Regia Deperdita and AM 556 a 4to respectively. Hallberg notes that six of the nine instances of *finna* he counts in "the longer version" of *Gísla saga* are at points where "the shorter version" has *hitta*, so there remain three instances of *finna* in the longer version without any equivalent in the shorter version. In conjunction with the fact that AM 445 c I 4to has been dated to c. 1390–1425 and thus is the oldest extant manuscript of *Gísla saga*, it is interesting to note that one of Hallberg's three examples of unparalleled instances of *finna* in the longer version is matched by a *hitta* in the fragmentary text in AM 445 c I 4to: while the significance of this may not be great, it would at least have supported Hallberg's hypothesis.

One last deficiency of Hallberg's statistics is that although they give the impression of being absolute, they are somewhat flawed on account of there being a considerable lacuna in the texts of the longer version. One *hitta* in the shorter-version text, for example, occurs at a point in the narrative that is not preserved in the longer version texts: we cannot know whether there was a *hitta* or *finna* equivalent here. Equally, we cannot know if the longer-version texts during this portion of narrative might have contained any instances of either *hitta* or *finna* that would have been without parallel in the shorter-version texts. It is striking that in one place in the longer-version texts, and in one place in the AM 445 c I 4to text, a number of attestations of *hitta* without parallel in AM 556 a 4to are found clustered together. One might speculate that if such clusters were also found in portions of the narrative in the longer- and fragmentary-version texts that do not survive, they too could have altered Hallberg's statistics.

Finally, some linguistic interest has centred on the purported age of certain words that occur in the longer and shorter version texts of the saga. The presence or absence in one or another text of later loan words or synonyms has been remarked on in passing by a few scholars: Schach, for example, comments that the vocabulary found in the longer-version texts is more modern than that of AM 556 a 4to (1986: 407; see also Guðbrandur Vigfússon and F. York Powell 1905: II, 194, on the word "buffeit"). There has been more substantial discussion with reference to the adverb "æva," which appears in the extra-diegetic narratorial introduction to Gísli's cryptic, self-incriminating verse uniquely in the AM 556 a 4to shorter-version text of *Gísla saga* ("þa G. q. v. er æfva skyllde"; see Kock 1911: 134–36 on the etymology of "æva"; de Vries 1962: 682; also La Farge 1992: 317).[5] Turville-Petre notes that the word "is archaic, and is hardly ever found in historical prose" (1944: 377); elsewhere, it appears in extant prose texts only in the late thirteenth-century AM 291 4to manuscript redaction of *Jómsvíkinga saga* (Petersens 1879: 14).[6] In Eddic poetry, however, the word is found in *Vǫluspá*, *Hávamál*, *Skírnismál*, *Vǫlundarkviða*, *Guðrúnarkviða* III, and *Atlakviða*, as well as in *Grógaldr* and *Getspeki Heiðreks* (Cleasby and Vigfússon 1957: 758); *Vǫlundarkviða* preserves the whole phrase "æva skyldi."

Björn M. Ólsen remarks that since scribes often updated the language of their exemplars, language cannot be taken seriously as a basis for assessing the age of a saga (1937–39: 129). Nonetheless, Björn does not dismiss the presence of the phrase "æva skyldi" in AM 556 a 4to and its implications out-of-hand: in fact, he rejects Finnur Jónsson's belief that the phrase is a later interpolation on the grounds that the word is such an archaic one that later scribes would not have been likely to insert it, and suggests that the sentence must have been in the "frumsaga" – which in turn "bendir hún til, að Gísla saga sje fremur gömul" (1937–39: 130) (suggests that *Gísla saga* is rather old). The use of a "poetic" word in a prose context has caught the attention of a number of critics; the context of Turville-Petre's discussion of the word is that of the "poetical tendencies" of the *Gísla saga* prose. Several scholars in addition to Turville-Petre (1944: 378 ff.) have explored the ways in which *Gísla saga* seems to bear the imprints of influence from certain heroic Eddic poems, especially those in the Burgundian cycle (see Ker 1908: 209–10; M. Olsen 1928; Clark 2007: especially at 496–500). Gordon (1949–50: 202–3) suggests that the phrase "æva skyldi" is a fossilized remnant of an

5 The standard formula "þa q(vat) G(isli) visu" (Loth 1960: 38) suffices as a preface to the poetic quotation in the AM 149 fol. and NKS 1181 fol. texts of the longer version of the saga. For further discussion of the phrase from a literary perspective, and about its editorial treatment, see Lethbridge 2010.

6 I am grateful to Chris Sanders of the ONP Dictionary at the Arnamagnæan Institute in Copenhagen for supplying me with this information.

earlier manifestation of the *Gísla saga* narrative, and that it might hark back to a "prose skeleton of a poetic work" whose tragic subject was Gísli's life, and which might have been a forerunner to the written saga as we know it. I will return to theories concerning such forerunners presently.

GÍSLA SAGA: POSITED SOURCES AND INFLUENCES

The identification of the sources, both written and oral, on which the hypothetical original author of the first written *Gísla saga* might have drawn, and the detection of various influences that may have shaped the written realization of the narrative, is a stratigraphic exercise akin in some ways to the detection of fossilized linguistic layers – the textual equivalent of archaeology. Whatever the true extent and nature of the imagined anecdotal traditions pertaining to Gísli Súrsson and his family that presumably underpin the written articulations of the narrative as we know it from extant manuscript copies, the structural and thematic organization of this written narrative has clearly been shaped by certain other discernible impulses and draws on other sources, both indigenous and learned, which may have been transmitted orally and/or in writing prior to their adaption into the written *Gísla saga* narrative.

Turville-Petre suggests that the *Gísla saga* author "was influenced, strongly though probably indirectly, by the changing artistic fashions of Europe" (1944: 390); it is for this reason, according to Turville-Petre, that *Gísla saga* "lacks the austerity which characterises many of the best Icelandic sagas ... [and] appeals especially to those trained to appreciate the romantic literatures of medieval and post-medieval Europe" (1944: 390). Whether or not one agrees with Turville-Petre's assessment of *Gísla saga* as lacking in austerity, and the extent to which the character of the saga has been shaped by European artistic fashions, some foreign influence on the written texts of the saga has been persuasively argued for. Carol Clover (1977), despite noting that *contra* Turville-Petre, *Gísla saga* "is, or appears to be, as 'native' a work as can be found in the prose production of thirteenth-century Iceland" (1977: 7), has argued convincingly that a central sequence of events in the narrative – the failed blood-brotherhood oath, Gísli Súrsson and Vésteinn Vésteinsson's final meeting, and Gísli's gift to Vésteinn of the broken coin, Þorkell's overhearing of Auðr and Ásgerðr's conversation about Vésteinn over their needlework, and Vésteinn's return to Iceland – constitutes an adaptation of a tale complex that combined the "Two Brothers," "Homecoming," and the "Faithless Wife" tale types, and that was popular throughout medieval Europe in both literary and folktale forms. Again, however, it is possible that the key motifs and themes here may have been combined with the Gísli material prior to the time when the narrative was set down in writing, thus while the unearthing of analogues is fascinating, it alone cannot shed much specific light on the question of the date of the saga's written composition.

The frequent deployment of proverbs in the context of the reported speech of individual characters is one distinctive indigenous strand or element in the written texts of the saga (see Hermann Pálsson 1984). It is impossible, though, to ascertain the stage at which these utterances might have been incorporated into the narrative as we know it. The way that narrative patterns at the heart of the pan-Germanic Vǫlsung legend seem to have moulded the expression of what Ida L. Gordon calls the "tragic theme" of the *Gísla saga* narrative (1949–50: 194–98) is more prominent. In addition to the direct reference to the Vǫlsung legend in the verse in which Gísli compares his sister Þórdís unfavourably to Guðrún Gjúkadóttir, the potent themes which run through the Vǫlsung narratives – the divisive force of adulterous love, and the paramount importance attached to family and personal honour and reputation, for example – are fully worked out in *Gísla saga,* where, together, these strands bring about the internally-directed destruction of Gísli's family (see Ker 1931: 209–10; M. Olsen 1928; Heinrichs 1958; and most recently Clark 2007). The detection of influence from the Vǫlsung legend alone, however, does not shed much light on the specific circumstances surrounding the written composition of *Gísla saga* though, since it is impossible to say whether the presumed incorporation of Vǫlsung tropes occurred prior to *Gísla saga*'s first written expression, assuming some coherent oral version of the narrative did exist beforehand, or whether this happened when the saga was first written down. Equally, it is impossible to ascertain whether the Vǫlsung legend patterns influenced the *Gísla saga* narrative – whether at an oral or written stage, via oral or written channels.

A second prominent and essential native thread in the tapestry of the written saga narrative is the body of verse woven into the prose: forty-odd poetic stanzas, mostly in *dróttkvætt*, are quoted over the course of *Gísla saga*, over two-thirds of which are attributed to Gísli himself. *Gísla saga* is not included amongst the so-called *skáldasögur* (i.e. *Bjarnar saga Hítdœlakappa, Kormáks saga, Gunnlaugs saga ormstungu, Hallfreðar saga vandræðaskálds*) but the artistic and rhetorical effects achieved by frequent poetic quotation throughout *Gísla saga* are various and have been productively examined (see, for example, Dronke 1978: especially 25–26 and most recently O'Donoghue 2005: 136–79). Nothing outside the saga suggests that the historical Gísli was known as a professional poet: he is not listed with other poets mentioned in the Kringla or Codex Upsaliensis versions of *Skáldatal*, for example. Early critics of the saga nevertheless believed the verses to be "genuine" (by which they meant they were the work of the eponymous tenth-century Gísli) on linguistic grounds such as the presence of uncontracted vowels in forms such as *áar*, *bráa*, *féi*, and *sæing*, and also on the basis of the (somewhat naive) conviction that no-one but Gísli himself could have conveyed the intensity of his tortured experiences in verse (see, for example, Finnur Jónsson 1903: xxi ff.).

Arguments for Gísli's authorship of the verses based on the detection of archaic linguistic forms do not stand, however, because although vowels in certain forms were contracted by the end of the twelfth century, they soon reappeared by analogy (see Björn K. Þórólfsson 1943: vi; Turville-Petre 1944: 388–89; Foote 1963: 116). As to the second point, Turville-Petre, for one, has noted that since certain of Gísli's dream-stanzas are prophetic, "they lead to the suspicion that Gísli did not compose them himself" (1944: 386). More seriously, the learned character of the Christian sentiment with which many of the verses are imbued (see Paasche 1928: 200–2) – albeit combined with native, pagan idioms such as *fylgjur*, *dísir*, and the figure of the valkyrie (see Foote 1963: 121–23) – renders the possibility that the verses were composed in the form in which they are extant by anyone during Gísli's pre-Conversion lifetime rather implausible (see, for example, Björn M. Ólsen 1937–39: 131; Björn K. Þórólfsson 1943: vii).[7] The spectrum of possibilities regarding the authorship of the *Gísla saga* verses is succinctly presented by Peter Foote (1963: 113–14): scholars have disagreed over whether the verses are contemporaneous with the prose and composed by one and the same individual in the thirteenth century, or whether, as certain contex-

7 It might be mentioned here that Hermann Pálsson (1973–74: 22–23) has drawn attention to a Biblical parallel for the two famous murder scenes – that of Vésteinn Vésteinsson, and then Þorgrímr goði Þorsteinsson – that act as dual fulcrums to the central part of the narrative: this is the killing of King Eglon of Moab (*Book of Judges*, 3).

tual discrepancies between individual verses and the prose in which they are embedded indicate, they were originally composed independently of the prose (Björn K. Þórólfsson 1943: v–vi; Turville-Petre 1944 and 1972 reprint; Gordon 1949–50: 186–89; Foote 1963: 114–15). In the case of the latter scenario, opinions diverge as to whether the poetic corpus as a whole represents the creative output of one individual, or is the work of several poets, working at different times in the period between Gísli's death and the postulated date of the saga's written composition. Guðbrandur Vigfússon and F. York Powell assign a range of different dates to individual verses, and suggest that while some must have been composed in the early thirteenth century, others have older origins but have been reworked by a twelfth-century "poetaster" (1905: II, 190–91; cf. their comments in 1883: II, 331. See also Björn K. Þórólfsson 1943: x–xi on likely dates of verses in metres other than *dróttkvætt*).

The way in which the verses in *Gísla saga* fall into two quite distinct categories is arresting. On the one hand, single stanzas or occasional clusters of two or three verses, spoken by Gísli in response to specific incidents, predominate in the first half of the narrative; in the second half of the narrative there are six lengthier sequences of verses in which Gísli describes the often violent dreams that trouble him once he has been outlawed. Sophie Krijn (1935) has seen these latter, extended sequences of verses as the remnants of three distinct poems composed not long after the historical Gísli's death; Björn M. Ólsen (1937–39: 122), on the other hand, believes them to be the work of the thirteenth-century saga author. Since the publication of Peter Foote's conclusions that the verses are largely the work of one poet working in the late twelfth century or around 1200 (1963: 113–23), most scholars have supported the theory of the single authorship of the majority of verses, on the basis of the perceived consistency of their stylistic expression across the whole corpus despite their diverging contexts and substance. Ida Gordon (1949–50: 185), for example, notes that "it is probably safer to assume that we are dealing here not with two different poets but with one poet whose purpose was different in the two parts" (see also, most recently, K. Olsen 1996).

If the theory that the majority of the *Gísla saga* verses are older than the prose in which they are embedded is accepted – and the balance of evidence makes this seem more likely than unlikely – then the question of the verses' transmisson prior to their use as a source and incorporation in the written saga must be pursued. Some critics have suggested that the posited thirteenth-century saga writer had access to the verses in written form (Finnur Jónsson 1903: xvii–xviii; Björn K. Þórólfsson 1943: xi). However likely or unlikely this is, it is not implausible to suppose that some kind of explanatory framework might have accompanied the verses whether they were transmitted orally, or in writing, as already noted earlier: Gordon (1949–50: 201ff.), Prinz (1935: 158–66), and Foote (1963: 124) are amongst those who have contemplated the likely nature of oral or written prosimetric forerunners to the written saga. While some sense of the events that constitute the written saga narrative can be construed from a reading or a hearing of the verses alone, when many of the verses are taken out of context, there is often little or no internal indication as to the occasion on which they are uttered; conversely, many episodes in the saga prose do not incorporate any verse at all.

Speculation over the likely existence of oral, prosimetric forerunners to the written sagas and the contours that these hypothetical oral narratives might have had is central to any consideration of the origins and development of the written *Íslendingasögur* genre (see especially Harris 1997, and further references therein). Elucidating the origins of the *Gísla saga* stanzas, and determining their relationship to the saga prose, is crucial in any attempt to establish the saga's genesis (see O'Donoghue 1991: 170–71). At the same time however, it must be remembered that – as Preben Meulengracht Sørensen (2001b: especially 188–89) and Guðrún Nordal (2007: 220) emphasize more generally with reference to the prosimetric form of the *Íslendingasögur* – in the context of the respective saga narrative itself and its transmission and reception, the range of possibilities regarding the origins of each stanza is not necessarily significant, as every verse is "authentic" first and foremost by sheer virtue of its incorporation into that prose narrative.

Appreciation of the intertextual dimensions of written saga texts is crucial in any attempt to come to an understanding of an individual saga; *Gísla saga* is no exception. Presumably, from the first date at which traditions about Gísli were transmitted in some coherent oral or written form, the narrative was not perceived or received as a self-contained, discrete unit, but appreciated and interpreted within the broader context of the medieval Icelandic literary milieu – the common inheritance of which is manifested in the frequent overlap between written sagas in the characters they present and the events they recount. Einar Ól. Sveinsson (1958: 76–95) regarded the identification of literary or written connections between sagas to be the most productive method of establishing dates for individual sagas: by arguing for direct borrowings from one text to another, scholars believe it is possible to establish theoretical *terminus post quem* and *terminus ante quem* dates for individual sagas, and to construct a relative chronology of extant sagas.

A number of motifs and details in *Gísla saga* have parallels elsewhere in saga literature: one striking example is the narrative treatment and function of the cursed swords Grásíða and Fótbítr in *Gísla saga* and *Laxdœla saga* respectively (see Mundal 1997; Heller 1966a; Gordon 1934: 93 lists other motifs in *Gísla saga* found elsewhere). More generally, the utilization of the same motifs or the appearance of the same characters in *Gísla saga* and elsewhere in the *Íslendingasögur* has led some scholars to posit tentative literary relations or the common use of a source such as a written genealogy (see Björn K. Þórólfsson 1943: xviii–xix with reference to *Kormáks saga*; 1943: xx with reference to *Bjarnar saga Hítdœlakappa*; and 1943: xxi with reference to *Snorra Edda*), despite Björn M. Ólsen's caution that "Aldur frumsögunnar er erfitt að ákveða, af því að hún kemur svo lítt við aðrar sögur" (1937–39: 129) (The age of the original saga is difficult to determine because of its negligible overlap with other sagas). There are intriguing correspondences between the account in *Gísla saga* of Gísli Þorkelsson's fateful fight with the slave Kolr which ends with both of their deaths, and that of the quarrel between, and subsequent deaths of, Végestr Bjartmarsson and the slave Bjǫrn Hjallkársson as recounted in the Hauksbók and Sturlubók versions of *Landnámabók*: it is interesting that Végestr is the uncle of Gísli Súrsson's wife, Auðr Vésteinsdóttir. Peter Foote notes that the *Landnámabók* account might be a "possible model for this story" (1963: 65–66) but *Gísla saga*'s potential textual relations with the different *Landnámabók* redactions are not altogether clear and there are a number of discrepancies between some of the details preserved in the extant texts of *Gísla saga* and those in the extant *Landnámabók* texts (Björn K. Þórólfsson 1943: xii–xvi). Critics generally assume that the posited author of the first written *Gísla saga* did not use *Landnámabók* as a source, but think that Sturla Þórðarson drew on *Gísla saga* in compiling his Sturlubók redaction of *Landnámabók*, thus a *terminus post quem* of c. 1270–80 is offered on the basis of Sturla's likely production of Sturlubók and ultimately his death (1284).

Leaving *Landnámabók* aside, two scenes in *Gísla saga* in particular have been examined in the light of posited literary relationships with other saga narratives. Firstly, close parallels have been noted between the structure and presentation of Gísli's murder of Þorgrímr goði, and the account in *Droplaugarsona saga* of the murder of Helgi Ásbjarnarson by Grímr Droplaugarson. Both murderers venture out to the farm in which their victim is sleeping clad very lightly in linen underclothes; both murderers tie together the tails of the cattle in the adjoining cowbyre in order to inhibit being pursued following their secret attack; both murderers wake their intended victim and/or his spouse in their bed-closet by touching them with a cold hand, for example. These and other similarities have led scholars to assert that "Greinileg tengsl eru með Gísla sögu og Droplaugarsona sögu" (Björn K. Þórólfsson 1943: xix) (there are clear [written] connections between *Gísla saga* and *Droplaugarsona saga*), and that "The similarity of the phrases and motives used in these two sagas is so close, that one of them must have copied directly from the other" (Turville-Petre 1944: 390). There has not been unanimous agreement, though, as to the most likely direction of this perceived borrowing.

Many of the arguments concerning the possible textual relationships between *Gísla saga* and *Droplaugarsona saga* exemplify the ways in which *rittengsl* conclusions are often highly subjective (see Finlay 1993: 143). Assumptions about *Droplaugarsona saga*'s age – that judging by its artistic style, on the basis of preconceived notions about the stylistic development of *Íslendingasögur* narratives, it must be one of the oldest *Íslendingasögur* – have informed some scholars' conjectures about the relative chronological precedence of *Droplaugarsona saga* and *Gísla saga*, and which saga must therefore have borrowed from the other (see, for example, Björn M. Ólsen 1937–39: 130). Arguments have also turned on attempts to explain perceived internal narrative inconsistencies, summed up usefully by Andersson (1968: 31–36). Gordon (1934), Björn M. Ólsen (1937–39: 125–27), Björn K. Þórólfsson (1943: xix–xx), Jón Jóhannesson (1950: lxxiii–iv), Hermann Pálsson (1977), and Foote (1963: 128–29) all conclude that *Gísla saga* has borrowed from *Droplaugarsona saga*, principally on the basis that the details of the murderers' light attire and their bovine tail-tying antics are illogical blind motifs in *Gísla saga* and make more sense in their *Droplaugarsona saga* context. Counter-arguments have been advanced by Guðbrandur Vigfússon and F. York Powell (1905: II, 193–94), Heusler (1943–69), Liestøl (1930), Björn K. Þórólfsson (1928: 55–62), and Andersson (1968: 31–36); it seems possible to argue the case from both sides, but no single nor cumulative line of reasoning is wholly convincing.

Secondly, connections between *Gísla saga* and *Eyrbyggja saga* have been adduced (see especially Einar Ól. Sveinsson and Matthías Þórðarson 1935: xxi–xxii; Björn K. Þórólfsson 1943: xvi–xviii; Andersson 1964: 168–72; Jónas Kristjánsson; and Guðni Kolbeinsson 1979: 144–47). The brief resumé in chapter 12 of *Eyrbyggja saga* (Einar Ól. Sveinsson and Matthías Þórðarson 1935: 19–20) concerning material that is treated in detail in *Gísla saga* (i.e. Þorgrímr Þorsteinsson's marriage, the circumstances surrounding his death, the birth of Snorri goði, Þórdís's divorce from Bǫrkr digri) is taken as evidence for the *Eyrbyggja saga* writer's familiarity with a written *Gísla saga* and thus for the latter saga's chronological precedence: "Höfundur Eyrbyggju gerir sýnilega ráð fyrir að efni þetta sé alkunnugt, og sýnir það að Gíslasaga er eldri" (The author of *Eyrbyggja saga* obviously assumes that the material is generally known, and this shows that *Gísla saga* is older), write Jónas Kristjánsson and Guðni Kolbeinsson (1979: 144). Certain discrepancies between the information in *Gísla saga* and in *Eyrbyggja saga* are explained as the consequence of the *Eyrbyggja saga* author having used *Ævi Snorra goða* as an additional source (Einar Ól. Sveinsson and Matthías Þórðarson 1935: xxii, xxxiii). One might wonder, however, whether this general outline of events could equally well have been preserved and transmitted orally, particularly in the localities in which the murders of Vésteinn Vésteinsson and Þorgrímr goði purportedly occurred.

The verbal parallels between the accounts of Þórdís's attempt to avenge Gísli in *Gísla saga* (Björn K. Þórólfsson 1943: 116–17; Agnete Loth 1960: 78–79) and those in chapter 13 of *Eyrbyggja saga* (Einar Ól. Sveinsson 1935: 23–24) are more compelling as evidence for some kind of "literary" relationship between the written texts of the two sagas. Knut Liestøl (1930: 38, 45) has suggested that the verbal overlap between the two sagas stems from the two written renditions of the same scene being independent realizations of an orally-transmitted narrative episode (cf. also Andersson 1964: 172). Otherwise, from the outset, assumptions regarding the chronological written precedence of *Gísla saga* over *Eyrbyggja saga* – which rest, partly, on *Eyrbyggja saga*'s posited textual relationships with other texts – have largely determined critics' opinions regarding the direction of the perceived borrowing. But an additional complication arises out of the fact that there are a number of textual divergences between the accounts of the scene as it is preserved in the shorter- and longer-version texts of *Gísla saga*, so that there are both correspondences and discrepancies between the *Gísla saga* renditions of the scene, on the one hand, and *Eyrbyggja saga*'s articulation on the other.[8]

It has been widely agreed that the professed author of *Eyrbyggja saga* made use of a shorter-version text of *Gísla saga* in the process of composing his version of the scene; subsequently, the individual thought to have been responsible for expanding a shorter-version text of *Gísla saga* and thereby producing the longer version was assumed to have had recourse to a text of *Eyrbyggja saga* (see Björn K. Þórólfsson 1943: xlvii; Heller 1958: 76–77; Andersson 1964: 168–69). This model, however, hinges on taking for granted the chronological precedence of the shorter version of *Gísla saga* over the longer version. Jónas Kristjánsson's and Guðni Kolbeinsson's 1979 reversal of the priority of the shorter and longer versions accordingly necessitated a revision of the conclusions regarding the two versions' alleged textual relationship with *Eyrbyggja saga*: they argue, therefore, that the rendering of Þórdís's vengeance scene in the longer version of *Gísla saga* stands behind the rendering in *Eyrbyggja saga*, which was then used by the individual who created the shorter version of *Gísla saga* (1979: 147; see also Schach 1972: 120–53 and 1986: 409–10).

Paul Schach (1972) has positively explored some of the ways in which the divergences between the so-called Helgafell episode as recounted in the longer and shorter *Gísla saga* versions and in *Eyrbyggja saga* might bear witness to the changing interpretations and intentions of those responsible for transmitting the narrative material, but he is in the minority. Critics have largely approached the question about *rittengsl* possibilities rather inflexibly, determined above all to identify direct literary debts in order to construct relative chronologies, and casting their conclusions somewhat anachronistically and negatively in terms of plagiarism, with all of the inherent negative connotations that accompany the notion in modern literary contexts.The possibility that influence from one tradition to the other may be manifested at an oral stage, for example, is most often disregarded (though see, recently, Gísli Sigurðsson 2004).

Finally, critics have claimed that passages unique to the longer-version texts of the saga are derivative of other written sources such as *Egils saga*,

8 The scene is not preserved amongst the surviving leaves of AM 445 c I 4to.

Íslendingabók, and *Heimskringla* (see Guðbrandur Vigfússon and F. York Powell 1905: II, 190, 194; Björn K. Þórólfsson 1943: xlv–xlvi). Guðbrandur Vigfússon and F. York Powell, for example, write that the scribe of the first longer-version text "brings in pieces from the Kings' Lives which have really nothing to do with Gisle's Saga" and call it "extraneous matter" (1905: II, 190). Again, these arguments build on prejudice against the longer-version texts and on the principle that the longer version is an amplified reworking of a shorter-version text; unenthusiastic opinions about the artistic style of the longer-version texts have led critics to frame such claims in negative terms of a posited "editor" interpolating additional material, perceived to be irrelevant, from these other sources. The rigidity of such approaches to the extant evidence for *Gísla saga*, and the insecure foundations on which these arguments are often constructed – i.e. subjective assumptions about the written transmission of texts and the stylistic development of *Íslendingasögur* narratives, for example, and the relationship between the longer and shorter versions of *Gísla saga* – obscure the fluidity inherent in medieval Icelandic texts and the processes of their transmission, as attested by the manuscript evidence.

The identification of historical events or connections that might have provided the stimulus for the writing of *Gísla saga*, or might have shaped its written expression and organization, can be seen as a complementary line of enquiry to that just discussed, of investigating posited *rittengsl* connections between texts in order to establish the date of individual sagas. The apparent evidence in *Íslendinga saga* for the thirteenth-century existence of a spear known as Grásíða, thought to be old at that time and explicitly associated with Gísli Súrsson, has been noted by a number of scholars (see Guðbrandur Vigfússon and F. York Powell 1905: II, 193, Björn M. Ólsen 1937–39: 127–29, Björn K. Þórólfsson 1943: xxv and xxxix–xl, Anne Holtsmark 1951: 10–17, and Richard Perkins 1989: 250–54). In *Íslendinga saga* chapter 39, we hear that Guðlaugr Eyjólfsson of Þingvellir uses this spear to kill Bjǫrn Þorvaldsson at the battle of Breiðabólsstaðir in 1221; later, in chapter 138, the spear appears again, this time in the hands of Sturla Sighvatsson on the occasion of his last battle, Ǫrlygsstaðir, which took place in 1238.[9] It is probably safe to assume that this spear was not a genuine

9 Chapter 39: "Hljóp Guðlaugr fram ok lagði til Bjarnar með spjóti því, er þeir kölluðu Grásíðu og sögðu átt hafa Gísla Súrsson. Lagit kom í óstinn, ok snerist Björn upp at

tenth-century artefact that once belonged to the historical Gísli Súrsson; these references thus beg the question "which came first, the spear or the written *Gísla saga*?," as put by Richard Perkins (1989: 251), and also whether the author of *Íslendinga saga*, Sturla Þórðarson, knew *Gísla saga*.

Peter Foote concludes that by 1221 some orally-transmitted narrative about Gísli and Grásíða was in circulation, and that the note in *Gísla saga* that describes Grásíða as having a "damascened" blade (Björn K. Þórólfsson 1943: 38[10]) is likely to have been informed by the appearance of the contemporary spear (see Holtsmark 1951: 16–17 on the meaning of ON *mál*). By 1221 the spear must have achieved "notoriety" and after this time, the "author of the saga we possess was moved ... to write the prehistory of [this] real weapon" (Foote 1963: 130; see also Holtsmark 1951: 12–13). Foote – and Perkins – think it unlikely that a written saga of Gísli existed prior to 1221 and thus that the thirteenth-century spear was named after the weapon in the written saga (Foote 1963: 130; Perkins 1989: 251). Rather, as Perkins suggests, the influence of the oral tradition about Gísli and Grásíða resulted in "someone [giving] the name Grásíða to a spear of some quite different origin and claim[ing] it was the spear that Gísli had owned" (1989: 251). An interesting argument has been made recently by Axel Kristinsson (2003: 10–11), who sees the fact that Sturla Sighvatsson chose to fight with "Gísli's"

kirkjunni ok settist niðr. Guðlaugr gekk til Lofts ok sagði honum, at Björn var sárr orðinn. Loftr spyrr, hverr því olli. 'Vit Grásíða', svarar hann" (Jón Jóhannesson et al. 1946: I, 282) (Guðlaugr ran forward and thrust at Bjǫrn with the spear that they called Grásíða, and claimed that Gísli Súrsson had owned. The stab hit him in the throat and Bjǫrn turned back up to the church and sat down. Guðlaugr went over to Loftr and said to him that Bjǫrn had been wounded. Loftr asked who had done that. 'Grásíða and I', he answered). Chapter 138: "Sturla varðist með spjóti því, er Grásíða hét, fornt ok ekki vel stinnt málaspjót" (Jón Jóhannesson et al. 1946: I, 435) (Sturla defended himself with the spear called Grásíða, an old and not very strong inlaid spear). A reference to the weapon is also found in the second *helmingr* of an anonymous verse quoted at the end of chapter 39, in which Grásíða is described as "rather sharp to kiss" ("hvöss vas hon heldr at kyssa," Jón Jóhannesson et al. 1946 I, 284). This verse picks up the line "harðmúlaðr vas Skúli" (Skúli was hard-mouthed) which is found first in a *helmingr* of Snorri Sturluson's *drápa* to Jarl Skúli as cited in chapter 38 of *Íslendinga saga*, and then in a stanza commissioned by a certain Þóroddr í Selvági which is quoted immediately after Snorri's verse as an example of the parodic verses that Snorri's encomium spawned (Jón Jóhannesson et al. 1946: I, 278–79).

10 It is interesting that while the spear is described as being damascened in the shorter-version AM 556a 4to text of *Gísla saga*, in the longer-version texts the spear is described only as being large, with a long shaft, "var spiotit mikit, var skeptit langt at spiotinu" (Loth 1960: 24–25).

spear at the battle of Ǫrlygsstaðir as highly significant. Despite the spear's age and feebleness – we are told that Sturla repeatedly has to straighten out the spear-head with his foot[11] – it is a symbolic choice, through which Sturla, who gained control of the principality of the Seldælir in 1225, was "identifying himself with the local hero Gísli Súrsson, and ... giving the message to the men of the Seldælir principality that he was Gísli's heir and their natural leader" (2003: 11; see also Axel Kristinsson 2009).

Correspondences between certain details of Gísli's outlawry as related in *Gísla saga* and the outlawry of the famous thirteenth-century outlaw Aron Hjǫrleifsson (1199–1255) as recounted in *Íslendinga saga* and *Arons saga Hjǫrleifssonar* have also been noted (see Heller 1966; Aðalgeir Kristjánsson 1965; Foote 1963: 130–31). Aron was involved in the conflict between bishop Guðmundr Arason of Hólar and Sighvatr Sturluson, and he was sentenced to outlawry in 1222 for his part in the killing of Túmi Sighvatsson, at Hólar, in February earlier that year. Aron escaped to Norway in 1225, but prior to this was on the run in Iceland from Sighvatr and Sturla Sighvatssynir, both of whom wanted to avenge Túmi's death. Aron received protection from his kinsmen, the sons of the chieftain, and physician Hrafn Sveinbjarnarson, who lived at Eyr on the northern side of Arnarfjǫrðr; he was also sheltered by a farmer at a second Eyr on the northern side of Geirþjǫfsfjǫrðr – very close to where Gísli Súrsson's secret hideouts and his wife Auðr's smallholding were located (see Map 4, "Gisli's Country," in Foote 1963: 138). Aron's outlawry is described in *Arons saga Hjǫrleifssonar*, in Sturla Þórðarson's *Íslendinga saga*, and in *Þorgils saga skarða*. In the accounts of both men's survival as outlaws, we are told how they sail from Barðastrandr across Breiðafjǫrðr in a boat they have taken or been given, how they subsequently abandon the vessel in order to create the impression they have been drowned (Björn K. Þórólfsson 1943: 78; Loth 1960: 52–53; Jón Jóhannesson et al. 1946: I, 306), and how they both make or repair boats for the farmers who are hiding them (Björn K. Þórólfsson 1943: 79; Loth 1960: 53; Jón Jóhannesson et al. 1946: I, 305 and II, 260), for example (see Aðalgeir Kristjánsson 1965: 149–57 for a detailed list of parallels). Foote suggests that Aron's concealment in Geirþjófsfjǫrðr might have renewed local interest in Gísli's story, and that this might have given rise to the composition of the

11 "Hann lagði svá hart með því jafnan, at menn fellu fyrir, en spjótit lagðist, ok brá hann því undir fót sér nökkurum sinnum" (Jón Jóhannesson et al. 1946: I, 435).

written saga: while "Gisli is not a literary portrait of Aron ... there are one or two features in his saga which we may regard as borrowed from Aron's career, or which, at any rate, have been given a sharper edge in the narrative as a result of Aron's experiences" (1963: 131).

Through exploring the possibility of connections between the written composition of *Gísla saga*, the existence of the thirteenth-century Grásíða, and the outlaw career of Aron Hjǫrleifsson, critics have attempted to establish a *terminus post quem* for *Gísla saga* and have argued that the saga must have been composed after the battle of Breiðabólsstaðir in 1221, and after Aron's period of outlawry in Iceland in the first half of the 1220s. Given the modern tendency to situate the commencement of *Íslendingasögur* writing around the beginning of the thirteenth century, the possibility that the dates of Aron's outlawry and of Breiðabólsstaðir might be *terminus ante quem* dates has been considered implausible (see Perkins 1989: 251). However, the assumption that *samtíðarsögur* are historically reliable and concurrently the hypothesis that the purported details of Aron Hjǫrleifsson's outlawry as recorded in *Íslendinga saga* and *Arons saga* might have influenced the written organization of the account of Gísli's outlawry can also be upturned. It is equally possible that a coherent narrative about Gísli's outlawry – which could have been either oral or written – might have shaped the literary account of Aron's outlawry, which may not necessarily have reflected the reality of his own outlawry that closely. With reference to Grásíða: *Íslendinga saga* is not thought to have been written before the latter years of Sturla Þórðarson's life (d. 1284), so it might also be possible that the spear used firstly by Guðlaugr Eyjólfsson in 1221, and then by Sturla Sighvatsson in 1238, could have been given the name Grásíða retrospectively after both men had fought with it, and after *Gísla saga* had been set down in writing, but before Sturla wrote *Íslendinga saga*. Mention might also be made of the vagueness surrounding the references in *Íslendinga saga* to the weapon and its provenance, especially in the context of its first mention, where it is not clear to whom, exactly, the third person-plural personal pronoun "þeir" refers in the phrase "er þeir kölluðu ... og sögðu ..." (which they called ... and they claimed ...); this, in itself, might caution us against using this as concrete evidence for the dating of *Gísla saga*.

THE AUTHORSHIP OF *GÍSLA SAGA* AND SOME CONCLUSIONS

Attempts to ascertain the date of *Gísla saga*'s production naturally have led scholars to ask who might have been responsible for the first written composition of the saga: "ever since N. F. S. Grundtvig proposed Snorri as the man behind *Egils saga*," notes Carol Clover, "the hunt for authors has been on" (2005: 245). Stefán Einarsson (1937: 69) remarks that "[i]t would be an interesting speculation to try to draw the picture of the author who in the troubled age of the Sturlungs wrote *Gísla saga*. Would not such a man be likely to be both heroic and soft as Gísli was?" The urge to establish the identity of the conjectured "author" of *Gísla saga* has thus been a prominent theme in twentieth-century scholarship on the saga, particularly in that scholarship which is influenced by bookprose principles (see Vésteinn Ólason 1999: 164–66). Most critics have gone no further than to speculate over this author's likely place of origin and have concluded that, on the basis of the detail and familiarity with the landscape in which the *Gísla saga* narrative is set, this was probably the Vestfirðir and maybe, more specifically, somewhere in Dýrafjǫrðr (e.g. Björn M. Ólsen 1937–39: 130; though cf. Guðbrandur Vigfússon and F. York Powell 1905: II, 189). On the basis of the strong Christian sentiment that is manifested particularly in Gísli's dreams, some of these same critics think it likely that this author was a cleric (Björn M. Ólsen 1937–39: 131; Finnur Jónsson 1903: xvi–xvii and 1929: xiii; Björn K. Þórólfsson 1943: xxxviii–xxxix; Aðalgeir Kristjánsson 1965: 148).

A handful of critics, however, have tried to attribute the written composition of *Gísla saga* to known individuals, notably Snorri Sturluson (1178/79–1241) and Sturla Bárðarson (born c. 1180). Einar Ól. Sveinsson has called Snorri the "king of saga-writers" (1937–38: 73–74) and the arguments for his authorship of *Gísla saga* exemplify the inclination to assign *Íslendingasögur* to him, largely on the basis of his reputation as one of the figureheads of Icelandic literature (see, for example, the discussion in Boulhosa 2005: 6–21). These attributions are, more often than not, speculative, based on insecure foundations, and characterized by circular logic: Snorri's posited – but ultimately unsubstantiable – authorship of *Egils saga*, for example, is taken either as the starting-point or deployed as the crowning evidence for such propositions (see, for example, Megaard 2006: especially at 696–97). This is epitomized in the claims for Snorri's authorship of *Gísla saga* – or more specifically, the theory that Snorri reworked a text of the longer version of the saga, thereby producing the shorter version which is generally held to be stylistically superior (see Stemshaug 1985: 86, note 7, and Jakobsen 1985: 96).

Aðalgeir Kristjánsson's arguments for Sturla Bárðarson's authorship of *Gísla saga* (1992; see also Sveinbjörn Beinteinsson 1991) are principally founded on facts about Sturla gleaned from *Sturlunga saga* – his religious education, that he was a poet, his close connections with the chieftain Hrafn Sveinbjarnarson (who lived at Eyr in Arnarfjǫrðr, died in 1213, and whose life is recounted in *Hrafns saga Sveinbjarnarsonar*) and the Sturlungar family. This is somewhat nebulous evidence to say the least; as with the lines of reasoning for Snorri's posited authorship of *Gísla saga*, the hypothesis is ultimately inconclusive. Peter Foote's suggestion (1963: 131–33) that Hrafn Sveinbjarnarson's life and career might illuminate the milieu in which the written *Gísla saga* could have been produced is an interesting one that has the potential for insights of a more general, but concurrently more plausible kind. Likewise, Axel Kristinsson's attempts to link the production of *Gísla saga* with political developments in the Seldœlir principality in the early decades of the thirteenth century is absorbing (2003, 2009). Axel's hypothesis that the writing down of *Gísla saga* might have been sponsored either by Sturla Sighvatsson (1199–1238) or by his successor, his brother Þórðr kakali Sighvatsson (d. 1256), as a means of consolidating their political power and identity in the Seldœlir principality (2003: 11, 2009: especially 4–5), is persuasive; the margin he suggests for the saga's composition, between 1242 and 1245 (2009: 8), is extremely narrow though, and similar objẹctions to those already expressed in this article concerning the limitations of using contemporary events to fix *terminus post* and *ante quem* dates apply.

Attempts to attribute the authorship of certain texts to specific individuals is sometimes found in medieval manuscripts: one well-known example is the attribution of *Gunnlaugs saga ormstungu* to Ari inn fróði in the fourteenth-century manuscript Sth perg 18 4to. The respective hypotheses concerning Sturla Sighvatsson and Þórðr kakali, Snorri Sturluson, and Sturla Bárðarson are not completely implausible, but they cannot be substantiated and are representative of the ways in which in modern saga scholarship the anachronistic desire to attribute a written narrative to an individual, thereby situating it firmly within an historical and ideological framework, often supersedes the evidence for that narrative itself and distorts our understanding of the distinctive nature of medieval and post-medieval Icelandic textuality. Not only are our modern assumptions about authorship as a creative process quite different to apparent attitudes towards the written composition and transmission of saga narratives in medieval Iceland, but with a few exceptions, we only know of a small number of the presumably more numerous literate individuals who would have been capable of producing and transmitting saga narratives; for this reason, scholarly efforts to "credit" individuals with the authorship of certain sagas often revolve around the same figures whose birth and death dates consequently impose a date for the individual narrative's written composition by default.

The very existence of the diverging texts of *Gísla saga*, each of which conveys distinctive emphases and interpretations of aspects of the narrative (see Lethbridge 2010), highlights the fact that medieval Icelanders did not conceive of the first written text of the saga as necessarily representing the definitive formulation of the saga. Attempting to pin the written composition of the saga onto one specific individual and thereby privileging one text of the saga – that irretrievably lost original – over others that exist shifts the critical focus away from this surviving evidence for the continuous, regenerative tradition of the saga narrative, to a single, hypothetical, irrecoverable articulation. The rhetorical questions Vésteinn Ólason and Þórður Ingi Guðjónsson pose in the conclusion to their study on *Gísla saga* are, to my mind, more stimulating and potentially profitable lines of enquiry: "Burde vi snakke om *Gísla sagas* tre forfattere? Eller kan vi slet ikke bruge ordet 'forfatter'?" (2000: 108) (Ought we talk about *Gísla saga*'s three authors? Or can we simply not use the word "author"?). "Dating the sagas" is an irrefutably important undertaking but certain fundamental questions must be asked, and key issues must be resolved, before significant progress can be made – to begin with, what exactly is being dated in individual cases?

As I hope I have demonstrated by taking *Gísla saga* as a case study, arguments for dating individual sagas by establishing *terminus post* and *ante quem* dates on the basis of such types of internal and external evidence as enumerated (a saga's linguistic and stylistic expression, and potential sources and influences both literary and historical) are often circular and insecure and founded on subjective presuppositions, although the conclusions pronounced by critics give the impression of being definitive. Especially problematic is the notion of *rittengsl* as the keystone in constructing arguments for the dating of individual sagas. As Gísli Sigurðsson has warned,

> we cannot automatically assume literary relations simply because two or more written sources describe or contain the same themes, motifs, formulas or clichés, names, genealogies, or events. All such features could have been passed on from one person to another without the aid of written books ... If it turns out that the accepted theories of literary relations prove unsustainable ... it would seem that the whole intricate edifice of ideas about the age of the sagas of Icelanders, lost older versions, the influences of one saga on another, and the connections between Landnámabók and the sagas – all the ideas that have been built upon the assumption that these relations were proven, unambiguous, and beyond dispute – will be in need of complete revision from the bottom up. (Gísli Sigurðsson 2004: 128)

The necessity for moving the debate on and conceiving of new approaches to the issue of dating the sagas is emphasized by Chris Callow in a recent article (2006: especially 297–300). Callow's line – that the texts of the *Íslendingasögur* must be seen as "meaningful for the people who constructed them" through their encoding not only of "an abstract message about morals or conduct, but one about local political relationships" (2006: 299) – is clearly congruent with Axel Kristinsson's social-historical approach to *Gísla saga* mentioned above. This cannot be said to represent an entirely new approach – Einar Ól. Sveinsson articulates the same basic idea in his 1937–38 article – but the way in which Callow's approach utilizes developments in other academic fields such as social anthropology, in conjunction with the way in which the focus and attitudes of scholars of Old Norse literature towards extant medieval and post-medieval textual evidence is undergoing various shifts in certain spheres, make it potentially rewarding. *Gísla saga* is an interesting case study because of the state of its preservation: the existence of three distinct versions (whose textual relationship is still not altogether clear despite the attention of numerous formidable scholars) forces us to think about the extent to which the exercise of dating the saga is viable – at the very least, we are induced to question how appropriate and reliable previous approaches to the question are, and we are prompted to err on the side of caution as far as making explicit statements about the saga's "date" is concerned in the absence of any concrete evidence.

Bibliography

Aðalgeir Kristjánsson 1965. "*Gísla saga* og samtíð höfundar." *Skírnir* 139: 148–58.

——— 1992. "Var Sturla Bárðarson höfundur *Gíslasögu*?" *Skáldskaparmál* 2: 107–23.

Andersson, Theodore M. 1964. *The Problem of Icelandic Saga Origins: A Historical Survey*. New Haven, CT, and London: Yale University Press.

——— 1968. "Some Ambiguities in *Gísla saga*: A Balance Sheet." *Bibliography of Old Norse-Icelandic Studies*: 7–42.

——— 1985. "Review of Paul Schach, *Icelandic Sagas* [1984]." *Speculum* 60: 1017–19.

Axel Kristinsson 2003. "Icelandic Sagas as Political and Social Instruments." *Scandinavian Journal of History* 28: 1–17.

——— 2009. "The Revered Outlaw: Gísli Súrsson and the Sturlungs." *The CAHD Papers* 4. Available online at www.akademia.is/CAHD.

Bjarni Guðnason 1993. *Túlkun Heiðarvígasögu* (Studia Islandica 50). Reykjavík: Bókmenntafræðistofnun Háskóla Íslands.

Björn M. Ólsen 1937–39. "Gísla saga Súrssonar." In Sigfús Blöndal and Einar Ólafur Sveinsson (eds.), *Um Íslendingasögur. Kaflar úr háskólafyrirlestrum* (Safn til sögu Íslands og íslenzkra bókmennta). Reykjavík: Hið íslenska bókmenntafélag, pp. 118–131.

Björn K. Þórólfsson 1928. "Droplaugarsona saga." In Johannes Brøndum-Nielsen et al. (eds.), *Festskrift til Finnur Jónsson. 28 Maj 1928*. Copenhagen: Levin & Munksgaard, pp. 45–66.

Björn K. Þórólfsson and Guðni Jónsson (eds.) 1943. *Vestfirðingasǫgur* (Íslenzk fornrit 6). Reykjavík: Hið íslenska fornritafélag.

Boulhosa, Patricia Pires 2005. *Icelanders and the Kings of Norway: Mediaeval Sagas and Legal Texts* (Northern World 17). Leiden: Brill.

Byock, Jesse L. 1984. "Saga Form, Oral Prehistory, and the Icelandic Social Context." *New Literary History* 16: 153–73.

Callow, Chris 2006. "Reconstructing the Past in Medieval Iceland." *Early Medieval Europe* 14: 297–324.

Clark, David 2007. "Revisiting *Gísla saga*: Sexual Themes and the Heroic Past." *Journal of English and Germanic Philology* 106: 492–515.

Cleasby, Richard, and Guðbrandur Vigfússon 1957. *An Icelandic-English*

Dictionary. With a Supplement by Sir William A. Craigie. 2nd ed. Oxford University Press.

Clover, Carol 1977. "Gísli's Coin." *Bibliography of Old Norse-Icelandic Studies* 7–37.

—— 2005. "Icelandic Family Sagas (*Íslendingasögur*)." In Carol J. Clover and John Lindow (eds.), *Old Norse-Icelandic Literature: A Critical Guide*. 2nd ed. (Medieval Academy Reprints for Teaching 42). Ithaca, NY, and London: University of Toronto Press in associaton with the Medieval Academy of America, pp. 239–315.

Danielsson, Tommy 2007. "On the Possibility of an Oral Background for *Gísla saga Súrssonar*." In Else Mundal and Jonas Wellendorf (eds.), *Oral Art Forms and their Passage into Writing*. Copenhagen: Museum Tusculanum Press, pp. 23–35.

Dronke, Ursula 1978. "The Poet's Persona in the Skalds' Sagas." *Parergon* 22: 23–28.

Einar Ól. Sveinsson 1937–38. "The Icelandic Family Sagas and the Period in which their Authors Lived." *Acta Philologica Scandinavica* 12: 71–90.

—— 1958. *Dating the Icelandic Sagas: An Essay in Method* (Viking Society for Northern Research Text Series 3). London, Viking Society for Northern Research.

Einar Ól. Sveinsson, and Matthías Þórðarson (eds.) 1935. *Eyrbyggja saga* (Íslenzk fornrit 4). Reykjavík: Hið íslenska fornritafélag.

La Farge, Beatrice 1992. *Glossary to the Poetic Edda. Based on Hans Kuhn's Kurzes Wörterbuch*. Heidelberg: Winter.

Finlay, Alison 1993. "*Droplaugarsona saga*." In Phillip Pulsiano (ed.), *Medieval Scandinavia: An Encyclopedia* (Garland Encyclopedias of the Middle Ages 1). New York and London: Garland, p. 143.

—— 2003. "Interpretation or Over-Interpretation: The Dating of Two *Íslendingasögur*." *Gripla* 14: 61–91.

Finnur Jónsson (ed.) 1903. *Gísla saga Súrssonar* (Altnordische Saga-Bibliothek 10). Halle: Niemeyer.

—— (ed.) 1929. *Gísla saga Súrssonar, udgiven efter håndskrifterne af det Kongelige nordiske Oldskrift-Selskab* (Kongelige Nordiske oldskriftselskab). Copenhagen: Gyldendal.

—— 1920–24. *Den oldnorske og oldislandske litteraturs historie*. 3 vols. 2nd ed. Copenhagen: Gad.

Foote, Peter 1955. "Notes on the Prepositions OF and UM(B) in Old Icelandic and Old Norwegian Prose." *Studia Islandica* 14. Reykjavík: H. F. Leiftur, pp. 41–83.

——— 1963. "An Essay on the Saga of Gisli and its Icelandic Background." In George Johnston (trans.), *The Saga of Gisli*. Toronto: Dent, pp. 93–134.

Fries, Ingegerd 1995. "När skrevs sagan? Om datering av isländska sagor, särskilt Heiðarvígasagan." *Scripta Islandica* 45: 21–41.

Gísli Sigurðsson 2004. *The Medieval Icelandic Saga and Oral Tradition. A Discourse on Method*. Translated by Nicholas Jones (Publications of the Milman Parry Collection of Oral Literature 2). Cambridge, MA: Milman Parry Collection, distributed by Harvard University Press.

Gordon, Ida L. 1934. "The Murder of Þorgrímr in *Gísla saga Súrssonar*." *Medium Ævum* 3: 79–94.

——— 1949–50. "The Origins of Gíslasaga." *Saga-Book of the Viking Society* 13: 183–205.

Guðbrandur Vigfússon 1856. "Um tímatal í íslendinga sögum í fornöld." *Safn til sögu Íslands og íslenzkra bókmennta* 1: 185–502.

——— 1858. "Um útgáfur af nokkrum Íslendingasögum." *Ný félagsrit*: 154–68.

Guðbrandur Vigfússon (ed.) 1878. *Sturlunga saga. Including the Islendinga Saga of Lawman Sturla Thordsson and other Works*. 2 vols. Oxford: Clarendon Press.

Guðbrandur Vigfússon and F. York Powell (eds. and trans.) 1883. *Corpus Poeticum Boreale: The Poetry of the Old Northern Tongue from the Earliest Times to the Thirteenth Century*. 2 vols. Oxford: Clarendon Press.

——— (eds. and trans.) 1905. *Origines Islandicæ: A Collection of the More Important Sagas and Other Native Writings Relating to the Settlement and Early History of Iceland*. 2 vols. Oxford: Clarendon Press.

Guðrún Nordal 2007. "The Art of Poetry and the Sagas of Icelanders." In Judy Quinn, Kate Heslop, and Tarrin Wills (eds.), *Learning and Understanding in the Old Norse World: Essays in Honour of Margaret Clunies Ross* (Medieval Texts and Cultures of Northern Europe 18). Turnhout: Brepols, pp. 219–37.

Hallberg, Peter 1965. "Om språkliga författarkriterier i isländska sagatexter." *Arkiv för nordisk filologi* 80: 157–86.

——— 1968. *Stilsignalement och författarskap i norrön sagalitteratur. Syn-*

punkter och exempel (Nordistica Gothoburgensia). Gothenburg: ACTA Universitatis Gothoburgensis.

——1994. "Ett och annat om dialogen i de isländska sagorna." In Gísli Sigurðsson, Guðrún Kvaran, and Sigurgeir Steingrímsson (eds.), *Sagnaþing. Helgað Jónasi Kristjánssyni sjötugum 10. apríl 1994*. 2 vols. Reykjavík: Hið íslenska bókmenntafélag, pp. 317–26.

Harris, Joseph 1997. "The Prosimetrum of Icelandic Saga and Some Relatives." In Joseph Harris and Karl Reichl (eds.), *Prosimetrum: Cross-cultural Perspectives on Narrative in Prose and Verse*. Woodbridge: D. S. Brewer, pp. 131–63.

Hast, Sture (ed.) 1960. *Harðar saga* (Editiones Arnamagnæanæ, Series A 6). Copenhagen: Munksgaard.

Heinrichs, Heinrich Matthias 1958. "Nibelungensaga und Gísla saga." In Hans Werner Seiffert (ed.), *Beiträge zur deutschen und nordischen Literatur. Festgabe für Leopold Magon zum 70. Geburtstag 3. April 1957*. Berlin: Deutsche Akademie der Wissenschaften zu Berlin, pp. 22–29.

Heller, Rolf 1958. *Die Literarische Darstellung der Frau in den Isländersagas* (Saga. Untersuchungen zur nordischen Literatur- und Sprachgeschichte 2). Halle: Max Niemeyer.

Heller, Rolf 1966a. "*Gísla saga Súrssonar* und *Laxdæla saga*." In Kurt Rudolph, Rolf Heller, and Ernst Walter (eds.), *Festschrift Walter Baetke: dargebracht zu seinem 80. Geburtstag am 28. März 1964*. Weimar: Hermann Böhlaus Nachfolger, pp. 181–90.

—— 1966b. "Aron Hjörleifssohn und Gisli Surssohn." *Arkiv för nordisk filologi* 81: 57–63.

Hermann Pálsson 1973–74. "Death in Autumn: Tragic Elements in Early Icelandic Fiction." *Bibliography of Old Norse-Icelandic Studies*, 7–39.

—— 1977. "Sögur bornar saman: *Gísla saga* og *Droplaugarsona saga*." *Skírnir* 151: 163–73.

——1984. "Minnisgreinar um *Gísla sögu Súrssonar*." In Bjarne Fidjestøl et al. (eds.), *Festskrift til Ludvig Holm-Olsen på hans 70-årsdag den 9. juni 1984*. Øvre Ervik: Alvheim & Eide, pp. 272–82.

Heusler, Andreas 1943–1969. "Berührungen zwischen den Isländergeschichten. Die Saga von Gisli und die von den Droplaugsöhnen." In Helga Ilse Reuschel and Stefan Sonderegger (eds.), *Kleine Schriften* 2, vol. I. Berlin: de Gruyter, pp. 321–46.

Hollander, Lee M. 1954. "Review of Ulrike Sprenger, *Praesens Historicum und Praeteritum in der Altisländschen Saga.*" *Scandinavian Studies* 26: 33–35.

Holtsmark, Anne 1951. "Studies in the *Gísla Saga.*" *Studia Norvegica: Ethnologica et Folkloristica* 6: 1–55.

Jakob Benediktsson 1951. "Review of Ulrike Sprenger, *Praesens historicum und Praeteritum in der Altisländischen Saga.*" *Skírnir* 125: 239–41.

Jakobsen, Alfred 1985. "Har Snorri Sturluson 'revidert' *Gísla saga Súrssonar?*" *Arkiv för nordisk filologi* 100: 89–96.

Jeffrey, Margaret 1934. "The Discourse in Seven Icelandic Sagas: Droplaugarsona saga, Hrafnkels saga Freysgoða, Víga-Glúms saga, Gísla saga Súrssonar, Fóstbræðra saga, Hávarðar saga Ísfirðings, Flóamanna saga." PhD thesis, Bryn Mawr College.

Jón Jóhannessson (ed.) 1950. *Austfirðinga sǫgur* (Íslenzk fornrit 11). Reykjavík: Hið íslenska fornritafélag.

Jón Jóhannesson, Magnús Finnbogason, and Kristján Eldjárn (eds.) 1946. *Sturlunga saga.* 2 vols. Reykjavík: Sturlunguútgáfan.

Jónas Kristjánsson 1988. *Eddas and Sagas: Iceland's Medieval Literature.* Translated by Peter Foote. Reykjavík: Hið íslenska bókmenntafélag.

Jónas Kristjánsson and Guðni Kolbeinsson 1979. "Gerðir Gíslasögu." *Gripla* 3: 128–62.

Ker, William Paton 1931. *Epic and Romance: Essays on Medieval Literature.* 2nd ed. London: Macmillan.

Kock, E. A. 1911. "Ordforskning i den äldre Eddan." *Arkiv för nordisk filologi* 27: 107–40.

Krijn, Sophie 1935. "Om Gíslasaga Súrssonar." *Arkiv för nordisk filologi* 51: 69–84.

Lethbridge, Emily 2010. "Gísla saga Súrssonar: Textual Variation, Editorial Constructions, and Critical Interpretations." In Judy Quinn and Emily Lethbridge (eds.), *Creating the Medieval Saga: Versions, Variability, and Editorial Interpretations of Old Norse Saga Literature* (The Viking Collection 18). Odense: University Press of Southern Denmark, pp. 123–152.

Lie, Hallvard 1939. "Noen metodologiske overveielser i anl. av et bind av 'Íslenzk fornrit.'" *Maal og Minne*: 97–138.

Liestøl, Knut 1930. *The Origin of the Icelandic Family Saga.* Translated by A. G. Jayne (Instituttet for sammenlignende kulturforskning, Serie A Forelesninger 10). Oslo: Aschehoug.

Loth, Agnete (ed.) 1960. *Membrana Regia Deperdita* (Editiones Arnamagnæanæ, Series A, vol. 5). Copenhagen: Munksgaard.

Ludvig, Werner 1934. *Untersuchungen über den Entwicklungsgang und die Funktion des Dialogs in der isländischen Sage* (Rheinische Beiträge und Hilfsbücher zur germanischen Philologie und Volkskunde 23). Halle: Niemeyer.

Magerøy, Hallvard 1978. "Kvar står sagaforskningen i dag?" *Nordisk tidskrift för vetenskap, konst och industri* 54: 164–75.

McKinnell, John 1970. "The Reconstruction of Pseudo-Vatnshyrna." *Opuscula* 4 (Bibliotheca Arnamagnæana 30): 304–37.

Megaard, John 2006. "Hva skrev Snorri?" In John McKinnell, David Ashurst, and Donata Kick (eds.), *The Fantastic in Old Norse/Icelandic Literature. Sagas and the British Isles. Preprint Papers of the 13th International Saga Conference, Durham and York, 6th–12th August, 2006*. 2 vols. Durham, vol. II, pp. 689–98.

Meulengracht Sørensen, Preben 2001a. "Næsten alle sagaer var skrevet. En kommentar til den såkaldte Sturlungaprolog." In *At fortælle Historien, Telling History: Studier i den gamle nordiske litteratur, Studies in Norse Literature* (Hesperides 16). Trieste, pp. 193–205.

—— 2001b. "The Prosimetrum Form 1: Verses as the Voice of the Past." In Russell Poole (ed.), *Skaldsagas: Text, Vocation, and Desire in the Icelandic Sagas of Poets* (Ergänzungsbände zum Reallexikon der germanischen Altertumskunde 27). Berlin: de Gruyter, pp. 172–90.

Müller, Peter Erasmus 1817–20. *Sagabibliothek med anmærkninger og indledende afhandlinger*. 3 vols. Copenhagen: I. F. Schultz.

Mundal, Else 1997. "Symbol og symbolhandlingar i sagalitteraturen." In Ann Christensson, Else Mundal, and Ingvild Øye (eds.), *Middelalderens symboler* (Kulturtekster 11). Bergen: Senter for europeiske kulturstudier, pp. 53–69.

O'Donoghue, Heather 1991. *Genesis of a Saga Narrative: Verse and Prose in Kormaks saga*. Oxford: Clarendon Press, Oxford University Press.

—— 2005. *Skaldic Verse and the Poetics of Saga Narrative*. Oxford and New York: Oxford University Press.

Olsen, Karin 1996. "Woman-kennings in the *Gísla saga Súrssonar*: A Study." In M. J. Toswell and E. M. Tyler (eds.), *Studies in English Language and Literature: "Doubt Wisely": Papers in Honour of E. G. Stanley*. London: Routledge, pp. 267–85.

Olsen, Magnus 1928. "Gísla saga og heltediktningen." In Johannes Brøndum-Nielsen et al. (eds.), *Festskrift til Finnur Jónsson 29. Maj 1928*. Copenhagen: Levin & Munksgaard, pp. 6–14.

Paasche, Fredrik 1928. "Esras aabenbaring og Pseudo-Cyprianus i norrøn litteratur." In Johannes Brøndum-Nielsen et al. (eds.), *Festskrift til Finnur Jónsson 29. Maj 1928*. Copenhagen: Levin & Munksgaard, pp. 199–205.

Perkins, Richard 1989. "Objects and Oral Tradition in Medieval Iceland." In Rory McTurk and Andrew Wawn (eds.), *Úr Dölum til Dala: Guðbrandur Vigfússon Centenary Essays* (Leeds Texts and Monographs, n.s., 11). Leeds: Leeds Studies in English, pp. 239–66.

Petersens, Carl af (ed.) 1879. *Jómsvíkinga saga (efter cod. AM 410 4to) samt Jómsvíkinga drápa*. Lund: Gleerup.

Prinz, Reinhard 1935. *Die Schöpfung der Gísla saga Súrssonar. Ein Beitrag zur Entstehungsgeschichte der Isländischen Saga*. Breslau: Ferdinand Hirt.

Rafn, Carl Christian, and Finnur Magnússon (eds.) 1838–45. *Grønlands historiske mindesmærker*. 3 vols. (Uddrag af Gisle Sursöns saga, især indeholdende Helge Vesteinsöns, een af Grönlands förste indbyggeres, levnet, vol. 2). Copenhagen: Det Kongelige Nordiske Oldskrift-selskab, pp. 576–608.

Roe, H. A. 1970. "Review of Peter Hallberg, *Stilsignalement och författerskap i norrön sagalitteratur*." *Scandinavian Studies* 42: 76–80.

Schach, Paul 1972. "Some Observations on the Helgafell Episode in *Eyrbyggja saga* and *Gísla saga*." In John M. Weinstock (ed.), *Saga og språk: Studies in Language and Literature*. Austin, TX: Jenkins, pp. 113–45.

——— 1986. "Instant Saga Style: The Evidence of the Manuscripts." *Journal of English and Germanic Philology* 85: 404–20.

Schier, Kurt 1970. *Sagaliteratur* (Sammlung Metzler 78). Stuttgart: Metzler.

Seewald, Franz 1934. *Die Gisla Saga Surssonar: Untersuchungen*. Göttingen: [s.n.].

Sigurður Nordal 1952. "Sagalitteraturen." In *Nordisk kultur VIII B, Litteraturhistorie Norge og Island*. Copenhagen: A. Bonniers, pp. 180–273.

Sprenger, Ulrike 1951. *Praesens Historicum und Praeteritum in der Altisländschen Saga* (Basler Studien zur Deutschen Sprache und Literatur 11). Basel: Benno Schwabe.

Stefán Einarsson 1937. "Review of Reinhard Prinz, *Die Schöpfung der Gísla saga Súrssonar*." *Modern Language Notes* 52: 68–69.

Stemshaug, Ola 1985. "Dei norske stadnamna i *Gislasaga*." *Arkiv för nordisk filologi* 100: 72–88.

Storm, Gustav (ed.) 1888. *Islandske Annaler indtil 1578* (Det norske historiske Kildeskriftfonds Skrifter 21). Christiania: Norsk historisk kildeskriftfond/Gröndal & søns bogtrykkeri.

Sveinbjörn Beinteinsson 1991. "Gíslasaga og höfundar hennar." *Morgunblaðið,* 12 January.

Turville-Petre, E. O. G. 1953. *Origins of Icelandic Literature.* Oxford: Clarendon Press.

——— 1944. "Gísli Súrsson and his Poetry: Traditions and Influences." *Modern Language Review* 39: 374–91. Reprinted in E. O. G. Turville-Petre (ed.), *Nine Norse Studies* (Viking Society for Northern Research Text Series 5). London: Viking Society for Northern Research, pp. 118–53.

Vésteinn Ólason 1993. "Íslendingasögur og þættir." In Vésteinn Ólason and Guðrún Nordal (eds.), *Íslensk bókmenntasaga.* 2 vols. Reykjavík: Mál og menning, vol. 2, pp. 23–163.

——— 1999. "Gísli Súrsson: A Flawless or Flawed Hero." In Stig Toftgaard Andersen (ed.), *Die Aktualität der Saga: Festschrift für Hans Schottman* (Reallexicon der germanischen Altertumskunde: Ergänzungsbände 21). Berlin and New York: de Gruyter, pp. 163–75.

——— 2005, "Family Sagas." In Rury McTurk (ed.), *A Companion to Old Norse-Icelandic Literature and Culture* (Blackwell Companions to Literature and Culture 31). Oxford: Blackwell Publishing, pp. 101–18.

Vésteinn Ólason and Þórður Ingi Guðjónsson 2000. "Sammenhængen mellem tolkninger og tekstversioner af *Gísla saga*." In Kristinn Jóhannesson, Karl G. Johansson, and Lars Lönnroth (eds.), *Den Fornnordiska texten i filologisk och litteraturvetenskaplig belysning: Studier och diskussionsinlägg* (Gothenburg Old Norse Studies 2). Gothenburg: Göteborgs universitet, pp. 96–120.

de Vries, Jan 1962. *Altnordisches etymologisches Wörterbuch.* Leiden: Brill.

Weenen, Andrea de Leeuw van 2000. *A Grammar of Möðruvallabók* (CNWS Publications 85). Leiden: Universiteit Leiden.

Örnólfur Thorsson 1990. "Leitin að landinu fagra": Hugleiðing um rannsóknir á íslenskum fornbókmenntun. *Skáldskaparmál* 1: 28–53.

DATING *EYRBYGGJA SAGA*

The Value of "Circumstantial" Evidence for Determining the Time of Composition of Sagas about Early Icelanders

Torfi H. Tulinius

Though much work has been done on many sagas since Einar Ólafur Sveinsson published his *Dating the Icelandic Sagas*, no one has attempted to theorize this highly speculative, difficult and in many ways perilous activity during the half a century that has elapsed since the English version of Einar Ólafur's book appeared in Gabriel Turville-Petre's translation (Einar Ólafur Sveinsson 1958). Exceptions to this are to be found in chapters on dating that serve as introductions to monographs on individual sagas. Such an exception is Bjarni Guðnason's eloquent chapter on the difficulties of dating the sagas in his book-length study of *Heiðarvíga saga*, in which he applies Einar Ólafur's method, even though he criticizes some of his conclusions (Bjarni Guðnason 1993). An exception of another sort is Theodore M. Andersson's recent book *The Growth of the Icelandic Saga*, in which he proposes to map out the development of the saga genre, with particular emphasis on the *Íslendingasögur* or "sagas about early Icelanders," which is the new English term he suggests for this group of sagas to replace the inaccurate "family saga" and the inelegant and imprecise "sagas of Icelanders" (Andersson 2006). This implies at least a relative dating for the sagas, with Andersson basing his approach on what knowledge is available as well as on some assumptions.

This article will provide a summary of Einar Ólafur's method, as well as a discussion of the value he gives to different types of proof – or at least evidence – for dating. A closer look will then be taken at the specific value of what will here be called "circumstantial evidence" – though Einar Ólafur calls it "historical evidence" – for the dating of individual sagas, i.e. whether they resonate with particular historical events or developments, and how this can be used as evidence of their date of composition. In a concluding section I will discuss whether dating the sagas is condemned to be an exercise in building "a house of cards," in the words of Bjarni Guðnason (Bjarni Guðnason 1993: 9), or whether attempts such as those made by Theodore M. Andersson do indeed have explanatory value, despite the inevitable uncertainties of saga dating.

DATING THE SAGAS

The subtitle of Einar Ólafur's book in its English language version is "An Essay on Method." It is however more than that, because he also gives an overview of the state of research in the field at the time of writing. He begins with an introductory chapter where he presents earlier views of saga origins and dating, concentrating on the work of P. E. Müller and Björn M. Ólsen. In Einar Ólafur's view, the latter's research into the relationship between sagas about early Icelanders and *Landnámabók* paved the way for what would become the method adopted by the editors of the Íslenzk fornrit series and which has led to important advances in the dating of individual sagas. Indeed, Einar Ólafur's book is largely an effort to describe and systematize the methods he and other editors of the series have used.

He also mentions the then-recently published synthesis by Sigurður Nordal about the saga literature, "Sagalitteraturen," and suggests that his work on the dating of the sagas might be considered a supplement to Nordal's, supplying the information on dating that the latter did not have room to include in his discussion. By this, Einar Ólafur could be implying that a discussion of the growth and development of the sagas should be accompanied by a lucid presentation of what we know about their dating and how we have arrived at that knowledge.

After these introductory remarks, Einar Ólafur goes on to present the earliest manuscripts containing sagas about early Icelanders, highlighting how badly preserved they are, none of them in original manuscripts or even in complete manuscripts dating from their time of composition, and so many existing only by virtue of late copies of copies, sometimes fragmentary. This is indeed the essence of the problem of dating the sagas: how to arrive at some kind of knowledge of when they were originally composed by using the scant and incomplete evidence provided by what manuscripts have survived.

Obviously, the manuscripts are the basis on which all further knowledge has to stand, but other things must also be considered. Einar Ólafur goes on to review the transmission history of each of the sagas about early Icelanders before devoting a separate chapter to "alterations in the texts" (Einar Ólafur Sveinsson 1958: 31–40), in which he draws attention to a difference of a certain type between sagas in the way they have been transmitted. While the text of some does not change significantly from one manuscript to another, others show considerable differences. In some cases, such as those of *Gísla saga* and *Bandamanna saga*, one can even talk about distinct versions of the same saga. There are different ways of explaining these differences. One is that later redactors were improving on a pre-existing text that they thought deficient: making better sagas in a way. Another is that they had a different opinion of the events or persons described in the saga. A third is that they reveal different attitudes to saga writing, one showing respect for the saga as a whole and more or less finished text, another – which Einar Ólafur ascribes preferentially to the North of Iceland – where it was considered acceptable to add "þættir" to a pre-existing saga, creating thereby a new version (Einar Ólafur Sveinsson 1958: 37–38).

EINAR ÓLAFUR'S METHOD

The result of this discussion is that we have to be very careful in making any judgements on the age of the sagas and especially beware of any subjective feelings we may have. It is at this point that Einar Ólafur begins to expose his method in a series of six chapters. The first is called "References to Saga-Writing in Early Texts" and enumerates the main passages in old texts where the activity of saga writing is actually mentioned. These references, scant and vague as they are, can however be used to determine a date before which there were no sagas about early Icelanders, i.e. when the First Grammarian describes what was written in the vernacular at the time he was composing his work in the mid-twelfth century. However, Einar Ólafur mainly devotes this chapter to disproving Björn M. Ólsen's understanding of the passage in *Sturlunga saga* where it is said that "nearly all the sagas whose stories were set in Iceland were written before Bishop Brandr Sæmundarson died" in 1201 (Einar Ólafur Sveinsson 1958: 43). By making a comparison with another manuscript of *Sturlunga*, Einar Ólafur feels confident that in fact the redactor of the saga meant that some sagas about early Icelanders had been written before Sturla Þórðarson (1214–1284) wrote his *Íslendingasaga*. This brings us to a timeframe in which the sagas appeared between the mid-twelfth and the second half of the thirteenth century, which is not very precise at all and therefore other evidence must be considered (Einar Ólafur Sveinsson 1958: 47).

The next two chapters deal with historical evidence. The longer one reviews the different types of information one can glean from a saga that could in one way or another indicate when it was composed. This ranges from the famous mention of who told the story at the end of *Droplaugarsona saga*, to allusions to descendants of saga characters living at the time of writing or shortly before. Since I will be addressing *Eyrbyggja saga* in more detail later in this article, I will take the example of Guðný Bǫðvarsdóttir, mother to Snorri Sturluson, who witnessed the exhumation of the bones of her husband's ancestor, Snorri goði, at the church of Sælingsdalr. In some manuscripts of the saga it is said that "she then had the charge of the household at Hvammr," which indicates that the saga could have been written anytime after the first decade of the thirteenth century, when she seems to have left that farm for good. However, as Einar Ólafur says, these words of the saga "could equally well have been written later" (Einar Ólafur Sveinsson 1958: 54).

Other types of historical evidence he discusses are genealogies of descendants of saga characters. The time at which they end could be indicative of the date of composition, but this is not necessarily the case, as shown by the differences between manuscripts in how far they go down the genealogical lines. Also, mention of buildings or landmarks from the saga period which still stand, or stood until recently, can help in determining the age of sagas, though discrepancies between versions also indicate here that such remarks can come from copyists and not authors, and are therefore to be handled carefully.

Einar Ólafur chooses to devote a separate, though very short, chapter to direct references to historical events, though it could be argued that they belong to the category of historical evidence. However, the type of references to contemporary events he has in mind is when the plot of the saga or particular saga characters is thought to be modelled on people or happenings from the saga writer's time. He mentions a few scholars who have attempted to establish links of this sort, among them himself. Quite a few authors have continued to do the same thing in the decades that have elapsed since Einar Ólafur wrote his book, among them my recent book on *Egils saga*, where I address the question of whether the theme of fratricide detected in the saga could resonate with the protracted conflict between Snorri Sturluson on one hand and his brother Sighvatur and nephew Sturla on the other (Torfi H. Tulinius 2004: 216–18). For all these efforts, including this last one, Einar Ólafur's warning is a word to the wise:

> There are many possibilities in cases like these, and the problem is tricky, and has not been fully studied from all aspects. It would, therefore, be wise not to use such things as the basis for dating the sagas but rather to look for other evidence. (Einar Ólafur Sveinsson 1958: 75)

One type of historical evidence Einar Ólafur deems quite valuable in order to determine at least whether a saga is from the Commonwealth period or whether it is younger is the legal terms and provisions it follows. Indeed, quite a few sagas betray poor knowledge of the law that existed before Norwegian kings imposed their laws – a clear indication of dating. This does not go very far, and is of no help in finding out the age of sagas from the Commonwealth period. However, legal historical evidence of another sort is given by Einar Ólafur in the following passage from *Laxdœla saga*:

> Ekki þóttusk heiðnir menn minna eiga í ábyrgð, þá er slíka hluti skyldi fremja, en nú þykkjask eiga kristnir menn, þá er skírslur eru görvar. (Íslenzk fornrit (ÍF) IV: 42–43)

He then says:

> The last sentence seems to imply that trials by ordeal were in force when the saga was written. It is known that they were held in Iceland in the twelfth century and the thirteenth, and last of all in 1237. The Lateran Council of 1215 forbade clerics to take part in them, although ordeals continued to be held in Norway after that. Cardinal William of Sabena forbade trials by ordeal in Norway in 1247, and mention is made in the Icelandic annals of a "change of ordinance" in 1248. It is

> most likely that trial by ordeal was then abolished in Iceland. It seems, then, that this passage gives excellent evidence of age. (Einar Ólafur Sveinsson 1958: 65)

Here we are not dealing with law set by lay institutions, such as the Althing or the Norwegian monarchy, but canon law having an impact on legal practice in society. This is Einar Ólafur's only example of this type of indication of age, and since others of a similar kind will be discussed below, it is important to underline the positive attitude he shows towards arguments of this type. Although he does not explain it, his example shows that the recorded intervention of a prelate and its subsequent mention in Icelandic annals are elements that enable us to arrive at a closer dating.

Before going further into this issue, let us examine the remaining three chapters in which Einar Ólafur describes his method. The next point is what he calls "literary relations," addressing what can be learned about the respective age of the sagas by identifying whether and how they refer to earlier writings (Einar Ólafur Sveinsson 1958: 76–95). This is the longest chapter and probably the most characteristic of the methods used by the Íslenzk fornrit editors and, one might add, of what has been called the Icelandic school in saga studies. It consists of examining whether a saga betrays knowledge of another saga or another text and using that to introduce a respective dating. For example, if one can establish that the author of *Eyrbyggja saga* is using *Gísla saga* in the chapter on Þórdís's attempt to take revenge on Eyjólfr grái for the slaying of Gísli, then that is a clear indication that the latter saga is older, even though it may be preserved in younger manuscripts. This is quite an effective way of constructing a respective dating of the sagas, especially if one can make it rest on the secure foundation of manuscript age.

The problem with this approach is that the result can be a bit like Bjarni Guðnason's "house of cards." If one element in the structure was incorrectly dated, it jeopardizes the whole construction that may sit on it. An example of this is Jónas Kristjánsson's conclusion of his 1972 doctoral dissertation that *Fóstbrœðra saga* must be ascribed to a later date than had been previously ascribed to it (Jónas Kristjánsson 1972) – a view challenged in the present volume by Theodore M. Andersson – or Bjarni Guðnason's own "trouble-making" when calling into doubt the great age of *Heiðarvíga saga* (Bjarni Guðnason 1993: 269). As yet, nobody seems to have examined the changes we must bring to our perception of the dating of the sagas about early Icelanders if Bjarni's proposed later dating of the saga is generally accepted. In the case of both Jónas and Bjarni, one could say that they have dealt heavy blows to Einar Ólafur's vision of the respective ages of the sagas. These blows have not been assimilated by the community of scholars other than by being acknowledged, as Vésteinn Ólason does, for example in his contribution on the sagas about early Icelanders in the recent *Blackwell Companion to Old Norse-Icelandic Literature and Culture*, that there is a lot of uncertainty concerning the age of the different representatives of the genre (Vésteinn Ólason 2005: 116).

The following chapter on method deals with linguistic evidence. This can of course be quite valuable, though it is also difficult to deal with, because copyists can adapt the language of their model to their usage, thereby obliterating the signs of earlier linguistic use. It is easier to date late sagas by using such evidence than it is to determine how early they may be. However, some indications can be of help, for example whether the preposition *um* has replaced *of*, a development that must have started in the twelfth century but had definitely been completed after the last third of the thirteenth century. Basing himself on an investigation made a few years earlier by Peter Foote, Einar Ólafur's remarks that very few sagas about early Icelanders use *of* in their prose. Interestingly, the ones who do so the most are *Þorsteins saga Síðu-Hallssonar*, only preserved in a seventeenth-century manuscript, and there are indications that the word was used rather more than the average in the lost part of *Heiðarvíga saga* (Einar Ólafur Sveinsson 1958: 100). It is noteworthy that Bjarni Guðnason does not take this into account when refuting Einar Ólafur's and others' claims that *Heiðarvíga saga* is from the early thirteenth century, rather than from the 1250s as he believes (Bjarni Guðnason 1993: 176–218). Coming to *Eyrbyggja saga*, this is of importance because this saga borrows from the former one and any changes to its dating have an impact on our ideas of the age of the latter. In the Icelandic version of his book, Einar Ólafur notes the fact that in some manuscripts of *Eyrbyggja saga of* appears in quite many stanzas, while it has been replaced by *um* in others. This may be an indication of an earlier dating for the saga (Einar Ólafur Sveinsson 1965: 118–19).

Ancient vocabulary and expressions may point to an earlier dating but this is very difficult to prove. Einar Ólafur mentions *Heiðarvíga saga* and *Eyrbyggja* specifically in this respect, but such archaisms are easy to explain away by personal idiosyncrasies, different milieus, or regionalisms

(Einar Ólafur Sveinsson 1958: 103–5). It is however interesting to note Bjarni Guðnason's new dating of these two sagas with respect to *Laxdœla saga*. He believes this last one to be the oldest, *Heiðarvíga saga* comes after that, and finally *Eyrbyggja* (Bjarni Guðnason 1993: 269). The impact of courtly behaviour, values, and above all vocabulary, is only visible in what Bjarni believes to be the oldest of the three.

This leads us into Einar Ólafur's next chapter on influences from clerical and romantic literature on the sagas about early Icelanders. Concerning the influence of clerical literature, he does not feel that anything conclusive can be used in dating the sagas until further research has been undertaken on the development of clerical style, but he points to problems that might be of help if they were adequately examined, such as phrases which might betray knowledge and use of Latin historiography by saga authors.

Whether influence from courtly literature can be used as a criterion for dating the sagas depends on how we solve two problems. On the one hand, does the date of 1226 given in the prologue to *Tristrams saga* herald the beginning of courtly influence on saga literature, or is it simply a milestone in a longer story where early oral retellings of the stuff of *chansons de geste* and romances are already having an impact in the North? On the other hand, how do we distinguish between purely literary borrowings and more general cultural influences? Courtly ways of behaving, presenting oneself, and even of conceiving of one's position in society were probably known and admired in Scandinavian courts and by the households of local magnates, even in Iceland, already in the twelfth century.

Using courtly influence as an indicator of age is indeed a tricky matter, as can be seen in an example from Bjarni Guðnason's book on *Heiðarvíga saga*, where he says that *Egils saga* betrays no influence from the knights' sagas, while *Laxdœla saga* does to a considerable extent. This is, says Bjarni, consistent with the idea that *Egils saga* is from around 1230, while *Laxdœla* is from around 1255 (Bjarni Guðnason 1993: 198, 269). There does not however seem to be any doubt that whoever wrote *Egils saga* uses an element of plot borrowed from Chrétien de Troyes's *Yvain* (Torfi H. Tulinius 2004: 99–101). Whether this is evidence that the saga must have been composed after 1226 is a different matter altogether, because we cannot be sure that Chrétien's romance was not known before that, either in an oral retelling or an early translation.

Finally, even more difficult, Einar Ólafur says, are considerations of artistry. Did the sagas evolve from clumsy beginnings to the polished mastery of works such as *Egils saga* or *Njáls saga*? He admits that such questions are difficult to answer and one can have examples of very well-composed early sagas and quite poorly written late ones (Einar Ólafur Sveinsson 1958: 115). It is therefore even more difficult to build an opinion of the dating of a saga on artistic criteria. However, he does expose on several pages examples of inelegant narrative in *Heiðarvíga saga*, which he believes may comfort those who are of the opinion that it is an early saga.

Bjarni Guðnason goes to great pains to improve our assessment of the artistry of the author of the saga. I will not go into this here, although it would be interesting to examine how Bjarni, while using Einar Ólafur's method, arrives at other conclusions. My feeling is that Bjarni's main intuition – i.e. that *Heiðarvíga saga* reflects criticism of and worries over the behaviour of chieftains during the civil strife of the Sturlung era, that is to say, around the middle of the thirteenth century – has an impact on the way he assesses the evidence for its age.

This shows perhaps that despite Einar Ólafur's effort to systematize the dating methods of the editors of the Íslenzk fornrit series, it is very difficult to arrive at any sort of definitive knowledge about their dating. After having stressed in his words of conclusion the importance of looking at the manuscripts, of intellectual rigour and the search of objective evidence, he ends by insisting on the fact that much of the evidence is not definite proof but probability that must be scrupulously and carefully weighed before a conclusive opinion can be formed (Einar Ólafur Sveinsson 1958: 127).

LEGAL-HISTORICAL EVIDENCE FOR DATING THE SAGAS

However, in his final words Einar Ólafur also says that much more research must be undertaken in order at least to decrease the margin of doubt about the age of the sagas. In the following paragraphs a possible avenue of research will be proposed that may have the potential to assist in dating at least some of the sagas about early Icelanders. It is an approach that I have already attempted in my book on *Egils saga* and involves identifying allusions to specific provisions of canon law and connecting them with what knowledge we can gather on the introduction of canon law, respectively in Europe, in the Nordic countries, and in Iceland.

Earlier in this article, mention was made of an example where the date

1248 is set as a last possible date for the composition of *Laxdœla saga* because it speaks of trials by ordeals as something that is commonly carried out by Christians. After the change of ordinance in Iceland in 1248, it is highly unlikely that such an attitude would have been expressed by an Icelander educated enough to compose a saga. It is difficult to understand why this element seems to have been ignored by scholars like Bjarni Guðnason and Rolf Heller.

It has been a constant of my research since my doctoral thesis to look for the link between the text and the historical reality it is part of. Assumptions about dating have customarily relied on the information on dating given by other means, but it may be possible in some cases to turn the process around and ask whether such circumstantial evidence can influence our opinion on the age of a saga. More than a hundred years ago, Konrad Maurer remarked that the trial about Ásgerðr's legitimacy – that the saga says took place in Gulaþing – seems to be a conflict over what in canon law is called *legitimatio per subsequens parentum coniugium*: a child born out of wedlock becomes legitimate if the parents get married (Konrad Maurer 1895: 114). Maurer thought that this was just a coincidence, but he believed *Egils saga* was composed before or around 1200 and he also knew that this particular article of canon law had only been adopted into Norwegian law by Magnús Hákonarson in the 1270s. He was not, however, alert to the fact that the article, though dating ultimately from a papal verdict in the twelfth century, was only taken into the books of canon law which then circulated in Europe in the year 1232, with the publication of the *Liber Extra*. Neither did Maurer seem to know that there was quite an adverse reaction among royalty in Europe to archbishops' attempts to enforce the article. Indeed, Robert Grosseteste, bishop of Lincoln, tried and had to desist, for the barons of England refused to include into secular law provisions that would split up their estates (R. W. Southern 1986: 252–57).

In Norway, Duke Skúli may have considered invoking *legitimatio per subsequens parentum coniugium* to pursue his own political goals. He had no legitimate son who could inherit his power over the part of Norway he ruled by agreement with his son-in-law King Hákon, who had married Skúli's legitimate daughter and therefore stood to inherit Skúli's holdings. However, Skúli had an illegitimate son, Pétr. This was only revealed after the mother's husband, Andrés skjaldarband, disappeared while on a trip to the Holy Land. Skúli tried to make Pétr his legitimate heir, but King Hákon refused to allow this, claiming that only his legitimate children would inherit him. He thereby not only fuelled the conflict between the two men but also probably weakened Skúli's position, since it would be more difficult for him to get long-time support from important figures in Norway if he could not show that his power would continue through his son.

It is unlikely – if indeed it was attempted – that Skúli's hypothetical invocation of *legitimatio per subsequens parentum coniugium* in order to make Pétr his heir would have been considered legal by the Church. Skúli's wife, Ragnhildr, was still alive, and if Pétr was indeed Skúli's son, he was the fruit of adultery. It must, however, be considered probable that every possible legal course of action was explored in order to build a case for Skúli's claim at a time when Snorri Sturluson and many other lay members of the dominant class in Iceland were at the Norwegian court. Snorri had a special relationship with Skúli and spent time both with him and his son Pétr. Irrespective of whether Snorri composed *Egils saga* himself or not, the echoing of political conflict involving datable elements of canon law comforts those who like Jónas Kristjánsson believe that the saga was composed in the late 1230s or even the early 1240s (Jónas Kristjánsson 1990).

DATING *EYRBYGGJA SAGA*

Most scholars writing recently have acknowledged that the saga's reference to *Laxdœla saga* in its closing chapter must be an indication of it having been composed after that saga, i.e. in the middle of the thirteenth century at the earliest. Forrest S. Scott summarizes the arguments for this dating in the introduction to his recent scholarly edition of the vellum tradition and deems it safe to say only that the saga is likely to have been composed sometime between 1230 and 1270.

Einar Ólafur Sveinsson was however quite sceptical about the value of the reference to *Laxdœla saga* in the final chapter, believing that it could have been an addition made by a later copyist. Mention is made of Guðrún Ósvífrsdóttir at two moments in *Eyrbyggja saga*, in chapters fifty-six and sixty-five. Why should the author have named *Laxdœla saga* only in the later chapter while events from the saga are alluded to in both? The same question also applies to *Heiðarvíga saga*, which visibly existed when *Eyrbyggja* was written, because the author does not bother to tell of events that are narrated by that saga, unless they serve the plot of his own saga.

Einar Ólafur believed in an early dating for *Eyrbyggja saga*. His understanding of the textual history of *Landnámabók* excluded the possibility that the saga could be younger than the version written by Styrmir Kárason who died in 1245, since it seems to rely on the saga. However, it is difficult to determine with exactitude what Styrmir's version was like. It is done by subtracting from the Hauksbók version what is already in the Sturlubók one. The remaining elements are thought to have been only in Styrmir's *Landnámabók* and not in the version compiled by Sturla Þórðarson. Both Jón Jóhannesson in his book on the different versions of *Landnáma* and Jakob Benediktsson in the introduction to his edition of *Íslendingabók* and *Landnámabók* (lxiii–lxvi) are doubtful of Einar Ólafur's conclusions. One of the conclusions to Jón Jóhannesson's authoritative work from 1941 (and therefore not available to Einar Ólafur when editing the saga) was that the Melabók version is very close to Styrmisbók. In the former, no borrowings can be detected from the saga. Their conclusion is that both Sturla and Haukr borrowed directly from the saga, while Styrmir, writing probably in the 1220s, did not use *Eyrbyggja saga*. This means that the saga was written after 1230 and before 1270, when Sturla is thought to have composed his version of *Landnámabók*.

Einar Ólafur also draws attention to a series of resemblances between poetry from the saga and stanzas attributed to the Sturlungar and their followers, mostly in the years around 1220. These are numerous and quite striking. He interprets this as a sign that the saga was already in circulation in Western Iceland by then and its poetry had an impact on the versifying of people from that region. This is a compelling point but impossible to prove. Jakob Benediktsson dismisses it in his introduction to *Landnámabók*, saying that the similarities are not quite as striking as Einar Ólafur would believe. He also remarks that if the poetry from the saga did indeed have an influence on contemporary skaldic efforts, it may just as well have been because it was circulating orally. Finally, he points to the fact that Sturla Þórðarson both knew *Eyrbyggja saga* and imitated one of the poems it contains, *Hrafnsmál*, when composing his own poem with the same title (*Íslendingabók. Landnámabók* 1968: lxiv).

This is of course a question of judgement, and although it is impossible not to recognize the value of Jakob's criticism of Einar Ólafur's position, it can still be argued that the number of resemblances between the poetry of the saga and the stanzas Einar Ólafur gathered in *Sturlunga saga* are sufficiently numerous and thus cannot be easily dismissed by Jakob. However, this cannot be considered to be a strong argument in favour of an earlier dating of the saga.

Other scholars have held various positions on this question. Writing in 1978, Rolf Heller needed to date *Laxdœla saga* later than hitherto has been done, because he believed it echoes certain Icelandic events from after the middle of the thirteenth century. He was therefore prepared to admit that the reference to *Laxdœla saga* in *Eyrbyggja* is a later interpolation, something Peter Hallberg was unwilling to do. Writing on the saga both in 1965 and 1978, he argued that the saga is the work of Sturla Þórðarson, basing this conclusion on a statistical analysis of the vocabulary of other works known to be by Sturla, as well as *Eyrbyggja* and *Kristni saga*. He also claimed that the overwhelming use of "finnask" rather than "hittask" in the saga points to a composition well into the second half of the thirteenth century. In a recent book on the saga, Klaus Böldl, after having reviewed the work of earlier scholars, decides on a later dating, putting the composition of the saga into the period between 1255 and 1265, believing it could not have been written later than that because of how close the author seems to be to the society of the Commonwealth period (Böldl 2005: 24–26).

POLITICAL ECHOES

There is a considerable amount of uncertainty here and it seems safer to follow the majority of scholars who believe in a later date, thereby dispensing with the awkward task of having to discard the reference to *Laxdœla saga* in chapter sixty-five. On the other hand, the lack of courtly influence, the archaisms in the vocabulary, and a few other points that now will be mentioned argues in favour of an earlier dating.

In a contribution to the volume *Learning and Understanding in the Old Norse World*, published in honour of Margaret Clunies Ross on her sixty-fifth birthday, I proposed that the way the saga tells us how the wonders at Fróðá were brought to an end should be understood in light of the political conflicts in early thirteenth century Iceland. Attention is drawn to the fact that three different means are used to make the revenants leave: the obvious one by burning the beautiful bed-clothes that had brought on the haunting, the religious one by having a priest sing mass, confess the surviving members of the household, and sprinkle holy water over the dwelling, and finally the legal and least obvious one, by prosecuting the revenants in order to force them to leave. This unique way of ridding a place of ghosts is relevant if one considers early thirteenth-century clashes in Iceland over the respective roles of the clergy and aristocracy.

Indeed, a long and protracted conflict took place between Kolbeinn Tumason, the principal magnate of Northern Iceland, and Guðmundr Arason, the newly elected bishop of the see of Hólar, culminating in Kolbeinn's death in 1208 when attacking Hólar. The reason for the argument was the bishop's determination to enforce an article of canon law that had been adopted in the law of most countries but not in Iceland. It is the canonical concept of *privilegium fori*, i.e. the Church's exclusive right to prosecute and judge members of the clergy, even in cases where they were breaking the law of the land. The lay chieftains, led by Kolbeinn, would not concede this to the Church, insisting on their exclusive right to prosecute cases in society. The conflict was made even more difficult to resolve because of Kolbeinn's untimely death, which spurred on a coalition of chieftains to take over the see of Hólar and drive the bishop away. He would spend almost all of the next thirty years as an exile from his own bishopric, dependent on the good will of certain chieftains, among them Þórðr Sturluson who dominated the region of Snæfellsnes, in which *Eyrbyggja saga* takes place.

In a saga as preoccupied with the social identity of the chieftain class, this distribution of roles between the lay chieftains and the clergy is not the fruit of coincidence, but is conveying a message about how these two separate parts of the dominant class of Iceland should share their power: the priests should take care of spiritual matters, such as confessing, singing masses, praying for sinners' souls, etc., leaving to the *goðar* to take care of legal matters.

If this intuition is correct, then it seems that the saga would have been addressing issues relevant to the first decades and not the middle or second half of the thirteenth century. Bishop Guðmundr only died in 1237 and members of the Sturlung family were directly involved in the mentioned conflict, some as vigorous foes of the prelate but others as his more or less enthusiastic sympathizers. As chieftains, they would also have been preoccupied with any infringement of their prerogatives.

This suggests that *Eyrbyggja saga* may have been composed in a milieu close to the Sturlungar, in the 1230s when the whole issue of *privilegium fori* is likely to have been on the table again. Indeed, Bishop Guðmundr was pleading his case before the archbishop in Niðarós at the time, and an envoy had even been sent to Rome to ask the pope what should be done. In this context, it is likely that the *goðar* would have wanted to produce some kind of narrative that would ground their social position in history. The so-called "Úlfljótslög" are thought to have been written in this period. They contain a description of the origins of the *goðar* and their social role which could well be a sort of manifesto for the institution of the *goði* at a moment in history when it was being called into question by increasing royal and ecclesiastical power (Gunnar Karlsson 2004: 383–89).

Scholars have long felt that there was a connection between *Eyrbyggja saga* and the "Úlfljótslög," a passage in some versions of *Landnámabók* that is believed to have originated in the lost version by Styrmir Kárason (ca. 1170–1245) (Olaf Olsen 1965: 34–49; Jón Hnefill Aðalsteinsson 1997: 163–87). This is especially thought to be the case in the description of the role of the *goðar*. It is as if they originate in a shared attitude to and image of the past. It is therefore surprising that Sturla Þórðarson (1214–1284) did not include the passage in his version of *Landnámabók*, while he borrowed a lot from *Eyrbyggja saga*. It is possible that he did not know the "Úlfljótslög" or that he did not believe in their historical validity. If the saga was written in the same milieu and from the same viewpoint as Styrmisbók, this would be an argument in favour of Einar Ólafur's early dating of the saga, i.e. before Sturla's career as a writer could have begun.

However, there is another moment in Icelandic history when the ideological attitude I detect in *Eyrbyggja saga* would have been just as relevant or perhaps even more relevant: around 1253. At this time the power and legitimacy of the *goðar* was even more beleaguered, since the overlords were fighting to bring Iceland under Norwegian rule. At this point in the conflict, Gizurr Þorvaldsson was the most powerful chieftain and in Sturla Þórðarson's *Íslendinga saga* it is said that he "decided everything at the Althing that summer." It is therefore quite interesting that a very strange decision was made at the Althing: canon law was declared to take precedence over the law of the land. Scholars have long seen the connection between Gizurr's support of this decision and his subsequent marriage to Gróa, his mistress of many years and mother to his three sons. He was separated from a daughter of Snorri Sturluson and therefore needed dispensation from the Church in order to marry Gróa. I believe that this was not a sentimental issue but that Gizurr needed to marry her in order for his sons to become legitimate. For reasons similar to those Duke Skúli may have had, he had to show – in order for him to be seen as a plausible earl of Iceland – that he would have heirs to succeed him. This may be why, in his case, it was an advantage for him to accept this precedence of canon law over the law of the land (Torfi H. Tulinius 1996).

In this period, Hrafn Oddsson and Sturla Þórðarson were active opponents of Gizurr. They were the main chieftains in western Iceland in the absence of Þórðr kakali. It is not unlikely at all that a saga that both grounds the power of the chieftains in history and also portrays the difficulties of a society in which chieftains compete for power would have been relevant to the concerns of an author and public in the 1250s. This would fit well with Peter Hallberg's theory that Sturla Þórðarson wrote the saga. However, the question then is why did not he include "Úlfljótslög" in his version of *Landnámabók*.

CONCLUSION

No new conclusion has been arrived at concerning the date of *Eyrbyggja saga*. Though some new arguments have been added to Einar Ólafur's early dating of the saga, a later date is also tempting, even though the reference to *Laxdœla saga* seems – according to some scholars – a clear indication of their relative ages.

This discussion has shown, however, that considerations of dating are useful. They make us look at the texts in a certain way. Not only do we have to examine methodically their manuscript preservation, linguistic status, and relationship to other texts, it also brings us to the fact that they are acts of communication. We are communicating on certain issues in a certain context, and by exploring this context in order to look for indications of dating, we may arrive at a better understanding of what the sagas are about. Of course, one must not ignore the dangers of circular reasoning. However, a disciplined dialectical approach to this dialogue that the sagas are immersed in the time they were written can build up a convincing argument for one date rather than another.

The way ahead would then be to continue to study the historical context of the period in which the sagas were written. It is reasonably certain that more can be done to find examples of references to contemporary changes such as in canon law. In a more general way, a careful study of the issues that were the objects of struggles at the time of writing is certain to yield some results. However, this does not necessarily mean building "houses of cards." Arriving at a reasoned opinion of the respective ages of the sagas about early Icelanders and how they are grounded in the social reality of their times will greatly enhance our understanding of how they developed as an art form.

Bibliography

Andersson, Theodore M. 2006. *The Growth of the Medieval Icelandic Sagas (1180–1280)*. Ithaca and London: Cornell University Press.

Bjarni Guðnason 1993. *Túlkun Heiðarvígasögu* (Studia islandica 50). Reykjavík: Bókmenntafræðistofnun Háskóla Íslands.

Böldl, Klaus 2005. *Eigi einhamr. Beiträge zum Weltbild der* Eyrbyggja *und anderer Isländersagas* (Ergänzungsbände zum Reallexikon der Germanischen Altertumskunde 48). Berlin and New York: Walter de Gruyter.

Einar Ólafur Sveinsson 1958. *Dating the Icelandic Sagas: An Essay in Method*. London: Viking Society for Northern Research.

—— 1965. *Ritunartími Íslendingasagna. Rök og rannsóknaraðferð*. Reykjavík: Hið íslenska bókmenntafélag.

Eyrbyggja saga 1935. Edited by Einar Ólafur Sveinsson (Íslenzk fornrit 4). Reykjavík: Hið íslenska fornritafélag.

Eyrbyggja saga. The Vellum Tradition 2003. Edited by Forrest S. Scott (Editiones Arnamagnæanæ, Series A, vol. 18). Copenhagen: C.A. Reitzels Forlag.

Gunnar Karlsson 2004. *Goðamenning. Staða og áhrif goðorðsmanna í þjóðveldi Íslendinga*. Reykjavík: Heimskringla. Háskólaforlag Máls og menningar.

Hallberg, Peter 1965. "Íslendinga saga och Egla, Laxdœla, Eyrbyggja, Njála, Grettla: Ett språktest." *Maal og Minne*: 89–105.

—— 1979. "Eyrbyggja sagas alder – än en gang." *Acta Philologica Scandinavica* 32: 196–219.

Heller, Rolf 1978. "Das Alter der Eyrbyggja saga im Licht der Sprachstatistik." *Acta Philologica Scandinavica* 32: 53–66.

Íslendingabók, Landnámabók 1968. Edited by Jakob Benediktsson (Íslenzk fornrit 1). Reykjavík: Hið íslenska fornritafélag.

Jón Hnefill Aðalsteinsson 1997. *Blót í norrænum sið. Rýnt í forn trúarbrögð með þjóðfræðilegri aðferð*. Reykjavík: Háskólaútgáfan.

Jónas Kristjánsson 1972. *Um Fóstbræðra sögu* (Stofnun Árna Magnússonar á Íslandi, Rit 1). Reykjavík: Stofnun Árna Magnússonar á Íslandi.

——— 1977. "Egils saga og konungasögur." *Sjötíu ritgerðir helgaðar Jakobi Benediktssyni 20. júlí 1977*. Reykjavík: Stofnun Árna Magnússonar á Íslandi, pp. 449–72.

——— 1990. "Var Snorri Sturluson upphafsmaður Íslendingasagna?" *Andvari*, New Series XXXII: 85–105.

Laxdœla saga 1934. Edited by Einar Ólafur Sveinsson (Íslenzk fornrit 5). Reykjavík: Hið íslenska fornritafélag.

Maurer, Konrad 1895. *Zwei Rechtsfälle in der Eigla*. Munich: F. Straub.

Olsen, Olaf 1965. *Hørg, hov og kirke. Historiske og arkæologiske vikingestudier*. Copenhagen: Aarbøger for nordisk oldkyndighed og historie.

Southern, Richard W. 1986. *Robert Grosseteste: The Growth of an English Mind in Medieval Europe*. Oxford: Clarendon Press, Oxford University Press.

Torfi H. Tulinius 1996. "Guðs lög í ævi og verkum Snorra Sturlusonar." *Ný Saga* 8. Reykjavík: Sögufélagið, 31–40.

——— 2004. *Skáldið í skriftinni. Snorri Sturluson og Egils saga* (Íslensk menning 3). Reykjavík: Hið íslenska bókmenntafélag.

——— 2007. "Political Echoes: Reading Eyrbyggja Saga in Light of Contemporary Conflicts." In Judy Quinn, Kate Heslop, and Tarrin Wills (eds.), *Learning and Understanding in the Old Norse World: Essays in Honour of Margaret Clunies Ross* (Medieval Texts and Cultures of Northern Europe 18). Turnhout: Brepols, pp. 49–62.

Vésteinn Ólason 2005. "Family Sagas." *A Companion to Old Norse-Icelandic Literature and Culture*. Edited by R. McTurk. Oxford: Blackwell, pp. 102–18.

DATING THE ARCHETYPE

Eyrbyggja saga and *Egils saga Skallagrímssonar*

Jonna Louis-Jensen

DATING THE ICELANDIC SAGAS

Fifty years ago Einar Ól. Sveinsson published a booklet entitled *Dating the Icelandic Sagas* for the Viking Society (English translation by G. Turville-Petre). Since then a good deal of editorial work has been done on Icelandic saga manuscripts, and the time may have come to re-assess some of the dating criteria suggested by the author. His booklet may conveniently serve as a starting-point for a discussion of some of the problems we encounter when trying to establish the age of a saga.

By the time he published the booklet, Einar Ól. Sveinsson had edited several sagas of Icelanders for the series Íslenzk fornrit (ÍF), notably *Laxdœla saga* (1934), *Eyrbyggja saga* (1935), and *Njáls saga* (1954), and he was one of the leading figures of the so-called Icelandic school of saga scholarship. The Icelandic school regarded the sagas about early Icelanders as the works of authors who had treated the oral and written traditions available to them much as modern novelists would do, and according to this school the most fruitful means of determining the relative age of the sagas was the study of the literary interrelations (so-called *rittengsl*) of the saga texts. The approach recommended in *Dating the Icelandic Sagas* is similar to that in the introductions to the editions in ÍF. In his conclusion (p. 127) Einar Ól. Sveinsson speaks of "the method," which "must be as soundly and solidly based as possible"; here he seems mainly to be referring to the study of literary relations, recommended above other approaches on p. 76.[1] The *rittengsl* approach has, however, disappointed later scholars, since the direction of borrowing is often uncertain, even in cases where the interrelations seem to be likely or even obvious.

Although Einar Ól. Sveinsson appears to attach less importance to linguistic evidence for dating the sagas than to the *rittengsl* approach, he notes with personal satisfaction Peter Foote's study of the distribution of the preposition forms *of* and *um(b)* (1955), which, as he mentions, was carried out at his own suggestion, and he adds that "there is urgent need of further investigation" (p. 101). This still holds true, but other linguistic touchstones of a similar kind to *of/um(b)* were identified in the 1960s, especially by Peter Hallberg. The verb *hitta* was gradually replaced by *finna* in most contexts in the course of the thirteenth century (Hallberg 1965: 163–64). Similarly, the temporal conjunction *unz*, well-known from Eddic and skaldic poetry and also used in early Icelandic prose, was replaced by the composite conjunctions *til þess er* and *þar til er* (Widding 1960: 17). I believe that the future will bring more investigations along these lines. The use of computers in saga research has greatly facilitated vocabulary studies of this kind, and checking results that once took weeks or months to produce is now a matter of minutes – provided of course that the texts in question are available in machine-readable form.

What I first and foremost miss in Einar Ól. Sveinsson's booklet is a clearer understanding of the services the genealogical (stemmatic) method of textual criticism can render to our attempts at dating the sagas. What is in fact the object of our investigation when we talk of dating a saga? It is not the individual manuscript, which may be many copies removed from its ultimate source and written decades or even centuries later than it. Nor is it the lost original itself, which in the case of the sagas about early Icelanders, where variation in form and content may be considerable between the extant manuscripts, is often an entity with vague contours. What we can hope to be able to date with reasonable certainty is not the lost original but the archetype, understood as the (lost) ancestor of all preserved manuscripts of

1 A sober note is, however, struck on p. 94: "much may be doubtful in such attempts, and criticism, contrary evidence, and discussion are very valuable." On Einar Ól. Sveinsson's method, see also Torfi Tulinius in the present volume.

a given text. The archetype may be identical with the original, but this is not guaranteed to be the case.[2]

In his book *Studies in the Manuscript Tradition of Njálssaga* (1953), Einar Ól. Sveinsson himself applied the genealogical method to the vellum manuscripts of *Njáls saga* and concluded that they were all descended from a single archetype, although there were several open questions connected with the stemma. He even tried to reconstruct the archetype for a brief stretch, but in doing so he proved the virtual impossibility of the task, at least when the stemma is two-pronged, as in the case in point. A two-pronged stemma repeatedly leaves the editor with two readings of equal stemmatic weight, and if he wants to choose between them he has to rely on more or less subjective criteria. No wonder that Einar Ól. Sveinsson gave it up after a few pages. Nevertheless, even though we cannot reconstruct an archetype in all particulars by applying the genealogical method, it will enable us to eliminate at least some secondary readings in the manuscripts, and thus to get a truer picture of the archetype, which again will give us a more reliable basis for our attempts at establishing its age. As the philosopher Paul Oskar Kristeller (1905–1999) said in 1981 in a remarkable essay on the genealogical method: "We should resist the temptation to think that no problems can be solved because some problems cannot be solved, or that the problems we can solve are trivial and only the problems we cannot solve are important" (1981: 19–20).

THE ARCHETYPE OF *EYRBYGGJA SAGA*

In *Dating the Icelandic Sagas*, Einar Ól. Sveinsson does not refer to the genealogical method except apparently once, in strangely opaque terms: "In considering quality [of the extant manuscripts] we have the help of the learning which scholars have gained by experience of textual criticism and from the technique of editing, such as may be found in manuals on the subject" (1958: 16). His comments on the textual history of *Eyrbyggja saga* (pp. 20–21) are surprisingly vague, considering that he had himself edited the saga some twenty years earlier (ÍF IV, 1935). The ÍF edition was based on the only complete text of the saga, a text that survives in seventeenth-cen-

2 For a definition of the archetype in the philological sense, see e.g. Vésteinn Ólason and Þórður Ingi Guðjónsson 2000: 97, note.

tury transcripts of a lost vellum (Vatnshyrna, destroyed in the Copenhagen fire of 1728). Apart from this there exist four quite extensive vellum fragments of the saga. Einar Ól. Sveinsson's edition was based on the Vatnshyrna transcripts, but like Guðbrandur Vigfússon (1864) he had noticed that the language of the fragments was in some respects more archaic than that of Vatnshyrna, characterized by what Guðbrandur Vigfússon called "old and quaint" words.[3] This observation caused him to replace a large number of neutral expressions in his main text with more colourful ones from the fragments, so that, for example, *til sjá* could become *um klappa*. This seems to have been done for aesthetic reasons mainly, rather than as a result of stemmatic reasoning. Like earlier editors of *Eyrbyggja saga,* Einar Ól. Sveinsson operates with three classes of manuscripts: 1) Vatnshyrna (*V), 2) the "B group" (the fragments E, W and G), and 3) the fragment Melabók (M). Although he does not attempt to construct a stemma for *Eyrbyggja saga* in the edition, it seems that he counts the three groups as stemmatically equal, but he does not draw the obvious conclusion from this, namely that wherever B and M concur against *V, the former two must have retained the more original reading.[4] If he had applied stemmatic thinking more stringently, he would not only have realized that the "polished" (*sléttmáll*) style of *V is the result of a more or less systematic modernization of idiom; he would also not have needed to question the authenticity of three passages which he discusses in connection with the age of the saga (ÍF IV: xlv–xlvii):

1. The last chapter of the saga quotes an observation made by Guðný Bǫðvarsdóttir, mother of the three Sturlusons (Sighvatr, Þórðr and Snorri), at the exhumation of the bones of Snorri goði. W and M both have the additional information about Guðný: "er þá var húsfreyja í Hvammi" (W; "hon var þá hústrú í Hvammi" M; the passage is lacking in *V, and the fragments E and G do not cover it). We know of Guðný in Hvammur from the 1180s until at least 1199 (ÍF IV: xlvi); she died in 1221. Einar Ól. Sveinsson thinks that the clause was either present in the original or else an old addition.[5]

3 "alterthümliche und seltne Worte" (1864: xxix).

4 In *Dating the Icelandic Sagas,* however, it is mentioned as a possibility worth considering that B and M may "in some particulars" be closer to the original than *V (1958: 20–21).

5 "Ég hygg, að þessi orð séu annaðhvort úr frumtextanum eða svo gömul, að þeim sé fulltreystandi," ÍF IV, xlv–vi.

Since this clause is found in both W and M, that is to say in two of the three branches of the tradition,[6] it must have belonged to the archetype (though it does not add anything to our understanding of the age of the saga).

2. A reference to *Laxdœla saga* in the same chapter is found in W, M and *V; E and G do not cover this part of the text. Einar Ól. Sveinsson is inclined to think that the reference is a later addition (ÍF IV: xlvii–viii). It is, however, quite clear for stemmatic reasons that the reference must have been in the archetype, and later scholars have been less reluctant than Einar Ól. Sveinsson to believe that *Laxdœla saga* with its conspicuous influence from courtly literature could be older than *Eyrbyggja saga*.[7]

3. The adjective *kurteiss* is used about a woman in ch. 50, and Einar Ól. Sveinsson feels that this word is too reminiscent of the *riddarasögur* of the late thirteenth century to fit with his early dating of *Eyrbyggja saga*. Instead of *kurteis* (thus E, W and *V; G is defective here), M has *oflátlig*, which Einar Ól. Sveinsson thinks may be the original word ("mun vera frumtextinn" ÍF IV, lii). This is clearly not possible if we go by the stemma. M could not have retained the more original reading against the concordant evidence of the B branch and *V (unless B and *V had made the same change independently of each other, but the noun *ofláti* is found elsewhere in the saga, used about one of the female characters and retained in all the manuscripts, and so can hardly have been felt as "old and quaint"). There can be little doubt that the replacement was made in M (or some lost intermediary between M and *C), and the explanation may be that in the fifteenth century the word *kurteis* had acquired its modern meaning ("courteous"), and did

6 The stemma drawn up in Forrest S. Scott's edition of *Eyrbyggja saga* (EdAM A18, 2003, p. 17*) has two branches, not three. According to Scott, Melabók and Vatnshyrna go back to the lost archetype through a common intermediary *C:

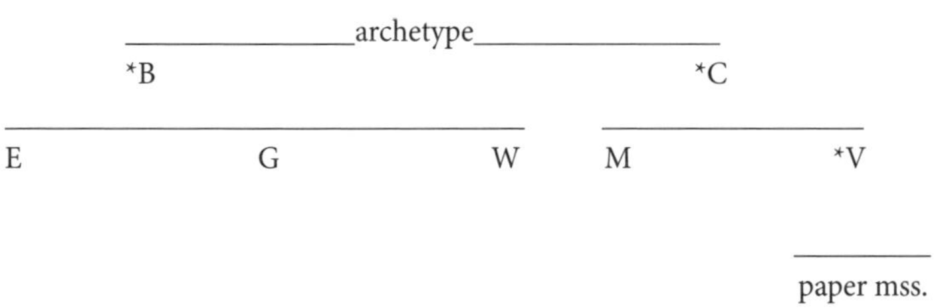

Whether the stemma is two-pronged or three-pronged makes no difference to the argument that a reading found in both W and M must be assumed to derive from the archetype.

7 See most recently Forrest S. Scott, EdAM A18, 19*–27*.

not seem applicable to a woman who expects a visitor to give up her luxurious bed-clothes to her, the lady of the house.

Einar Ól. Sveinsson may have felt that his arguments for an early dating of *Eyrbyggja saga* were not strong, since he did not repeat them in *Dating the Icelandic Sagas*, and later he seems to have changed his mind on the subject (Scott 2003, 19*). The new edition of the vellum fragments of *Eyrbyggja saga* (Scott 2003) with its important realization that M belongs to the same branch of the stemma as *V, not to the B branch, should make it clear that W is the single manuscript that gives the best picture of the archetype of *Eyrbyggja saga*, even in some respects better than the old fragment E (AM 162 E fol.), which is both very short and marred by scribal errors (Scott 2003: 10*–11*).

It is noteworthy that E, which has been dated to c. 1300, was written by the same scribe as one of the old fragments of the B-redaction of *Egils saga*, delta (AM 162 A fol. δ). The two fragments share a great many features as far as their palaeography and orthography is concerned (Kjeldsen 2005: 97–100), but occasionally in delta archaic spellings occur with no counterparts in E, such as the old Latin spelling *qv-* (especially in the name *Kveldúlfr*, but also in *kvikfé* and *kvómu*) (on archaisms in the fragments of *Egils saga* see further below, pp. 143–44), and the verb forms *hnykðe* and *øpðv* vs. *kipto* in E. Since the scribe apparently faithfully reproduced these archaisms in *Egils saga*, he would probably have done the same had he found any in his exemplar of *Eyrbyggja saga*. The archaic conjunction *unz* occurs eight times in delta, six of which reappear in their appropriate places in the *Egils saga* text of the much later Wolfenbüttel manuscript (W), and there can be little doubt that they go back to the archetype, and that they have been replaced with later synonyms in other manuscripts of the saga. The fragment E is unfortunately too short to contain any clauses beginning with *unz*, *til þess er* or *þar til er*, but *Eyrbyggja saga* in W, unlike *Egils saga*, has no examples of *unz* (nor has W's sister manuscript G). In the B-redaction (i.e. G and W combined) *þar til er* is far more frequent than *til þess er* (17:2), and this is likely to reflect the situation in the archetype. Peter Hallberg's dating of *Eyrbyggja saga* to well into the latter half of the thirteenth century, based mainly on *hitta/finna* statistics, seems reasonable enough if taken to apply to the archetype, even though Hallberg takes his figures from the ÍF edition (Scott 2003: 20*), but it may be added that a similar absence of archaisms is characteristic of *Heimskringla*, whose original(s) we would prefer for external reasons to date to the first half of the thirteenth century. Peter Foote warns us never to argue from the absence of archaisms (*in casu* the preposition *of*) (1955: 79), and of course it is not impossible that the archetype of *Eyrbyggja saga* was a thoroughly modernized redaction of an early thirteenth-century text, but there is neither internal nor external evidence to substantiate such a hypothesis.

SNORRI STURLUSON AND *EGILS SAGA*

The idea that Snorri Sturluson was the author of *Egils saga* was first proposed in the early nineteenth century, but there has been an ever-growing consensus about it in later years, reaching a splendid climax in the inclusion of *Egils saga* in the deluxe edition of Snorri's *Ritsafn* (Reykjavík 2002), sponsored by the Icelandic parliament. The arguments for and against Snorri's authorship have mostly been of a historical and/or literary nature; the first scholar to adduce linguistic evidence was Per Wieselgren (1927), who maintained that the linguistic and stylistic differences between *Egils saga* and *Óláfs saga helga* (the "*Heimskringla* version") were too great for both works to have come from the same author's pen. Wieselgren's conclusion was promptly rejected by Sigurður Nordal, who pointed out that what Wieselgren had taken to be the style of *Egils saga* was in fact that of the relatively late manuscript Möðruvallabók, and that he had not taken into account the theta fragment, dated to c. 1250 and thus presumably only a few decades younger than the original of *Egils saga*. Despite its late date, the Möðruvallabók text in Sigurður Nordal's edition of the saga (ÍF II, 1933) was to become the textual basis of Peter Hallberg's statistical research from the 1960s, especially his studies of "pair words." In the first of these studies Hallberg announced his findings in a tone of unmistakable triumph:

> If such an outcome cannot be accepted as proving beyond doubt that Snorri Sturluson dictated Egla, there seems to be little hope left that a linguistic study will ever lead to conclusive results in this or similar questions of authorship. (1962: 186)

Most scholars, including the editors of Snorri's *Ritsafn*, seem to have accepted Hallberg's ultimatum, and for the following forty years the prevailing discussion theme was whether Snorri had written *Egils saga before* or *after Heimskringla* (Jónas Kristjánsson 1977, Berman 1982). One of the difficulties with Hallberg's theory is, however, that it is chiefly based on a comparison of *Egils saga* with the saga of St Olaf, the central section of *Heimskringla*, not with the whole work.

SNORRI STURLUSON AND *THE SEPARATE SAGA OF ST OLAF*

In an earlier article (Louis-Jensen 1997, rpt. 2006) I have argued that there is no basis in the manuscript transmission of *Heimskringla* for assuming that the saga of St Olaf in Kringla (ÓH) was descended from the same archetype as the rest of the *Heimskringla* text; it is equally possible, from a text-critical point of view, to regard Kringla as an *ad hoc* combination of the first and last "thirds" of *Heimskringla* (Hkr I and Hkr III) with the *Separate Saga* of St Olaf, a combination made ten or twenty years after Snorri Sturluson's death. My argument has been misunderstood to the effect that I denied Snorri any share in *Heimskringla* whatsoever, but that was far from my intention. At the time I even subscribed to Sigurður Nordal's thesis (1914) that the *Separate Saga* of St Olaf was an earlier work by Snorri which he later had incorporated in *Heimskringla* with some well-chosen alterations. A renewed study of Nordal's book has convinced me that while he has proved conclusively that the *Separate Saga* is an earlier work than *Heimskringla*, his reasons for maintaining that Snorri himself must have incorporated it in *Heimskringla* are inadequate. It only gradually became clear to me that this inadequacy also applies to Snorri's authorship of the *Separate Saga*. While it was still believed that the *Separate Saga* was derived from *Heimskringla*, it was taken for granted that the three parts of *Heimskringla* shared the same author, but once Sigurður Nordal had reversed the stemma, the *Separate Saga* had become like any other anonymous work (*Egils saga*, for instance) – with the burden of proof lying with whoever would claim that it was written by Snorri Sturluson.

No doubt Hkr I and III were written in order to supplement an existing saga of St Olaf, most likely the one we know as the *Separate Saga*, but this does not in itself make the *Separate Saga* a work by Snorri. A thorough comparison of the language and style of the *Separate Saga* with the parts of *Heimskringla* that are ascribed to Snorri Sturluson with valid arguments (i.e. Hkr I and III) is certainly called for. If such an undertaking should lead to the hypothesis that the work we know as Snorri Sturluson's *Heimskrin-*

gla is in fact a combination of two works, only one of which it is reasonable to identify as Snorri's, we may ask whether the author of *Egils saga* should be identified as Snorri Sturluson or as the author of the *Separate Saga* ("Pseudo-Snorri") or as neither of these two. In order to throw some light on this question we may again turn to Peter Hallberg and his statistical research.

Besides the "pair word" statistics mentioned above Hallberg made a number of more conventional examinations of the vocabulary of *Heimskringla* and *Egils saga*, the results of which in his view confirmed Snorri's authorship of *Egils saga* (Hallberg 1968: 18). At least in two cases, however, Hallberg's statements about *Heimskringla* conceal distinct differences between ÓH (the "*Heimskringla* version") on one hand and Hkr I + III on the other. One of these cases is that of the relative frequencies of the verbs *hitta(sk)* vs. *finna(sk)*; the other is that of the composite temporal subjunctions *til þess er* vs. *þar til er*.

According to Peter Hallberg the percentages of *hitta(sk)* vs. *finna(sk)* in *Heimskringla* and *Egils saga* are strikingly similar, i.e. over 75 per cent *hitta(sk)* in both works. Unfortunately this part of Hallberg's study covers ÓH only, and the situation in Hkr I + III is very different: *finna(sk)* is more than twice as frequent as *hitta(sk)* throughout Hkr I and in the first two thirds of Hkr III. Only in the last third of Hkr III does the percentage of *hitta(sk)* reach a similar frequency as in ÓH, but this part of Heimskringla may in most respects be regarded as a copy of older works (*Morkinskinna* and *Hryggjarstykki*).

Peter Hallberg has further shown that a high proportion of the verb *hitta(sk)* is correlated with a high proportion of the conjunction *til þess er* in some sagas of Icelanders (1968: 172–73), and this he interprets in terms of chronology. *Egils saga* with its high percentages of *hitta(sk)* (76% in the ÍF text) and *til þess er* (85% in the ÍF text) fits very well into the chronological scheme, "not least if it is counted a work of Snorri!" says Hallberg, who has found similar percentages in ÓH: 76% of both *hitta(sk)* and *til þess er*. Hallberg does note, in passing and with some surprise, that Óláfs saga Tryggvasonar in *Heimskringla* shows completely different figures (12% *hitta(sk)*, 25% *til þess er*) and finds this difference difficult to explain ("svårförklarlig"). The explanation is, however quite simple: ÓH and Hkr I (including ÓT) do not share the same archetype. ÓH should be seen as an offshot of the manuscript tradition of the *Separate Saga*, whose archetype evidently belongs to a somewhat older stratum of saga literature than the archetype(s) of Hkr I and III. The perfect accordance found by Peter Hallberg between the percentages of *hitta(sk)* and *til þess er* in *Egils saga* and ÓH are not, as Hallberg claims, yet another proof that both are works by Snorri Sturluson, but rather that both are works belonging to a slightly older period than his.

THE ARCHETYPE OF *EGILS SAGA*

With *Egils saga* we are relatively well off as far as medieval manuscripts are concerned; the saga is preserved in thirteen medieval manuscripts, none of which are, however, complete, and in several later paper manuscripts that go back to partly or entirely lost medieval manuscripts. In 1956 Jón Helgason published an important article on the transmission of *Egils saga*; it is now accessible in an English translation by Michael Chesnutt. Jón Helgason also worked on a three-volume critical edition of *Egils saga* in the 1950s, and it has now been possible to publish the first and third volumes of this edition.[8] Our ideas about the style and language of *Egils saga* have hitherto been more or less determined by the fourteenth-century manuscript Möðruvallabók that has been the basis of all earlier editions, and the traditional dating of *Egils saga* has depended on the supposition that it was written by Snorri Sturluson. As I have tried to show in an earlier article (Louis-Jensen 2009) and hope to be able to substantiate further in a forthcoming paper, the arguments put forward by Peter Hallberg are not convincing, partly because figures for *Egils saga* are taken from the ÍF text, which in all essentials is that of Möðruvallabók. Hallberg ignores Jón Helgason's 1956 paper, where the following stemma is proposed:

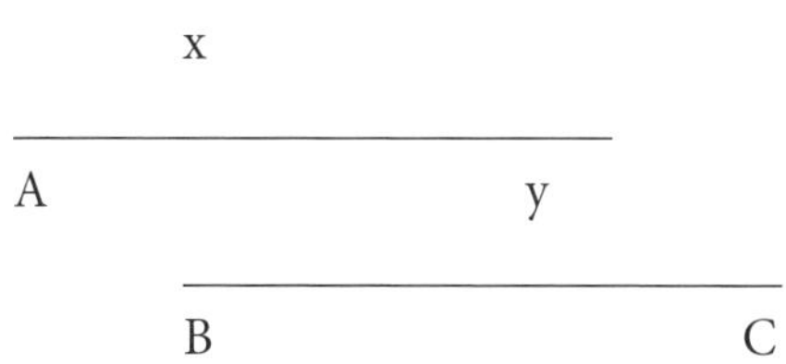

A, B, and C in this somewhat simplified version of Jón Helgason's stemma

8 EdAM A19 (edited by Bjarni Einarsson) and A21 (edited by Michael Chesnutt). A20 is expected within the next few years.

denotes redactions, not single manuscripts; the most complete representative of the A-redaction is Möðruvallabók. The fragment theta does not figure in the stemma; it belongs either to the A-redaction or to a higher node in the stemma (Chesnutt 2005: 228–29 with references).

The fragment theta is the oldest preserved fragment of an *Íslendingasaga* and has a long-standing reputation for having preserved the most authentic text of *Egils saga*. Thus Einar Ól. Sveinsson (1958: 19) declared that theta "is only a few decades younger than the original text and *appears to follow it very closely*" (my italics). Einar Ól. Sveinsson is not the only saga scholar to express himself as if he believed that practically every single word in theta must be a faithful rendition of the original of *Egils saga*, but in fact theta has a number of readings of its own which may or may not reflect the archetype, and this is precisely what makes it so difficult to place the fragment in the stemma (for a thought-provoking note see Ólafur Halldórsson 1991[9]). And yet at the same time Einar Ól. Sveinsson, referring to Peter Foote's study of the preposition *of/um*, notes that theta has not preserved the original wording in every particular:

> The scribe who wrote θ of *Egils saga* changed *of* to *um* in every case except one, but in ζ the proportion of *of-umb* to *um* is 43.3 per cent. (Einar Ól. Sveinsson 1958: 100)

At least in this respect theta must have followed the original less closely than the fragment zeta (AM 162 A fol. ζ), the oldest of a handful of fragments belonging to the B-redaction. Zeta was probably written c. 1275–1300 (Kjeldsen 2005: 167 with references), by which time the old preposition form *of* was no longer part of the spoken language and was in large measure replaced with *um* by scribes copying old manuscripts. The thirteen occurrences of *of* were without doubt copied from the scribe's exemplar, and it is equally certain that they were in the text from the beginning and have been copied faithfully by one scribe after another. Einar Ól. Sveinsson puts it very well: "although we know that copyists modernized the language, we do not know that they archaized it" (1958: 96). It is less certain whether the

9 Here Ólafur Halldórsson points out a phrase in theta that seems to be lifted from a Norwegian law-book, or perhaps from one of the Icelandic law-books Járnsíða or Jónsbók from the period after 1262. Such a phrase is unlikely to have come from the original of the saga.

seventeen occurrences of *um* in zeta are replacements made somewhere along the line, or whether the mixed usage goes back to the original. The period of transition seems to have been from c. 1200 to c. 1260 (Foote 1955: 59–60), which is precisely the period during which we may expect that *Egils saga* was first written.

Zeta is not the only fragment of the B class that displays archaisms which have been suppressed in the A- and C-redactions. In the fragment delta (AM 162 A fol. δ, written around 1300), the conjunction *unz* occurs eight times, and six of these occurrences reappear in the Wolfenbüttel manuscript, also a manuscript of the B-redaction – the absence of one of them being due to a minor omission in W, while another is replaced with *til þess er*. In Möðruvallabók (A-redaction) *unz* is replaced with *til þess er* in six of the eight instances and with other near-synonyms in the last two, and in the C-redaction the distribution is almost the same as in Möðruvallabók, in so far as all eight instances of *unz* are replaced with other conjunctions, mainly *til þess er*. The fragment delta even boasts an isolated occurrence of the adverb *umb*, extremely rare after c. 1225 according to Peter Foote (1955: 58).

A natural implication of this is that the percentages of the preposition *of* and the conjunction *unz* were at least as high in the archetype of *Egils saga* as in the late thirteenth-century fragments of the B-redaction, perhaps considerably higher. This would seem to place the probable date of origin of *Egils saga* in the time range of works written perhaps a generation before *Heimskringla* (*Orkneyinga saga*, the "Oldest *Morkinskinna*"), cf. Foote 1955: 64. Peter Foote summarizes his chronology as follows in his conclusion (1955: 78–79):

> Where a text shows a high proportion of OF, it may be safe to use this as evidence in assessing the date of a work. A high proportion will suggest that it was written before c. 1250, possibly before c. 1235 (the form UMB is important in this respect) [...] The possibility of dialect usage must however be taken into account. Finally, it must be remembered that we can only argue from the presence of OF in a text, never from its absence.

In *Heimskringla* (including *Ólafs saga helga* in the Kringla version[10]) there

10 The same seems to be true of the *Separate Saga of St Olaf*, but I have so far not had access to a machine-readable text of this work and am therefore less certain about the non-occurrence of these archaisms.

are no instances of *unz* or *of* in a prose context, and even if Peter Foote's warning against drawing conclusions from negative evidence is a point well taken, this does not, at the very least, constitute a positive argument for *Heimskringla* and *Egils saga* sharing the same author.

CONCLUSION

My conclusion must necessarily be preliminary, since we are still waiting for some of the source material to be published. In both ÓH and (some fragments of) *Egils saga* the language shows certain archaisms that are absent in Hkr I+III. Therefore, if it is true that Snorri Sturluson is the author of Hkr I+III, the linguistic evidence suggests that neither ÓH nor *Egils saga* was written or dictated by him. Nor do there seem to be any linguistic indications of ÓH and *Egils saga* sharing the same author. The relatively high percentages of *of/um* and *unz/til þess er* in fragments of *Egils saga* must derive from the archetype. They suggest a date of origin before 1235, cf. Foote as cited above. While this is in keeping with the traditional dating to c. 1230, based on the idea that Snorri Sturluson authored *Egils saga*, the absence of the same archaisms from the archetype(s) of Hkr I+III – or at least from the parts of Hkr I+III that have not demonstrably been copied from older works – speaks very strongly against that idea.

Bibliography

Berman, Melissa 1982. "Egils saga and Heimskringla." *Scandinavian Studies* 54: 21–50.

Bjarni Aðalbjarnarson (ed.) 1951. *Heimskringla* III (Íslenzk fornrit XXVIII). Reykjavík: Hið íslenzka fornritafélag.

Chesnutt, Michael 2005. "Tekstkritiske bemærkninger til C-redaktionen af Egils saga." *Opuscula* XII (Bibliotheca Arnamagnæana 44). Copenhagen; C.A. Reitzels forlag, pp. 228–62.

Einar Ól. Sveinsson (ed.) 1935. *Eyrbyggja saga* (Íslenzk fornrit 4). Reykjavík: Hið íslenzka fornritafélag.

—— 1953. *Studies in the Manuscript Tradition of Njáls saga* (Studia Islandica 13). Reykjavík: H. F. Leiftur.

——— 1958. *Dating the Icelandic Sagas: An Essay in Method.* London: Viking Society for Northern Research.

Foote, Peter 1955. "Notes on the Prepositions OF and UM(B) in Old Icelandic and Old Norwegian Prose" (Studia Islandica 14). Reykjavík: H. F. Leiftur, pp. 41–83.

Guðbrandur Vigfusson (ed.) 1864. *Eyrbyggja saga.* Leipzig: Vogel.

Hallberg, Peter 1962. *Snorri Sturluson och Egils saga Skallagrímssonar. Ett försök till språklig författarbestämning* (Studia Islandica 20). Reykjavík: Bókmenntafræðistofnun Háskóla Íslands.

——— 1963. *Ólafr Þórðarson hvítaskáld, Knýtlinga saga och Laxdæla saga. Ett försök till språklig författarbestämning* (Studia Islandica 22). Reykjavík: Bókmenntafræðistofnun Háskóla Íslands.

——— 1965. "Om språkliga författarkriterier i isländska sagatexter." *Arkiv för nordisk filologi* 80: 157–86.

——— 1968. *Stilsignalement och författarskap i norrön sagalitteratur.* Gothenburg.

Jón Helgason [1956] 2005. "Observations on Some Manuscripts of Egils saga" *Opuscula* XII (Bibliotheca Arnamagnæana 44). Copenhagen: C.A. Reitzels forlag, pp. 3–47.

Jónas Kristjánsson 1977. "Egilssaga og konungasögur." *Sjötíu ritgerðir helgaðar Jakobi Benediktssyni.* Reykjavík: Stofnun Árna Magnússonar, pp. 449–72.

Jørgensen, Jon Gunnar 2007. *The Lost Vellum Kringla* (Bibliotheca Arnamagnæana 45). Copenhagen: C.A. Reitzels forlag.

Kjeldsen, Alex Speed (ed.) 2005. "AM 162 A δ fol." (Reykjavík). *Opuscula* XII (Bibliotheca Arnamagnæana 44). Copenhagen: C.A. Reitzels forlag, pp. 71–153.

——— 2005 (ed.). "AM 162 A ζ fol." (Reykjavík). *Opuscula* XII (Bibliotheca Arnamagnæana 44). Copenhagen: C.A. Reitzels forlag, pp. 154–82.

Kristeller, Paul Oskar 1981. "The Lachmann Method: Merits and Limitations." *Text: Transactions of the Society for Textual Scholarship* I. New York, pp. 11–20.

Louis-Jensen, Jonna 1977. *Kongesagastudier: Kompilationen Hulda-Hrokkinskinna* (Bibliotheca Arnamagnæana 32). Copenhagen C.A. Reitzels Boghandel.

——— [1997] 2006. "Heimskringla – et værk af Snorri Sturluson?" *Nordica Bergensia* 14. [Bergen]: Nordisk institutt, Universitetet i Bergen. Reprinted in *Con Amore*. Copenhagen, pp. 217–32.

——— 2009. "Heimskringla og Egils saga – samme forfatter?" *Studier i Nordisk 2006–2007. Selskab for Nordisk Filologi. Foredrag og Årsberetning.* Copenhagen, pp. 103–11.

Ólafur Halldórsson 1991. "Nema skyld nauðsyn banni." *Lygisögur sagðar Sverri Tómassyni fimmtugum 5. apríl 1991.* Reykjavík, pp. 73–77.

Sigurður Nordal 1914. *Om Olaf den helliges saga*. Copenhagen: G.E.C. Gad.

——— (ed.) 1933. *Egils saga Skallagrímssonar* (Íslenzk fornrit II). Reykjavík: Hið íslenzka fornritafélag.

Vésteinn Ólason, and Þórður Ingi Guðjónsson 2000. "Sammenhængen mellem tolkninger og tekstversioner af *Gísla saga*." *Den fornnordiska texten i filologisk och litteraturvetenskaplig belysning* (Gothenburg Old Norse Studies, 2). Gothenburg: University of Gothenburg, pp. 96–120.

Widding, Ole 1960. "Nogle problemer omkring sagaen om Gudmund den gode." *Maal og Minne*: 13–26.

Wieselgren, Per 1927. *Författarskapet till Eigla.* Lund: Carl Blom.

THE TEMPORALITY OF THE (IMMANENT) SAGA

Tinkering with Formulas

Slavica Ranković

THE SAGAS' COMPLEX MEDIALITY: THE IMPLICATIONS FOR DATING

There seem to be such things in the world as *Egils saga, Njáls saga, Laxdœla saga* (*Íslendingasǫgur* we call them), but then there are also things such as AM 162 fol., fragm. theta, AM 132 fol., Lbs 1421 8vo, GKS 1003 fol., ÍB 226 4to. etc., which are supposed to be parts of the aforementioned sagas, or which contain them as parts instead. Then, over the sea of editions forgotten and new, diplomatic, normalized, translated, digitized, there tower the Íslenzk fornrit volumes which, for all intents and purposes, are the *Íslendingasǫgur*, or very quickly become so, once one engages with matters of interpretation. Speaking of seas, we must also take into account "det muntliga havet" (the open sea of orality) (Tommy Danielsson in Andersson 2006: 5). It was in such a sea, scholars now agree, that the sagas first began to take their many and variously sized protean shapes, only to dissolve the next moment and reassemble again, in always different yet increasingly stable forms. Eventually, some such formations found themselves entangled in the inky, spidery webs of ambitious authors and expert scribes, imbued further with learned lore and fused with imported narrative yarns – some more cognate, others less familiar. Yet these fragile snares could not hold them trapped for long. Fluid as they were at the oral stage, the sagas continued to be so in this new medium too, spilling over the manuscript pages as they were read aloud and retold, seeping through the lines and replenishing the sea of orality in novel ways. Finally,[1] unlike the familiar bulk of the AM 132 fol. for example, equipped with a concretizing paraphernalia of letters and numbers and comfortably furnished with a name that (apparently) locates it – Möðruvallabók – there are those precious "first," and very much lost folios, 4tos and 8vos, exuding such a strong puzzle-appeal from the murky depths of oblivion that one would be hard pressed to find a saga scholar who did not, at one time or another, ponder the mystery of their creation. Who wrote them? Or, more pertinently to the present volume, when were they written?

As a way of facilitating a better understanding of the beginnings of the sagas as a written genre, an attempt to answer these questions can hardly be considered futile. As Guðrún Nordal states in her contribution, such effort is never "an idle pursuit" (p. 196) for precisely the reason that she identifies: a date places a text within a historical context, which equips us with important ways of appreciating it. However, while it is often these first written renderings of the sagas that we hope to date (indeed, they once were things one could actually date), a problem occurs when this also comes to mean that what we are dating are the sagas themselves – *Egils saga, Njáls saga, Laxdœla saga* and so on. As was suggested in the opening passage, if things at all, these narratives have a different kind of "thingness" or objecthood – one that does not presume their being in one place in the exact same form and at the exact same time, but that rather reveals them as continuously evolving "multiforms" (cf. Lord 2000 [1960]: 100) and spatiotemporally distributed objects (cf. Gell 1998; Ranković 2007). If this multiformity is taken into account, it is inevitable that, as Gísli Sigurðsson notes, "the age of the written sagas becomes considerably less significant" (2004: 331), in particular when a search for the date betrays a desire for 'The Original' and its creative 'Genius.'" Such a desire is anachronistic in two respects: firstly, because of its Romantic, post-medieval origins tied to rather different types of text, and secondly, because it has by now become part of an outdated critical paradigm that is no longer applied to modern texts either. Paradoxically, it is both too modern and yet already passé at one and the same time.

This is not to deny the first written saga realizations their special status. It is possible – even likely – that such renderings, if for no better reason than

1 The word is here applied for the purposes of emphasis, not to say that there are not any more guises in which to encounter the sagas.

that they were first of their kind,[2] were likely to significantly influence subsequent redactions, revisions, and copies of the sagas. At the same time, it is impossible to determine precisely just how significant this influence was and in what way it was exerted. The purpose of the present contribution, however, is to suggest that, in addition to dating manuscripts (both extant and lost), there are other alluring temporal puzzles that are worth exploring and tinkering with once the sagas are considered in their multiformity and their complex oral-written-aural mediality. More specifically, if they resist dating as something applicable only to particular renderings, then what notions of temporality apply to the sagas as distributed or immanent narratives (cf. Clover 1986; Foley 1991)? Furthermore, where does the immanent saga stand in relation to its various orally and/or textually performed instances or concretizations?

These questions resonate with some of the concerns expressed by other contributors to this volume, most notably Jürg Glauser and Emily Lethbridge, who ask what is dated and why, and what constitutes the "final form," or even simply "the whole" of a saga, as well as addressing the problems of privileging one text over another. In addition, the present study takes up the questions posed by Gísli Sigurðsson (2004: 44) regarding the implications for our interpretations of the sagas – as well as major problems of saga scholarship (dating included) – if we assume a live oral tradition in the background of saga writing and take into account the fluidity (*mouvance*) inherent in the manuscript culture itself. Engaging with the question of what kind of temporality applies to the sagas as immanent narratives thus inevitably leads to the problem of origins, which is why we need to address the concept of the immanent saga.

2 Of course, it is possible that there was more than one "first" rendering per saga. Beyond the classic examples of several versions of the saga narratives (for example, see Lethbridge in this volume on *Gísla saga*), it might be instructive to consider the following hypothetical scenario as envisaged by Gísli Sigurðsson (2012: 233): "Such a major project as the writing of *Njáls saga* might well have evoked the idea of sponsors, with more than one individual being interested in securing for himself or herself a personal copy of the final product by sending and funding a scribe to work in the scriptorium. Consequently, when it came to the final act of writing there may, for all we know, have been three or more scribes working at the same time with one dictator, thus creating three different originals of the saga at the same time."

WHAT IS AN IMMANENT SAGA?

One of the most influential and relatively recent saga origin scenarios is Carol Clover's inventive revision of the "*þáttr* theory," where a pivotal role is given to the concept of the "immanent saga" (1986: 34):

> [A] whole saga existed at the preliterary stage not as a performed but as an immanent or potential entity, a collectively envisaged "whole" to which performed parts of *þættir* of various sizes and shapes were understood to belong, no matter what the sequence or the frequency of their presentation. I emphasize that I am here using the term *þáttr* not in its generic but etymological sense – to refer to any shorter bit of narrative (anecdotes, scenes, and episodes, as well as generic *þættir*) that a contemporary audience would have perceived as a "part."

But then, as literacy enters the stage (1986: 35):

> It was, I suggest, only when literary authors set about assembling the variety of oral traditions and literary sources available to them that the immanent whole was fully realized.

Firmly grounded in comparative folkloristics, the theory owes its success to its extraordinary explanatory potential, as well as, to an extent, its conciliatory effect with regard to the bookprose-freeprose rift, an effect which Clover anticipates (1986: 39):

> [T]he value of the immanent saga lies in its harmonization of the whole-saga and the standard *þáttr* hypotheses in such a way as to retain the advantages of both and the disadvantages of neither… It offers, in short, the most precise answer so far to the basic question of saga studies: where "oral" ends, and "literary" begins […] at the level of composition.

This desire to "give to Cesar what is Cesar's and to God what is God's" – i.e., give due credit to the oral traditional background while taking care to preserve the sanctity of the saga writers' personal ingenuities and account for literary influences – reveals itself in the quoted passages in both a positive and a negative light: positive inasmuch as it gives the theory its wings, negative inasmuch as it enforces a somewhat too sharply delineated distribution of the oral and the written contributions.

While the concept of immanence is potentially very useful, as described in the passages above, it seems to raise as many questions as it answers. For instance, in what sense can it be said that something immanent "existed"? What does it mean for something to be "collectively envisaged"? Does this collective (or, for that matter, any particular individual's) vision change over time, or does it always remains the same? Or is the constant change, paradoxically, the only way of remaining the same in oral tradition, the vital part of its homeostasis (cf. Ong 1982: 46–49)? What is the relation between the never-performed "whole" and its performed "parts" of various sizes?[3] Do they simply "belong" to the immanent saga, or are they in fact the only channel through which the immanent saga announces its existence or can be glimpsed at all, as well as the sites where the "collective vision" gets negotiated (cf. Ranković 2010)? Is the immanent saga "a sum of its parts" (Gísli Sigurðsson 2004: 45), and if so, how is one ever to add them up, even hypothetically, when they themselves are not one thing but clouds of evolving variants, dispersed in time and in space? Does then the immanent saga come before its performed parts as a "general narrative outline" (Andersson 2006: 4) or a "conceptual saga" (Gísli Sigurðsson 2004: 45), or are the outlines and concepts something that can only be derived *a posteriori*, following the performed stories?

While the questions that are addressed in first paragraph quoted from Carol Clover above express the need to further probe and develop the notion of the immanent saga, those that will be raised in the following discussion (pertaining to the second paragraph quoted from Carol Clover's work) adopt a distinctly critical approach inasmuch as Clover, led astray by the desire to identify "where 'oral' ends, and 'literary' begins," leaves the immanent saga bereft of its immanence and its perpetual potentiality, as the tentative "whole" of the first citation becomes a fully fledged, "fully realized" whole[4] in the second citation. This conceptual move opens up another list of questions: does the written commitment of some whole (made whole only provisionally, by that very act of commitment) immediately

3 For a useful discussion on possible lengths of the immanent sagas' performed "parts," see Andersson (2002).

4 Note that in this part of the discussion Clover also ceases to place scare quotes around the word "whole," thus imbuing it further with the sense of concreteness and finality.

translate into a fully realized whole? How can something that is immanent ever be fully realized when, by definition, immanent is something amorphous, something lacking a concrete shape, without a clear beginning and end? How can we ever know that, at the time of its first written rendering, what we now refer to as *Gísla saga* was not indeed one man's "fully realized" whole, while to another it might have only been a prequel to what is now *Eyrbyggja saga*?

Equally, is it not possible that what for us now are the first thirty chapters of *Egils saga* could have ended up as some "fully realized" Þórólfs saga? If we allow for the possibility that "the immanent whole was fully realized" by the saga writers and had thus lost its immanence, how can we account for the common phenomenon of the manuscript culture continuing to draw on the oral tradition and feeding back into it in turn, with the stories being recycled in both media (see, for example, Kellogg 1979), thus puncturing any notion of finality and wholeness? In what relation do these written, manuscript "performances" stand in respect to the immanent saga? Would not they too, just as with oral performances of the "parts," be "takes" on the immanent saga with which they would remain in constant dialogue, while replenishing and reshaping it at the same time?

As these questions suggest, far from being fully understood, the immanent saga and its peculiar temporality merit further study. An obvious way to engage with it would be to explore the manuscript variability of the sagas in a way in which each rendering would be regarded as both "a unique event," "an original" (Lord 1960: 102), datable and ascribable to particular (anonymous or named) authors, and simultaneously only as an instance of its "multiform" (Lord 1960: 100), immanent self. As such, a rendering is nothing in itself, in the sense that it is not even "a rendering" before it is read as such, as an instance "of," by which time it has already left the flatness of the page and its clockwork chronology. Of course, in this sense, every instance has always already left the reassuring stability and the well-tempered simultaneity of a localized form to join the formless (but formative) life of meaning in the edgeless volume of content, to join the ongoing dialogue between the others of its kind. As such, "a rendering" defies simple attributions of authorship because it is always more than itself, because it is a story that is "telling itself" (Spearing 2001: 728) and because it is, according to this difficult logic of evolutionary temporality, its own (distributed) author.[5]

THE EVOLUTIONARY TEMPORALITY OF THE IMMANENT SAGA

This way of studying a story "in the circle of variants" is something that folklorists have been doing for a long time, moving away from the hierarchical and stemmatic view of the relationship between the variants that they inherited initially from "text criticism, the art of comparing manuscripts" (Honko 2000: 6). Thus, for example, many a book or paper title dedicated to Serbian epic poetry reads as follows: *"Banović Strahinja" in the Circle of Variants and Themes about the Wife's Betrayal in the Folk Epic* (Medenica 1965), "'Little Radojica' in the Circle of Variants and Themes about the Shaman" (Kleut 2005) and *The Life of an Epic Song: "The Wedding of King Vukašin" in the Circle of Variants* (Delić 2006).[6] Studying the saga manuscripts in a similar way would allow each to tell its own stories of the shifting horizons of expectation of the saga writers, scribes, compilers, and their audiences over time. A comparison of their similarities as well as their divergences and idiosyncrasies that each text engenders, the varying codicological contexts in which we find them,[7] material features of their

5 Although as radical today as they ever were, the intuitions expressed here and throughout this article have a long and difficult history as the philosophy of difference, contingency, and adaptation: from Aristotle and Heraclitus, through to Thomas Aquinas, and on to Darwin, Nietzsche, Freud, and Heidegger. Although now widespread throughout the arts and humanities, they remain hotly disputed, but also habitually resisted or ignored, their tentative formulations programmatically misinterpreted, especially as they are (to date most rigorously) articulated in Derrida's work. This is perhaps most evident in the persistent portrayals of Derrida as the thinker of negativity, even as the difficulty of Derrida's message is precisely in that he leaves us with no easy oppositions. In *Writing and Difference* (1978: 19–20), for example, Derrida explicitly states: "Our intention here is not, through the simple motions of balancing, equilibration or overturning, to oppose duration to space, quality to quantity, force [read "content, which is the living energy of meaning," ibid., 5] to form, the depth of meaning or value to the surface of figures. Quite the contrary. To counter this simple alternative, to counter the simple choice of one of the terms or one of the series against the other, we maintain that it is necessary to seek new concepts and new models, an economy escaping this system of metaphysical oppositions."

6 The translation of these works' titles (originally in Serbian) is mine.

7 It cannot be all the same whether we find, say, *Grettis saga* as freestanding, or in company with other *Íslendingasǫgur*, with *fornaldarsǫgur*, or with stories of great international heroes such as *Ectors saga* and *Karlamagnús saga*. Such placements can speak volumes about the compilers' attitudes towards *Grettis saga*.

manuscripts (such as layout and illumination) might provide glimpses into evolutionary trends and currents in the development of the immanent saga.

This, of course, is not a revolutionary idea: something similar is championed by the proponents of "new" philology, even if here the emphasis is more on the uniqueness of each "material embodiment" (Driscoll 2010) rather than the relationships between the manuscripts, lest one should lapse back into the entanglements and the controversies of stemmas and textual hierarchies. The risk of this approach, however, is that in an endeavour to atone for "old" philology's major sin of treating the extant manuscripts as the poor, corrupt relations of the lost (and therefore perfect) originals, scholars might end up reifying each manuscript in turn as "The Original," thus neglecting the mutual interrelations and the echoic nature of the sagas that the manuscripts bear. While this approach in principle allows for the evolution of language at the micro-scale and the evolution of the saga texts at the macro-scale, there is still a danger that at the scale in-between (the mezzo-scale; i.e. that of an individual manuscript) this evolutionary time dimension might be entirely lost. It is precisely because a manuscript is a tangible, dateable object that its historical/chronological placement could easily be (mis)understood as also referring to the dating of a saga, albeit with a caveat that it is this particular *realization* of the saga that is dated and hence should be possible to capture in some temporal synchronicity. To be sure, the specific time, place, and purpose for which the manuscript is made are all fed into the meaning of the text at hand, and it is therefore of the utmost importance that they are studied. If it were not for such changing contextual specificities, there would be no evolution of the sagas to begin with. However, there is a perspective from which every notion of the synchronic, unproblematically datable origin story becomes moot, even when we talk about dating a specific realization, having to do with the fact that the sagas are traditional narratives.

As traditional narratives – both in the sense that the stories and the ways of telling them are inherited *and* in the sense that their writers and scribes lay no claims of authorship to them (cf. Vésteinn Ólason 1998: 21) – the sagas abound in formulaic expressions, themes and motifs,[8] so that each

8 As a counteraction to the overzealous and indiscriminate application of the Parry-Lord method, it has nowadays become commonplace in scholarly circles to say that formulas cannot be taken as evidence of their oral origins because they "can all equally appear in works produced with pen in hand" (Gísli Sigurðsson 2004: 48). There is a good reason

rendering, inasmuch as it is a rendering *of* a saga at all – of its immanent "formula" – has always already punctured the synchronic flatness of the manuscript form. According to John Miles Foley (1991: 7), formulas are able to facilitate this because of their role as conduits of "traditional referentiality," the capacity of oral and orally-derived narratives to reach out of their particular orally *and/or* textually performed instances and draw "on the fecund totality of the entire tradition."[9] Rather than regarding them merely in their role as mnemonic and compositional aids, or dismissing them as clichés empty of meaning, Foley argues that formulaic phrases, recurrent themes, motifs, etc., are instead laden with metonymic "word-power" (cf. Foley 2002) and endowed with a rich "expressive ecology" (Foley 2005: 27) through which they are able to convey subtle and complex meanings. Traditional narratives, then, demand to be read not in isolation, but as being in constant dialogue with their "silent but ever-present partner" (Foley 1991: 60), the tradition. In this context, the formulas act as channels that enable that communication. When the tradition is no longer alive (as is the case here), the extant renderings continue to call out to one another through their shared hoard of expressions and narrative patterns, creating an abundance of interpretational possibilities across the saga corpus and beyond the immediate wording of any given text. In this way they also defy chronological linearity and point to the more complex, diachronic or evolutionary temporality of each saga text.

Of course, studying the ways in which traditional idiomatic structures appear in the sagas – how their usage in specific contexts makes them adapt

for being cautious, and consequently I am not treating the formulas as evidence of oral composition of the sagas. Rather, they are treated as markers of their traditionality in that they point to a literary culture that nevertheless adheres and aesthetically responds to the precepts of oral poetics. At the same time, we need to be aware that every counteraction is often a bit of an overreaction too, and if we permit for any sort of oral tradition behind and around the written sagas, it becomes hard to explain why the saga writers would only draw on the story material and not tap into the rich reservoir of idiomatic phrases, motifs, themes, and general ways of constructing stories. What would motivate them to do so? Not only would that constitute an unjustifiable waste (of which hardly any other tradition can be found guilty), but if indeed these stories were written to be read aloud, enjoyed in company rather than only in solitude and silence, what would act as the social glue and how would the audience recognize they are indeed listening to a saga?

9 Foley here builds on the important groundwork laid by Lord (1960) in *The Singer of Tales,* and also adopts the notion of immanence from Clover (1986).

and change – can potentially contribute to saga dating in the classical sense (i.e., the dating of the envisaged first written renderings), since, for instance, radical and persistent experimentations with formulas tend to be later developments. However, as suggested by the qualifier "tend," this contribution would be rather limited and only of use in conjunction with methods that are deemed more solid and "objective" than style and "artistry" (cf. Einar Ól. Sveinsson 1958: 39–40; 115–23). To my mind, the greater value of a close, systematic study of formulaic patterns in the sagas lies in its potential to provide us with a better, more intuitive understanding of this important yet difficult notion of evolutionary temporality that characterizes the sagas as well as other orally derived traditional narratives. The rest of this article will therefore be dedicated to an attempt at such a study.

The formula that will serve as the case study will be that of a hero wearing blue-black (*blár*) clothing, which often happens when he sets off to seek vengeance. Ideally, one should examine how the formula is used across the extant corpus, as well as how it appears "in the circle of manuscript variants" of each saga. The two perspectives should then be superimposed in order to allow a fuller picture to emerge. In addition, as the sagas share their idiomatic heritage with other Old Norse genres, it would be illuminating to further compare how *blár* clothing is featured in those. A cursory and a slightly arbitrary search (purely driven by the availability of online texts) of how *blár* clothing is treated in *Heimskringla* (http://www.snerpa.is/net/snorri/heimskri.htm) and the *fornaldarsǫgur* (http://www.snerpa.is/net/forn/forn/htm) seems to reveal the common mythological connection of *blár* to the underworld (cf. Wolf 2006: 61), even if the formula as described above seems peculiar to the sagas of Icelanders. This is of potentially great consequence for the study of evolutionary temporality: one formula seems to have given birth to another. Even if the new "daughter" formula now has its own role to perform, it still continues to resound with the semantic echoes of its "mother." At the same time, the more the "daughter" formula is used, the more potential it has to change the meaning of the "mother" formula, making it, in a feedback loop, its "daughter" in turn. (For an example, see the discussion below on Geirríðr from *Eyrbyggja saga* as a sorceress and avenger.) This is something well worth exploring. However, at present, I can only offer a detailed discussion of the formula's usage across the saga corpus as represented by the Íslenzk fornrit editions. While this is a clear limitation, the method still yields data that is suggestive of the sagas' evolutionary dynamic/time, enhancing our intuition, which, as already noted, is the goal of the present study.

For convenience, speed, and ease of searching I have used the digitized Modern Icelandic texts of the *Íslendingasǫgur* and *þættir* as they appear at http://www.snerpa.is/net/isl/isl.htm and http://www.snerpa.is/net/isl/isl-th.htm, although all the chapter references and quotations are given from the Íslenzk fornrit editions, as is customary. I have further made use of an exceptionally easy-to-operate search programme devised by Miloš Ranković[10] and available to anyone wanting to engage in a similar study at http://sagasearch.appspot.com.

THE TEMPORALITY OF FORMULAS: THE CASE OF *BLÁR* CLOTHING

As the colour of both dyed cloth and otherworldly regions, the hellish realms of the departed, blue-black (*blár*) connotes both costliness / preciousness and death, a combination that in the saga literature blossoms into the formula of heroes wearing *blár* clothing "when they are off to kill" (Wolf 2006: 71).[11] Even though the formulation *hann var í blári kápu* (he was in a blue-black cloak) may be the most recognizable one, the actual type of clothing worn during a vengeful slaying does not seem to play the most important role, as many an avenger is featured in a blue-black *kyrtill* (tunic), *kufl* (cowl), or *hekla* (hooded cloak), or is described as *bláklæddr* (blue-black-clothed). The gravity of the situation calls for grand clothing[12] and the colour seems to further endow the wearer with almost shamanic properties: as the killing is usually exacted in revenge, beyond simply rectifying a personal injury, the hero often seems to officiate in restoring the cosmic justice by punishing the offender who has put it at an imbalance.[13]

10 I am further indebted to Miloš for the invaluable advice he has offered, both with regard to the searching methods and the theoretical underpinnings of this paper.

11 Kirsten Wolf (2006: 71) points out that *blár* clothing is worn by Óðinn in *Grímnismál*. In footnote 21 on the same page, Wolf suggests a possible connection between the formula and an ancient custom of the Celts and Germans who "dyed their bodies blue in order to scare their enemies." She also draws attention to the expression *blár sem hel* (2006: 61).

12 Note the parallel in epic poetry where the description of a hero's preparation for combat featuring splendid clothing and war gear takes up as much (if not more) space than the description of the combat itself.

13 The irony (often explored by the saga writers) is that by rectifying one injustice the hero sometimes ends up committing another, as when Gísli Súrrson kills one brother-in-law

This description can be said to encapsulate the core usage of the formula as long as "the core" is not conceived in terms of the immutable essence of the formula, but rather as an emergent common point through which all the examined instances can be seen to relate to one another. In other words, the core is the core because other instances treat it as such. Unsurprisingly, then, a thorough examination of the appearance of *blár* clothing across the saga corpus reveals that, no sooner than we can establish some rules of regular usage, the concrete contexts of application instigate the formula's boundaries to slide across each "established" dimension, whether pertaining to the role/qualities of the wearer, his (or, for that matter, her) intentions, the purpose of the killing, or the very nature and outcome of the pending conflict.

Thus, instead of a sharply defined entity, a picture of the formula that emerges is something resembling a cloud, with a tentative, burgeoning core and smaller or larger masses that diverge (as variations themselves show common characteristics and group) to the point of tearing themselves away from the fuzzy fringes (of usage), on their way to fusing with a neighbouring bulk or becoming another cloud, another formula. The sense of direction and purpose implied in this metaphor, i.e. that the "cloud" and its separating "masses" are somehow "on their way" to become this or that, is something that can, like in the cases of biological speciation, be identified and speculated about in retrospect only.[14] This seems to suggest a dynamism of evolutionary temporality: every rendering is a snapshot of a formula caught in movement (not that the formula can be said to exist at all prior to these "snapshots"), a movement that is played out by our reading

to avenge the death of another, or when, in blind adherence to a perverse oath, Hrafnkell kills a boy for riding his horse Freyfaxi.

14 As Miloš Ranković explains: "Speciation, for example, is an evolutionary event that has no determinable member event, such as a first human, or a first lion. Crucially, there is absolutely nothing about, say, a family of people that lived half a million years ago to suggest that they are at the branching point of *Homo neanderthalensis* and *Homo sapiens*. It is not that they did not know this, it is not that we would find it difficult to decide which individuals in a lineage belong to one and which to the other species, but that there is absolutely nothing about them that contains or predicts a speciation, whether hidden or conspicuous. And yet, there would have never been any Neanderthals as distinct from humans but for such families that were both and neither." (Unpublished paper available online at: http://milos-and-slavica.net/papers/developing-homunculicide-resistance.pdf.)

that makes the "snapshots" relate to one another like the frozen images in flick books, animated by the vigorous movement of a thumb.

I have grouped the results of my investigation of the *blár* clothing in the *Íslendingasǫgur* and *þættir* as follows:

I. *Blár* worn in the context of revenge (17)
I a) killing in revenge (10)
I b) killing, but not in revenge (1)
I c) killing with revenge intended, but thwarted, or legal redress achieved (3)
I d) the wearer effects, but does not execute the killing (1)
I e) inversion: the wearer killed instead (2)

II. *Blár* worn in anticipation of hostilities or for emphasis (14)
II a) negative: anticipation of attack/intimidation/showiness (9)
II b) positive: seeking settlement/peace/support (5)

III. *Blár* taken off /worn in disguise, sometimes with comic effects (7)
III a) *blár* taken off (3)
III b) *blár* worn (4)

IV. Metatextual comments/use (6)
IV a) awareness of the formula directly expressed (3)
IV b) awareness of the formula implied (3)

V. Misapplication (2)

VI. Unsorted fringes of the formula (6)

VII. Negative results

This is a list and therefore not a cloud, but the ensuing discussion of the instances in which *blár* clothing appears in the sagas and the role it plays there will hopefully allow for a fuller, more accurate image of the formula to emerge. These instances have been grouped according to their closeness to "the core" usage as described above, with the increase of each roman numeral signifying the increase in distance. Similarly, each alphabetically labelled subgroup marks further distances within the group itself and indicates directions of the departures. This is one general ordering criterion and, as such, it is necessarily rough. The formula features many different dimensions (discussed below), which cut across the groups and cause them to spill over into each other, thus some of the instances examined will belong to more than one group. For example, the whole subgroup I e) featuring inversion of the formula ("the wearer of *blár* killed") also exemplifies a particular kind of metatextual use (group IV) in that it counts on there being an informed audience whose expectations are consciously betrayed for the surprise effect to be achieved. The group is, however, placed within "the core" because it closely adheres to the context of its application and is conceived in direct opposite symmetry to what emerges as the regular usage of the formula. It is important to stress that neither the groups nor the dimensions are to be understood here as freestanding, immutable categories that somehow come before the instances of the text examined. Rather, they are derived *a posteriori*, from the way these instances relate to one another.

Each group heading features the number of instances exemplifying it in brackets, but these numbers should be taken as provisional inasmuch as some examples share characteristics with other groups and also combine with other formulas. That the "core" examples are cumulatively outnumbered by the "divergent" ones should not surprise us, even if it feels counterintuitive at first. To invoke (and distort) Tolstoy's famous distinction from *Anna Karenina*: all regular usages resemble one another, every irregular one is irregular in its own way, i.e. while there is only one way of being regular, there are many more ways of diverging. At the same time, precisely because there are more ways of differing, the number of instances representing each divergent group tends to be smaller the more radical the divergence. When viewed from this perspective, the number ratios change in favour of the "core" group.[15]

Each instance examined is referenced by a chapter and page number as it appears in the Íslenzk fornrit editions (henceforth referred to as ÍF), and also, for convenience, the reference to the English translations from *The Complete Sagas of Icelanders* vols. I–V (henceforth CSI) is provided, followed by the number of the volume and the page number.

15 I am grateful to Ted Andersson for prompting me to consider the statistics of the results fom my searches.

I. *Blár* worn in the context of revenge (17)

While this group emerges as one with the most straightforward application of the *blár* clothing formula (a hero donning blue-black to kill in revenge), it also already features some departures and variations along particular dimensions. So, for example, a character might set off to kill, but his intention might not be so clearly vengeful (I b), or it can be modified so that redress is achieved through legal means (I c). The hero might be intercepted and prevented from carrying out his intent (I c), or he might end up getting killed himself (I e). Then, as with Geirríðr in *Eyrbyggja saga* (I d) and Þorgils Hǫlluson in *Laxdœla saga* (I a), the wearer of *blár* may not be the most injured party in the attack, but he or she may nevertheless be instrumental in exacting revenge. Thus one finds variations along the "who," "what," "when," "how" and "why" dimensions of the formula already within its very "core."

I a) Killing in revenge (10)

The instances listed in this group may be said to represent "the core of the core" usage of the formula, with the first six (listed in alphabetical order) being straightforward, and the following four (from *Laxdœla saga* and *Fóstbrœðra saga* respectively) requiring a closer analysis on account of their complexity. This kind of structure will be maintained for each of the discussed groups.

1. *Brennu-Njáls saga*, ÍF XII, ch. 92, 231 (CSI III, 111): Skarphéðinn kills Þráinn Sigfússon in revenge for his knavish conduct towards the Njálssons in Norway and the further insults he made back in Iceland when asked for compensation. As the one dealing the deathblow, Skarphéðinn is dressed "in a black jacket" ("í blám stakki"), but note that all the Njálssons and their brother-in-law Kári wear dyed clothing during the attack ("allir váru þeir í litklæðum"): as mentioned earlier, the general solemnity of the occasion calls for the best attire.

2. *Gísla saga Súrssonar*, ÍF VI, ch. 16, 52 (CSI II, 18): Dressed "in a black cloak" ("í kápu blári") Gísli kills one brother-in-law (his sister's husband, Þorgímr goði) to avenge another (his wife's brother and his close friend Vésteinn).

3. *Hrafnkels saga Freysgoða*, ÍF XI, ch. 3, 104 (CSI V, 265): Wearing "black clothes" ("í blám klæðum"), Hrafnkell kills Einarr Þorbjarnarson in revenge

for the boy riding his beloved horse Freyfaxi, thus breaking the oath he gave to his master and forcing Hrafnkell to keep the one he made.

4. *Hrafnkels saga Freysgoða*, ÍF XI, ch. 8, 128 (CSI V, 278): Hrafnkell, again "í blám klæðum," kills the brother of Sámr (Einarr Þorbjarnarson's cousin) who, through legal manoeuvring and the use of force, managed to expel Hrafnkell from his farm, humiliating him in the process.

5. *Valla-Ljóts saga*, ÍF IX, ch. 4, 245 (CSI IV, 137): Valla-Ljótr kills the overbearing Halli in revenge for Halli's catching him on a legal technicality, compelling him to pay a hefty fee for a minor offence and then bragging about it. He is dressed "in black tunic" ("í blám kyrtli").

6. *Víga-Glúms saga*, ÍF IX, ch. 8, 27 (CSI II, 279): Víga-Glúmr puts on "the black cloak" ("feldinn blá") that he received from his grandfather and then kills Sigmundr Þorkelsson, an insolent neighbour who continuously imposed on his property and bullied his widowed mother while he was in Norway.

7, 8, 9. *Laxdœla saga*, ÍF V, 3 instances in ch. 63, 187–188 (CSI V, 97): This example features a young shepherd giving a detailed account of approaching riders in a classical manner of an epic catalogue. To his attentive master, Helgi Harðbeinsson, however, this beautiful description must sound like a litany of doom, confirming all the forebodings of his troubled dream,[16] as he recognizes the described riders and their blue-black clothing as an avenging party on their way to seek redress for the killing of Bolli Þorleiksson. While the scene develops in the expected way, and Helgi indeed gets killed (thus its inclusion in this group), it is interesting to note that the riders wearing blue-black (*kápa*, *kyrtill*, *hekla*,[17] respectively) are Þorgils Hǫlluson (the leader of the group whom Guðrún Ósvífrsdóttir duped into helping her sons effect revenge with a false promise of marriage), Þórðr the Cat (Guðrún's son from her first marriage), and Þorsteinn the Black (Helgi's brother-in-law forced to join the avengers to save his own skin). What is

16 Note that, as in the example from *Bjarnar saga Hítdœlakappa* discussed below, the premonitory dream formula appears in conjunction with *blár* clothing. Formulas often cluster in this way to create larger formulaic complexes.

17 It is in the Möðruvallabók version of the saga that Þorsteinn the Black is said to have "heklu blá" on. In his edition of the saga, Einar Ól. Sveinsson notes (ÍF V, 188, footnote 6) that the colour in two other manuscripts is *grábla* instead. This further shows how the study of variability of the formula across the manuscripts of each saga separately would be a useful companion to the approach applied here.

conspicuous, however, is the absence of *blár* garments on the young Þorleik and Bolli, the very people whom Helgi injured the most by killing their father and then treating their mother cruelly by wiping his bloodied spear on her shawl. This can perhaps partly be explained by their youth – they obviously require the leadership of a man such as Þorgils to exact revenge, even if it was Bolli who dealt the already wounded Helgi his final death-blow. However, as the saga shows a definite awareness of the *blár* clothing convention, it is tempting to interpret the exemption of the two brothers from wearing it as a deliberate move, a metatextual twist, that is supposed to tell us something, most likely that Þorleikr and Bolli belong to a new heroic breed, one that is more in line with the chivalric model. This interpretation is not too farfetched, as the continental influences on the saga have long been noted (cf. Einar Ól. Sveinsson, 1934: xvii–xviii), and the adjective *kurteiss* (courteous) transplanted from the milieu of courtly literature is only applied to the main heroes and heroines of the saga such as Óláfr Peacock, Kjartan and his wife Hrefna, Guðrún Ósvífrsdóttir, Bolli and the brothers. What is striking about this particular example, however, is how organic it is. The new outlook is not communicated merely by reaching for imported vocabulary and narrative paradigms, but by using the traditional idiom in a particular way, in this case by assigning *blár* clothing to one group of avengers, but not to the other. In this way the formula points at its past and potential future usage at the same time, defying the strict bonds of linear time.

This example from *Laxdœla saga* is not an isolated case either. A separate investigation of a different formula – that of heroes showing no immediate reaction to an insult to their honour or an incitement[18] – offers another example of a departure of this kind. Unlike the young sons of Droplaug, for instance, who, on being urged by their mother to avenge an insult to her and to their honour, initially "acted as if they did not hear what she said" ("létu sem þeir heyrði eigi þat, er hon talaði") (CSI IV, 359; ÍF XI, 145), Þorleikr and Bolli are instead "greatly shaken" ("brá mjǫk") (CSI V, 92; ÍF V, 179) by Guðrún's display of their father's bloodstained clothes and her reproachful words. Instead of suppressing their emotions in emulation of

18 The formula is most often expressed in the following way: *hann gaf sér ekki*, or *lét sem hann heyrði/viti/vissi eigi/ekki*. In this way men in the sagas (often women too) show their stamina and ability to keep their temper under control, but they take revenge very soon afterwards, when a good opportunity presents itself.

the heroes of old, the new breed lets them show, not as a sign of weakness, but rather as the impetus that spurs them on to great deeds. In this way, the saga does not only rely on the imported lexis and the narrative conventions of chivalry to communicate subtle transitions in the heroic ideal, but richly exploits the formulaic acumen of the indigenous tradition itself, bearing witness to its remarkable plasticity.

10. *Fóstbrœðra saga*, ÍF VI, ch. 23, 231, 239 (CSI II, 377, 381): the placing of this example in this group is problematic, if not entirely unjustified, and so warrants a closer look. When Þormóðr effects his first killing in Greenland in retaliation for his foster-brother's death, he is not *í blári kápu*. Rather, he turns his reversible fur cloak so that the brown-black side shows on the outside ("snýr út inu svarta á feldinum"),[19] and then, after the deed is done, he turns it back to white so as to trick his pursuers. A few pages later in the same chapter we find Þormóðr, still on the run, exchanging cloaks with the vagrant Oddr (again, so that he might not be recognized by his enemies), only, this time, the cloak is described as *blár* ("tekr Oddi við blári kápu en fær Torráði[20] verjuna ok ferr hann í"). At no point in between the two instances are we informed that Þormóðr ever changed, even if we can speculate whether, in theory, he could have done so during the brief stop at Skúfi's and Bjarni's farm. This transmogrification of a brown-black into a blue-black cloak could be a simple inconsistency or mistake, or an omission on the part of the storyteller/ writer/scribe (at whatever point it happened) to tell us that Þormóðr changed. Alternatively, it could be (as I believe) a result of the clash between two needs of the narrative: to tell a funny story about the reversible fur cloak while at the same time presenting Þormóðr as an avenger, in which case he needs to be *í blári kápu*. Whatever the case, it is the ease with which one garment becomes another that is notable, most likely brought about by the shared context of revenge. In other words, for all intents and purposes, the two cloaks *are* one and the same in that they perform the same function. Note in particular that the reversible cloak is initially worn with the white on the outside and that Þormóðr only turns it to black when he learns that an opportunity has presented itself for him to take revenge. The reversibility of the cloak alone is, then, not all there is to

19 Víga-Skúta wears a similar cloak when he ambushes his father-in-law, Víga-Glúmr (*Víga-Glúms saga*, ch. 16). This is discussed in more detail in the section "Metonymic migration of the formula."

20 This is a false name Þormóðr gives to Oddr.

this scene (otherwise the hero could have killed his enemy while wearing white on the outside (this would have been easier as he was already dressed this way) and then turned it to black when deluding the pursuing party. The fact that he does the opposite (albeit that the black is brown-black) in preparation for revenge-taking reads as though Þormóðr improvises *blár* by wearing the closest colour available to him under the circumstances. This active move, then, places *svartr* in such close semantic proximity to *blár*, that it is perhaps no great wonder the cloak later literally turns to *blár*.

If it were not for the second part of this example, the first would only feature in the discussion of the semantic permeability of *svartr* and *blár* in the context of revenge-taking (see the section "Metonymic migration of the formula"). Vice versa, if it were not for the first part, the second would be placed among the III a) group below where we find avengers (often in similarly comical circumstances) getting rid of their cloaks to cover their tracks.[21] It is, however, when these two instances are viewed together that the placement in the "core" group seems justified, even if only tentatively so.

I b) Killing, but not in revenge (1)

1. *Bjarnar saga Hítdœlakappa*, ÍF III, ch. 25, 177 (CSI I, 288): Bjǫrn has a premonitory dream about being attacked, so he sets out dressed for a fight. The hero manages to kill one of his assailants and lightly wounds the leader of the attack, his long-standing enemy, Þórðr. This example fits well in the group II a) too, as the hero is "í blári kápu" in anticipation of attack. Nevertheless, it is placed here because of the immediacy of action and the expected outcome that follows the wearing of blue-black. Furthermore, without stretching the circumstances too far, the killing could be construed as a revenge of sorts, since, being revealed in Bjǫrn's dream as an inevitability, the attack already warrants retaliation. The usage of *blár* here also combines with another formula frequently encountered in the sagas: that of heroes refusing to change their route when warned about impending danger in dreams and/or by the loved ones who, unlike heroes, interpret these dreams pessimistically and often correctly. When the formulas are nested within one another, or combined into larger complexes, they also act as multiple

21 Note in particular how irresistibly reminiscent this scene is of the one in *Gísla saga*, ch. 20, in which the hero exchanges his *blár* clothing with a gullible servant in order to fool his enemies.

sites of the sagas' non-linear temporalities. Each formula harks back to its previous usages, and also points to future functions as a part of the common complex, which can in turn have a bearing on how formulas will be used separately thereafter.

I c) Killing with revenge intended, but thwarted, or legal redress achieved (3)

1. *Egils saga*, ÍF II, ch. 81, 284 (CSI I, 169): Egill rides to the Þing "í blári kápu,"[22] ready to kill Steinarr Ǫnundarson for the offences he committed against his son Þorsteinn, including legal machinations in order to proclaim Þorsteinn an outlaw. Egill is appeased, however, by being allowed to arbitrate the case. The example combines with group II a) (people wearing *blár* in anticipation of hostilities, or to intimidate the enemy) but is placed here because the readiness to kill is in this scene imbued with a greater sense of urgency and imminence.

2. *Eyrbyggja saga*, ÍF IV, ch. 47, 134 (CSI V, 194): Snorri goði sets off "í blári kápu" to kill his sister's illicit lover Bjǫrn Ásbrandsson, but the attempt is unsuccessful as Bjǫrn manages to restrain Snorri and hold him at knifepoint until a tentative settlement is achieved, according to which Bjǫrn will stop his visits and leave the district.

3. *Hávarðar saga Ísfirðings*, ÍF VI, ch. 11, 327 (CSI V, 331): fresh from defeating an enemy and uncertain as to whether the two figures approaching him are friends or foes, Torfi Valbrandsson dressed "in a black shirt" ("í blám stakki") runs at them with a raised axe, only to recognize his companions. The example combines with group II a), but is placed here for the same reason as the one from *Egils saga* above.

I d) The wearer effects, but does not execute the vengeful killing (1)

1. *Eyrbyggja saga*, ÍF IV, ch. 20, 53 (CSI V, 154): this example is particularly interesting as it casts women in the unlikely roles of assailant and avenger in addition to the more conventional role of victim and peacemaker. Namely, because of the sorcery of Katla, Arnkell goði is unable to seek redress from

22 A brief glance at the A (Bjarni Einarsson 2001: 159) and C (Chesnutt 2006: 156) redactions of the saga shows that manuscripts from both groups have Egill riding "í blári kápu." To reiterate once again the point made at the outset of the discussion on the formula, it would be useful to combine the survey of the usage of the formula across the corpus with how it appears in the manuscripts of each saga separately.

her scoundrel son Oddr who has cut off the hand of his noble wife Auðr as she attempted (and succeeded) in pacifying the embattled sides by placing herself in the middle. Seeing that he is getting nowhere, Arnkell enlists help from a good housewife, Geirríðr, in the hope that her white magic will be able to neutralize Katla's dark incantations. As they ride to Katla's, it is Geirríðr rather than Arnkell who puts on a blue-black cloak ("blá skikkju"), and the attack this time succeeds, ending in Oddr's death. Even though she is not the one dealing the actual blow (being a woman this would have been inappropriate), Geirríðr is still the crucial figure in this retaliating mission in that she facilitates it by defeating the most powerful enemy, which in this case is Katla, and not her son. Thus the main participants in this conflict (the victim, offender, and avenger) all turn out to be women.

While the *blár* cloak casts Geirríðr in the role of an avenger in effect if not in deed, it also harks to an older mythological layer of meaning that ties this colour to the underworld (*hel*) thus further highlighting Geirríðr's magic powers.[23] This is a good example of the potential feedback loop mentioned at the outset of the discussion of the evolution of formulas: it is not only the avengers that are endowed with otherworldly characteristics by wearing the colour of *hel*, as the soothsayers and sorcerers can employ their skills as avengers too. In this way, what is supposed to be the newer layer of meaning feeds back into the older, thus effectively changing it and making it the newer in turn.

I e) Inversion: the wearer killed instead (2)

1. *Svarfdœla saga*, ÍF IX, ch. 5, 136 (CSI IV, 153): Ljótr the viking wears "heklu blá" but dies defending his ships, rather than launching an attack himself. This example fits within the II a) category too, in that the colour signals Ljótr's distinguished status as well as his menacing behaviour as a viking. It is placed here because of the close proximity of his slaying and the description of his *blár* attire in the saga.

2. *Valla-Ljóts saga*, ÍF IX, ch. 1, 235 (CSI IV, 133): Torfi is dressed "í blári kápu" when ambushed and killed by Halli. He may have wanted to seek redress for Halli's insolent behaviour earlier at his farm (Halli obviously expected to be pursued since he stopped and waited in the forest), but having

23 Note that in *Eíríks saga rauða* (ch. 4) the female soothsayer who foretells a great future to Guðríðr also wears *blár*.

made some scathing remarks about Halli himself, Torfi has also provided his enemy with a pretext for revenge. This, in fact, is all Halli wanted in the first place in order to prevent his widowed mother from marrying a man of a lower social rank such as Torfi. Although both men may have sought vengeance, the one signalling his intent by wearing *blár* ends up dead.

II. *Blár* worn in anticipation of hostilities or for emphasis (14)

The following group exemplifies a usage in which the semantic power of the formula has been tapped into, but put to different service, sublimated. Instead of signifying an intention to kill, *blár* is worn in anticipation of an attack, or for emphasis, to underline the gravity of the situation described. This emphasis is of two basic kinds: negative, when heroes use *blár* to flaunt their high status, intimidate and provoke their enemies, or a combination of these; and positive, when *blár* is worn to underline the solemnity of a plea for support, or the offer of peace and a settlement. There is a certain edginess pertaining to both kinds of emphases that keeps this variation only a hair's breadth from the "core" of the formula: a provocation can easily flare into an armed confrontation, as indeed can the failure of negotiations and good intentions. Unsurprisingly then, the two kinds of emphases are often intertwined themselves.

II a) Anticipation of conflict, intimidation/showiness (9)

1. *Brennu-Njáls saga*, ÍF XII, ch. 13, 44 (CSI III, 19): this is a particularly interesting instance since once again it involves a woman as an unlikely wearer of *blár*. On the occasion of her second betrothal, the saga's villainous leading lady, Hallgerðr, appears wearing "a woven [blue-]black cloak" ("vefjarmǫttul blán"). It is possible to conceive that this was intended to be read as a threat or a warning to the men involved in arranging her new marriage not to mishandle the affair as happened the first time round, and hence avoid the same result: a dead husband for whom her father and uncle would be forced to pay compensation. Considering that, throughout, the saga exhibits not only a keen awareness of the "core" usage of this formula but also shows a great propensity for a divergence and exploration of the formula's expressive possibilities,[24] it is difficult to disregard this instance as

24 Perhaps this confident command over the traditional idiom, combined with experimentation and departures from it, goes some way towards explaining the great appeal of *Njála* to modern as much as medieval audiences (cf. Einar Ól. Sveinsson 1953).

coincidence or a mere show of Hallgerðr's wealth and elegance. This example, then, also potentially qualifies for inclusion in the metatextual group (IV).

2. *Brennu-Njáls saga*, ÍF XII, ch. 91, 227 (CSI III, 109): upon learning of the Njálssons' intentions to avenge their treatment in Norway, Þráinn Sigfússon takes to riding "í blári kápu" all the time, fully armed and surrounded with a band of men. While this is done in anticipation of an attack, it might also point to his general bullishness and menacing behaviour (in the context of the formula his clothing could signal that he wants people to fear him). Þráinn is further described as "a showy person" ("skrautmenni"), but even though this is meant to relate to his liking of finery, there is reason to believe that this also relates to his general arrogant demeanour, as a few other characters listed below share both characteristics.

It is also interesting to notice that Þráinn takes his cloak off just before being killed by Skarphéðinn, which seems to point further to a thorough understanding of the traditional idiom shown by the saga: it is the avenger, not the offender, that should wear *blár* at the point of redress.

3. *Brennu-Njáls saga*, ÍF XII, ch. 120, 304 (CSI III, 143): the fact that Skarphéðinn appears in a blue-black tunic ("í blám kyrtli") at the Þing further casts into relief his general resistance to his father's settlement-seeking efforts and reads as his wish to provoke and intimidate the opposition. This way of interpreting the text is supported when viewed against the fact that the trousers[25] that he later hurls at Flosi, along with the accusation of effeminacy, are also coloured *blár*. What he effectively seems to be saying to Flosi with this gesture is not only: "be a man" (that much is clear from the actual words he utters), but also: "be a man and take revenge" (see IV b, below).

4. *Fljótsdœla saga*, ÍF XI, ch. 21, 286 (CSI IV, 427): Gunnarr Þiðrandabani is "í blám kyrtli" while hiding in the household of Guðrún Ósvífrsdóttir. While this may be a reminder of the action that has led to his nickname, it can also be read in terms of Gunnarr's anticipation of an attack. It is also an inversion of sorts, or perhaps even the case of misapplication, since the circumstances call for his pursuers, the would-be-avengers of Þiðrandi, to be dressed in *blár*. At face value, this seems to suggest a later development in the evolution of the formula, but it can equally be read as harking back

25 They were intended as a part of the compensation that Njáll and his sons were to pay to Flosi.

to the mythological connotations of *blár* (Wolf 2006: 61), which then makes this kind of usage older than the one tied to the saga-specific layer. The fact that it is impossible to determine with certainty what exactly is the case here (or whether in fact both things are taking place simultaneously) exemplifies the non-linearity of the evolutionary time of the formulas (and, by extension, the sagas).

5. *Harðar saga ok Hólmverja*, ÍF XIII, ch. 13, 35 (CSI II, 206): in terms of the outcome, this example belongs to I e) group as it constitutes an inversion: i.e. it is queen Gunnhildr's treasurer who appears on the scene "í blári kápu," and it is he who ends up killed. However, *blár* is here emphasized more in relation to the status symbol of the wearer, while also underscoring the character's arrogance and menacing demeanour.

6. *Víga-Glúms saga*, ÍF IX, ch. 6, 16 (CSI II, 275): Víga-Glúmr's first sighting of his Norwegian grandfather Vigfúss is while the latter is presiding over the games and entertainment in his lofty household at Voss, wrapped in a blue-black cloak ("í skautfeldi blám") and playing with a gold-inlaid spear.[26] As in examples 2 and 5 (above) *blár* is worn to emphasize the wearer's noble status, but it also goes hand in hand with his personal characteristics. Consider, for instance, the sense of superiority with which he greets Glúmr, and also his name (Vigfúss, "eager to kill"), suggesting a violent disposition.

7. *Þórðar saga hreðu*, ÍF XIV, ch. 3, 176 (CSI III, 368): the beautiful sister of Þórðr the Menace, Sigríðr, is wrapped in a blue-black cloak ("í blá yfirhǫfn") when she is noticed by Ásbjǫrn, the nephew of Miðfjarðar-Skeggi (Þórðr's enemy). As in the case of Hallgerðr, the cloak is a part of Sigríðr's elegant attire, but it could also be seen to prefigure the conflict that will spawn from this ill-fated encounter and her refusal to marry Ásbjǫrn.

8, 9. *Bjarnar saga Hítdœlakappa*, ÍF III, two instances in ch. 11, 136–137 (CSI I, 268): these two instances are discussed at the end because they are on the borderline with the next featured group (II b). Dressed "í blári kápu," Þórðr tries to persuade Bjǫrn to visit him, apparently as an offer of friendship to make amends for cheating him while in Norway and marrying his intended. However, the motives of both men become suspect in hindsight, as things turn sour immediately after Bjǫrn accepts the offer. The visit pro-

26 Both objects will be given as a parting present to Víga-Glúmr. Note also that a gold-inlaid spear often features among the equipment of the *blár*-clothing wearer.

vides Þórðr with an opportunity to flaunt his rights as a husband in front of Bjǫrn, while Bjǫrn in turn flirts with his former lover and composes compromising verses so as to incense Þórðr. This seems to confirm that the reading of the scene according to Bjǫrn's mother may have been correct and that Þórðr's intentions were not peaceful to begin with. She saw Þórðr's attire as an expression of hostility: "There is a man riding there," she said, "in a black cloak, looking very much like Thord Kolbeinsson; it is him too, and his business would be best left undone" ("Maðr ríðr þar," segir hon, "í blári kápu ok er alllíkr Þórði Kolbeinssyni, ok hann er ok, ok mun hans ørendi óþarft"). While bordering between II a) and II b), the example also fulfils the criteria for metatextual use and could be featured in group IV too.

II b) Positive: seeking settlement/peace/support (5)

1. *Brennu-Njáls saga*, ÍF XII, ch. 118, 296 (CSI III, 139): when, contrary to Njáll's advice, his sons slay Þráinn Sigfússon, Njáll realizes that he will need as many men as he can muster to defend the case at the Þing. He sets off "í blári kápu" to enlist support of his friend Ásgrímr Elliða-Grímsson. This can be seen as a way of emphasizing the gravity of the situation and also serving to remind others of the violent deeds that will ensue if the opportunity to resolve things peacefully is missed.

2. *Brennu-Njáls saga*, ÍF XII, ch. 147, 421 (CSI III, 200): Síðu-Hallr is featured "í blári kápu" when he meets with Þorgeirr Skorargeirr and Kári Sǫlmundarson to procure a settlement for his son-in-law Flosi after the burning of Njáll and his family. The scene closely parallels the one described above since, like Njáll, Síðu-Hallr is a man of peace and is, again like Njáll, ready to help his relatives even if he does not condone their actions.

3. *Ljósvetninga saga*, ÍF X, ch. 17(27), 88 (CSI IV, 245): Beard-Broddi comes to the Þing dressed "í blári kápu" and ready for hostilities (note the affinities with II a group), but argues in favour of a settlement and manages to negotiate one.

4. *Ljósvetninga saga/Ófeigs þáttr*, ÍF X, ch. 1(6), 119 (CSI IV, 203): Ófeigr Járngerðarson comes "í blári kápu" to deliver a friendly rebuke to Guðmundr the Powerful who mercilessly imposed on the hospitality and limited resources of his thingmen. Ófeigr's intentions are here recognized as peaceful, even if Guðmundr is not as pliable as some of the characters discussed above, and even if the saga also features an unfriendly exchange between the two (ch. 11 (21), 58–59).

5. *Laxdœla saga/Bolla þáttr*, ÍF V, ch. 83 (5), 237 (CSI V, 124): Bolli rides "í blári kápu" during his friendly rounds in the north of the country. Here, as elsewhere, *blár* is a part of the hero's splendid equipment, but is also more than that. When warned by his host against the disgruntled Hjaltasons, Bolli states that, while his intentions are peaceful (hence the example's placement in this group), if attacked, he and his companions would be more than ready to "repay them in kind for their trouble" ("leikim þá enn nǫkkut í mót"). This readiness for hostilities shows affinities with II a) group above.

III. *Blár* taken off /worn in disguise, often with comic effects (7)

The following group takes us another step away from the "regular" usage of the formula, as *blár* clothing is either worn or taken off to conceal the wearers and/or their intentions. This treatment of the formula is often (but not always) meant to have a comical effect. Even though this is a departure from the traditional meaning, in most cases its effectiveness directly depends on the audience's familiarity with the convention. In such cases we can also talk about a metatextual use of the formula.

III a) *Blár* taken off (3)

1, 2. *Gísla saga Súrssonar*, two instances in ÍF VI, ch. 20, 64, 65 (CSI II, 24): while on the run, Gísli is still *í blári kápu* in which he killed Þorgímr goði. To put his pursuers off track, he gives the cloak to a gullible, cowardly servant, making him his decoy.

3. *Laxdœla saga*, ÍF V, ch. 62, 185 (CSI V, 95): Þorgils Hǫlluson takes his blue-black cloak off ("steypir af sér kápu blári") in order to obtain information about Helgi Harðbeinsson's whereabouts. The cloak is taken off so that its symbolism does not reveal Þorgils's true intentions and thus put Helgi's servant on the alert. That this is nowhere explicitly stated points to the saga's reliance on its audience's knowledge of the convention.

III a) *Blár* put on (4)

1, 2. *Víglundar saga*, two instances in ÍF XIV, ch. 8, 78 (II, 419): with none of the men at home and two troublemakers intent on dishonouring her at her doorstep, the resourceful housewife Ólof appears dressed in blue-black ("maðr bláklæddr") while brandishing a sword. She thus manages to scare off the two blockheads just as they start paying unwanted attentions to her maid, whom they mistook for the mistress of the house. For the comical effects to be fully appreciated the saga must count on its audience's tacit familiarity with the convention. As a result, this instance can also be seen to exemplify a metatextual use of the formula.

3. *Króka-Refs saga*, ÍF XIV, ch. 16, 151 (CSI III, 415–416): upon his arrival in Norway, Refr "had a [blue-]black, hooded cape made for himself" ("hann lét gera sér kufl bláan") as a part of other steps he takes to conceal his identity (for instance, he also gives a false name and profession, wears a fake beard, etc.). Even though this is soon followed by his killing of one of the king's followers who attempted to rape his wife, the instance cannot be easily classified as killing in revenge, as Refr catches the man in the act and hence the emphasis is more on saving, or rather, helping his wife (who, incidentally, was not doing a bad job of fighting the assailant off herself). It is very difficult to assess to what degree the saga draws on the connotative reservoir of the *blár* clothing formula. On the one hand, there is a connection here between wearing *blár* and a killing, and on the other hand, earlier in the saga there were clear opportunities for a more straightforward application of the formula (such as when Refr avenges a grave insult by Þorgils Víkarskalli in Greenland) in which this potential is, however, left entirely unexploited.

In the earlier discussion of an example from *Fóstbrœðra saga*, I have argued (as I will in the next section too) that *svartr* occasionally seems to take on the traditional characteristics of *blár*. Here (and in the example to follow), the opposite seems to have taken place, in that *blár* is worn as *svartr*, more for disguise than anything else. The purpose to which Refr puts his "kufl bláan" resembles that of Grettir the Strong who also wears a *kufl* (only *svartan*) when pronounced an outlaw and forced into hiding. This testifies to the semantic permeability of the two black colour adjectives (Wolf 2006: 55–57).

4. *Króka-Refs saga*, ÍF XIV, ch. 17, 154 (CSI III, 417): again, being "í blám kufli" is a part of Refr's disguise as he appears in front of the king Haraldr Sigurðsson. Ironically, instead of hiding him, the cloak makes him stand out in the crowd, enough for the king to point him out and inquire about him, which was, in fact, probably Refr's intention to begin with. Consequently, the cloak is used to shield him from being recognized as Refr (and

this only temporarily, since he wants the king to eventually solve his riddles and recognize them as his, once he is out of harm's way), and also to inspire curiosity.

IV. Metatextual comments/use (6)

This group features examples that testify to an awareness of the *blár* clothing formula *as* a formula/convention, whether this is expressed in relatively declarative terms (as in IV a, or implied through departures from and conscious subversions of the convention, as in the group IV b and a good number of previously discussed (overlapping) examples. Unsurprisingly perhaps, metatextual twists and departures of this sort are more commonly fostered in highly literate cultures: with no recourse to a fixed record, oral singers and storytellers tend to be too busy using the code, relying on its mnemonic scaffolding, to comment (implicitly or otherwise) on its usage "from the outside," as it were. We should, however, resist a temptation to treat these instances as points at which "'oral' ends and 'literary' begins," as they can (and do) occur in oral literature, even if they tend to survive as such more rarely.[27] The point that John Foley makes about the differences in attitudes towards the traditional idiom of the two otherwise closely related South Slavic oral epics is instructive (1991: 97):

> No feature so tellingly differentiates the two forms as the relative measure of tradition versus textuality. Whereas the Moslem epic depends directly, crucially, and nearly exclusively on the immanent, unspoken tradition for the quickening of any given performance into narrative life, the Christian epic – generally short, spare, and integral enough to allow the poet a greater exercise of individual artistic sense – combines the referentiality inherent in its traditional structures with the signature of its most immediate maker. The Christian songs, which some have understood as memorized and then "worked on" or "revised" as mental palimpsests, are, to put it somewhat more suggestively, in certain ways more like our familiar literary works.[28]

27 This is in line with another common misapprehension: that oral literature is bereft of novelty. Good oral singers and storytellers are inventive (cf. Ranković and Ranković 2012), but the more divergent their rendering from the norm, the harder it is for it to survive the transmission process. It is also often the case that, by the time learned people decide that the oral lore is worth recording, the pool of the practitioners of oral art has become considerably smaller and depleted.

28 I have discussed elsewhere (e.g. Ranković 2006) that the length of the Christian

While writing may indeed be considered as particularly conducive to these sorts of narrative opportunities, they can and are exploited in cultures that have no access to writing. Thus it is not literacy as such that is crucial for these kind of departures to take place, but rather some notion of fixity (whether on parchment, paper, magnetic or digital recording, or indeed in sound), which releases the more complex notion of "textuality" from the strict shackles of the alphabet.[29] Another important point to bear in mind is that however "original" we consider these subtle metatextual narrative effects to be, their very originality is utterly dependent on traditional meanings and can only be achieved and appreciated against the background of the established code, with the help and active participation of the initiated audience. If anything, these instances in the sagas testify to the richness of the aesthetic potential that the interaction between the oral and written media facilitates, and put into further relief the evolutionary temporality of these texts.

IV a) Awareness of the formula directly expressed (3)

1. *Laxdœla saga/Bolla þáttr*, ÍF V, ch. 87 (9), 245 (CSI V, 129): it is said of Valla-Ljótr here that "for everyday pursuits he wore a [brown-]black tunic and carried a light pole axe, while if he were preparing for a fight he had a [blue-]black tunic and a broad-bladed axe, with which he appeared more than a little intimidating" ("Þat var búningr hans hversdagliga, at hann hafði svartan kyrtil ok refði í hendi, en ef hann bjósk til víga, þá hafði hann blán kyrtil ok øxi snaghyrnda; var hann þá heldur ófrýnligr"). Although we are not informed which of the two outfits he wore while intervening between

(Serbian) epic songs is not the only factor that can account for this effect of "a greater exercise of individual artistic sense." The period at which the songs were collected is one of the uprisings marking the beginning of the end of the Ottoman Empire's rule over the Balkans, a period that elicited a redefinition of identity of the Serbian people and was thus conducive to experimentation in oral epic singing as the main platform for negotiating communal identity. Furthermore, the main aesthetic criterion of the collector of the most famous body of published songs, Vuk Stefanović Karadžić, was that the best song is the one that "both the learned man can read and the simple man can listen to" (1969: 47–48), which may have resulted in those featuring song-specific inventions to be selected for publication more frequently than others.

29 This is, in fact, inherent in Jacques Derrida's (1974) concept of *écriture*, which tends to get confused with "physical writing systems" (Taylor 2005) thus resulting in unnecessary annoyance of scholars who then find the notion of writing as preceding orality a preposterous one.

the embattled Bolli and Þorsteinn, we can only guess that Ljótr needed all the ability to intimidate he could muster for the two valiant men to obey him and stop fighting on pain of having to face him in combat personally. Whatever the case, the example testifies to a clear awareness of the connection between *blár* clothing and fighting, as well as the difference between the two colour adjectives *blár* and *svartr* (cf. Wolf 2006: 71), but also to their proximity, as will be discussed in the next section. This explicit awareness may also extend to countless other examples of the formula with "regular" or "core" usage, over and above those listed here from what remain of the medieval sagas, both oral and written.

2. *Laxdœla saga*, ÍF V, ch. 67, 198 (CSI V, 103): Þorgils Hǫlluson is said to have had a blue-black cloak ("blá heklu"), which spoke verses portending his doom while potentially also reflecting on its purpose: "knows of wiles, this hood" ("veit hattkilan bragð"). The placement of the example in this group is, however, rather tentative and it was moved to the Unsorted/Fringes of the formula group (VI) and back again several times.

3. *Valla-Ljóts saga*, ÍF IX, ch. 2, 240 (CSI IV, 135): the description of Valla-Ljótr here closely resembles the one from *Bolla þáttr*, and has the same effects as those discussed above, except that instead of a *svartan kyrtil*, Ljótr is said to wear *brúnan*[30] when in good mood and *blán* "when the killing mood was upon him" ("er víghugr var á honum").

IV b) Awareness of the formula implied (3)

1. *Brennu-Njáls saga*, ÍF XII, ch. 123, 314 (CSI III, 148): by throwing blue-black trousers ("brókum blám") at Flosi while accusing him of effeminacy, Skarphéðinn does not merely insult his manhood, but invites him, albeit covertly, to take revenge (see II a above), which is precisely what Flosi does in the end.

2. *Gísla saga Súrssonar*, ÍF VI, ch. 12, 41 (CSI II, 13): Þorgrímr-goði's servant-woman Rannveig reports to her master that she has seen someone, most likely Vésteinn Vésteinsson, riding past their farm "í blári kápu," while her fellow herdsman Geirmundr, eager to protect Vésteinn, lies and says that it was only Ǫnundr's servant carrying a fishing spear and wrapped in Gísli's cloak. Even though he ultimately fails, Geirmundr does his best to

30 For a discussion of the possibility that *brúnan* and *svartan kyrtil* may be interchangeable in *Valla-Ljóts saga*, see the next section "Metonymic migration of the formula."

prevent his master from interpreting the colour of the cloak as Vésteinn's declaration of hostile intentions, lest this provides Þorgrímr with a pretext to act violently himself. In addition, after identifying the cloak as belonging to neutral parties, Geirmundr proceeds to disqualify the weapon as one used for peaceful pursuits such as fishing, rather than killing people. A number of things testify to the extent to which the saga relies for its effects on the audience's tacit knowledge about the symbolism of *blár* clothing: this extraordinary effort on Geirmundr's part to explain the cloak away and diminish its potential meaning, and, conversely, the ease with which Rannveig infers from it that it was Vésteinn whom she saw riding past their farm (she knows of the discord between him and her master and so readily jumps to this conclusion); Þorgrímr's readiness to believe Rannveig and not Geirmundr (hers is the version he prefers and so he entrusts her with a mission of going to Gísli's to ensure it was Vésteinn indeed); as well as the fact that none of the above motivations is explicitly stated anywhere.

3. *Vatnsdœla saga*, ÍF VIII, ch. 22, 60 (CSI IV, 29): this example features one of the most complex employments of the formula in the saga corpus. At first glance this seems to be a straightforward case of inversion (I e), as the old, *í blári kápu*-clad Ingimundr, seemingly seeking redress from the villain Hrolleifr, ends up getting killed himself. Later, when dying in his high seat, Ingimundr sends his servant to warn the culprit, advising him to flee before his avenging sons pursue him. It is only at this point that Ingimundr's act can be read as one of self-sacrifice, for his death is not a result of a revenge attempt gone wrong, but the successful outcome of a ploy devised by a willing victim. Bound to Hrolleifr by bonds of hospitality that the villain has abused long enough and unable to restrain his sons from breaking those bonds by killing the troublemaker, Ingimundr appears wearing *blár* on the scene of his sons' clash with Hrolleifr, just as it reaches boiling point. With the benefit of hindsight, it is possible to argue that Ingimundr does so in hope that his intentions will be read (and so ultimately *misread*) from his cloak by his sons and his killer alike, in the way that tradition dictates and in the way that we, as readers of the saga, did at first. It is only such a drastic gesture that would persuade his sons that he means business and reassure them enough to withdraw from the scene, leaving him to handle the situation as it befits a chieftain. Similarly, it is only this gesture that would induce Hrolleifr to actually kill him, forcing the villain to leave the district in fear of revenge, and without endangering the lives of Ingimundr's sons in the

process. In this way Ingimundr manages to ensure that the bonds of hospitality have not been trespassed against and that the villain will go without Ingimundr's sons risking their lives to expel him. There are some extra benefits to be reaped as well: by dying in such a selfless way, Ingimundr can hope to enjoy the favour of the Christian god whose existence, like all the "noble heathens" in the sagas, he already intuits, while also meeting a warrior's end rather than suffering the humiliating death of old age. Just as the old and new religions and ideologies fruitfully merge, so the formulaic and metatextual elements combine here to produce a storytelling gem.

V. Misapplication (2)

The examples in this group preserve a connection between *blár* clothing and armed confrontation, but only show a vague awareness of how things are supposed to play out. The formula thus seems either misapplied, or a clumsy attempt at a departure from its traditional form, or else is used inertly (as when in some Serbian epic songs even an adulteress is introduced as the idiomatic "faithful wife" (*vjerna ljuba*); cf. Maretić 1966: 134). At the same time, we must always be wary of passing definite judgements of this sort, as what may strike us today as mere debris of the formula, what feels generally strange, obscure, confused, unskilful, or difficult to interpret, may not have come across as such to the intended audiences.

1. *Flóamanna saga*, ÍF XIII, ch. 9, 246–247 (CSI III, 277): instead of the young Þórðr, it is the man he slays in revenge for the killing of his father (Hrafn) who is depicted "í blári kápu." While this could have been meant to emphasize Hrafn's warrior status (note the affinities with II a and I e), it seems more likely to be a case of misapplication. This possibility is further highlighted by the description of Hrafn as armed to the teeth, yet "not prepared for a battle" ("hann hafði eigi við bardaga búizt").[31]

2. *Þorskfirðinga saga* (*Gull-Þóris saga*), ÍF XIII, ch. 18, 220 (CSI III, 357): while it is Gull-Þórir who seeks redress for his burnt friend, it is one of the culprits who rides "í blári kápu" that he kills (Hallr). It is not quite clear here whether this is a case of misapplication of the formula, or an inversion (which would place it within the I e group), or whether the cloak worn by

31 It is possible that what is meant here is not that Hrafn was not prepared for battle, but rather for the surprise attack that the young man will launch. If this indeed is the case, it is still rather clumsily expressed and points to someone not very skilled at storytelling.

Hallr in anticipation of an attack is to be seen as the part of equipment he used during the attack on Ketilbjǫrn's farm (note the affinities with II a here).

VI. Unsorted/fringes of the formula (6)

The examples listed below only form a group inasmuch as they cannot be grouped: each is unique, although they remain in the semantic vicinity of the *blár* clothing formula. The instances either feature some elements of the formula that have not quite coagulated, or the conditions for the application are not all present. It might also be that they show a potentially metatextual employment, but in such a way that it is impossible to argue for it with any strong degree of certainty. Furthermore, the items of clothing featured are sometimes only partially coloured *blár*, or are accessories more than clothes as such (for instance, hats and shawls), or they are not clothes at all but other objects such as Kári Sǫlmundarson's sword. These potentially pre- and post-formulaic employments can be understood to constitute the fringes of the *blár* clothing formulaic cloud, blurring its edges and pointing to its constant, multidirectional movement and its potential for always being "on the way" to become this or that, thus reshuffling its centre-fringe relationships and defying any notion of temporal synchronicity.

1. *Bjarnar saga Hítdœlakappa* ÍF III, ch. 17, 154 (CSI I, 276): one of the scorn-pole figures that Bjǫrn raises to shame Þórðr is said to wear a black hat ("hǫtt blán"), but it is not clear whether it is the figure being humiliated (i.e. Þórðr, if he is for some reason meant to be recognized by this hat, in which case the instance should probably be disregarded), or actually the one doing the humiliating (i.e. Bjǫrn, to be recognized as an avenger of sorts).

2. *Brennu-Njáls saga*, ÍF XII, ch. 130, 335 (CSI III, 158): here it is not an item of clothing that is described as *blár*, but rather the edge of Kári Sǫlmundarson's sword, said to have lost its temper ("var blánaðr annarr eggteinninn á") during the burning of his father-in-law, Njáll, and his household. When this is remarked upon by the people helping the singed Kári escape, he says that "he would harden it with the blood of the Sigfussons and the other burners" ("hann skyldi herða sverðit í blóði Sigfússona eða annarra brennumanna"). In light of this comment, it seems likely that the scene should be read in terms of the sword's own craving for revenge,

in which case the properties of *blár* clothing along with the emotions of its wearer have been metonymically transferred to another, the most important part of the avenger's equipment: his weapon. The result is an exceptionally strong scene.

3. *Gísla Saga Súrssonar*, ÍF VI, ch. 21, 68 (CSI II, 24): in the verses Gísli is described as *bláserkjar* ("blue-armoured warrior"). Is this meant to further emphasize his role as an avenger?

4. *Harðar saga ok Hólmverja*, ÍF XIII, ch. 15, 39 (CSI II, 208): the reader wonders here whether there is any significance in Hǫrðr's unknown helper's wearing a cloak that is only striped in blue-black ("blárendri"). Could it be that this is meant to highlight his role as a facilitator rather than the executor of the killing of the undead viking Sóti and the plunder of his mound? Or is *blár* only meant to symbolize the man's connection with the underworld, thus highlighting the mythological layer of meaning? Perhaps the very difficulty in disentangling these two notions is telling of the saga's complex temporality.

5. *Laxdœla saga*, ÍF V, ch. 55, 168 (CSI V, 87): this example features another garment partially coloured *blár*, for Guðrún's shawl is said to be decorated with blue-black stitching ("í mǫrk blá"). It is on this shawl that Helgi Harðbeinsson wipes his spear smeared in Bolli's blood, but when rebuked by Halldór he states: "something tells me that my death lies under the end of that shawl" ("ek hygg þat [...] at undir þessu blæjuhorni búi minn hǫfuðsbani"). Is the colour of the stitching significant in this context, symbolizing Guðrún's role as the planner, but not the exactor of revenge, or is this sheer coincidence?

6. *Víga-Glúms saga*, ÍF IX, ch. 25, 86 (II, 308): Víga-Glúmr gives his blue-black cape ("feldin blá") to Gizurr the White as a token of friendship and gratitude for his support at the Þing. It is possible that the cape is presented here only in its capacity as a valuable object. At the same time, in giving away this family heirloom (along with the gold-inlaid spear which goes to Ásgrímr Elliða-Grímsson) Víga-Glúmr breaks the oath he made to his grandfather, and things go badly for him as a result. In particular, the fact that he is unable to get adequate redress for the killing of his brother-in-law may be potentially significant in the light of his parting with this important part of the avenger's equipment.

VII. Negative results

Out of the thirty-nine sagas and fifty-one *þættir* searched at Snerpa, eighteen sagas and all of the *þættir* save for the *Bolla þáttr* and *Ófeigs þáttr*[32] do not feature the formula. To be sure, *blár* clothing occurs in this group too, such as when the seeress in *Eiríks saga rauða* comes in "a black mantle" ("tuglamǫttul blán") (CSI I, 6; ÍF IV, 206) to prophesy a great future to Guðríðr, or when in *Halldórs þáttr Snorrasonar inn fyrri* the deceased king Óláfr Tryggvason appears "dressed like a monk in a black cloak" ("búinn sem munkr í blám kufli") (CSI V, 221; ÍF V, 257) to buy the freedom of his warriors captured after the battle of Svǫlðr and sold as slaves. However, in cases such as these it is invariably the mythological connotations that are exploited – the connection between *blár* and the underworld and otherworldly experiences – rather than those pertaining more narrowly to the formula as discussed in the examples above. While the list of *þættir* not featuring the formula is too long to be of any value, a list of the sagas that do not include this formula is potentially useful and is thus included below:

1. *Bandamanna saga*
2. *Bárðar saga Snæfelsáss*
3. *Droplaugarsona saga*
4. *Eiríks saga rauða*
5. *Finnboga saga ramma*
6. *Grettis saga*
7. *Grœnlendinga saga*
8. *Gunnars saga Keldugnúpsfífls*
9. *Gunnlaugs saga ormstungu*
10. *Hallfreðar saga vandræðaskálds*
11. *Heiðarvíga saga*
12. *Hœnsa-Þóris saga*
13. *Kjalnesinga saga*
14. *Kormáks saga*
15. *Reykdœla saga ok Víga-Skútu*
16. *Vápnfirðinga saga*
17. *Þorsteins saga Síðu-Hallssonar*
18. *Þorsteins saga hvíta*

32 Note the especially dependent status of these *þættir* on *Laxdœla* and *Ljósvetninga saga* respectively.

Looking at the sagas listed here I am as yet unable to detect any clear patterns that would suggest a valid explanation as to why the *blár* clothing formula does not appear in them. For instance, if the supposed dates of the "first" written saga renderings (say, those suggested by the editors and translators of *The Complete Sagas of Icelanders*) are taken as a potential criterion, then we find in the above list both the sagas considered to be "early" (such as *Eiríks saga rauða*, *Grœnlendinga saga*, and *Kormáks saga*) and those usually deemed "late" (including *Grettis saga*, *Kjalnesinga saga* and *Gunnars saga Keldugnúpsfífls*). If, on the other hand, one hopes that regional differences are more likely to be significant, then one is again in for a disappointment. In the east, for example, we find both *Hrafnkels saga* that features the formula and *Droplaugarsona saga* that does not; in the west we have *Egils saga* and *Bjarnar saga Hítdœlakappa* that have it, and *Gunnlaugs saga* that does not; in the north, *Vatnsdœla saga* and *Víga-Glúms saga* have it, but *Finnboga saga ramma* and *Reykdœla saga ok Víga-Skútu* do not. The situation is similar in the south, where we find *Njáls saga* featuring the formula, but not *Gunnars saga Keldugnúpsfífls*.

Identifying thematic and generic differences between texts that feature the formula and those that do not could be another potentially telling criterion: generic difference at least seems to play a role when the sagas and *þættir* are considered, even if one continues to wonder why this is the case (for example, *Þorsteins þáttr stangarhǫggs* features at least two scenes[33] in which the formula would find its natural place). When it comes to the sagas' subgenres, the situation is even less clear. For instance, at the first glance, it would be tempting to suggest that, revenge not being the most prominent theme in the so-called *skáld* sagas, it is no great wonder that three of these (*Gunnlaugs saga ormstungu*, *Hallfreðar saga vandræðaskálds*, and *Kormáks saga*) are found in the "Negative Results" group. However, it is perhaps notable that the four other texts belonging to this category (*Bjarnar saga Hítdœlakappa*, *Egils saga*, *Fóstbrœðra saga*, and *Víga-Glúms saga*) do feature the formula. Furthermore, even the sagas in which feuding

33 For example, Þorsteinn could have been depicted wearing *blár* when he sets off to avenge the injury that has earned him the shameful nickname. If his relatively modest social status is taken as a possible explanation for this, then the question is why Bjarni (who, as the district's chieftain, could have certainly afforded such a precious garment) does not wear the colour when seeking redress from Þorsteinn for the slaying of his farmhands. Note that *Vopnfirðinga saga* does not feature *blár* clothing either.

is a central theme (such as *Vápnfirðinga saga*, *Heiðarvíga saga*, and *Droplaugarsona saga*) and which would therefore be the most likely candidates to make use of the formula are in fact listed among the "Negative Results." Then there are the sagas in this list with a pronounced interest in the supernatural (such as *Bárðar saga Snæfelsáss*, *Kjalnesinga saga*, *Grettis saga*), in which case we would expect that *blár* would only be exploited for its otherworldly connotations, but *Flóamanna* and *Gull-Þóris saga* share their interest in the supernatural, yet feature the formula, even if misapplied, at least in a recognizable context.

The fact that I have not found any patterns and explanations does not mean that they might not yet emerge. This is the very kind of problem that could be usefully illuminated if the analysis of the formula variability over the saga corpus (as represented by the online and *ÍF* editions used here) were to be combined with the analysis of the formula variability in the separate surviving manuscript renderings of each saga. For instance, it would be interesting to see whether any (and if so, which) of the extant manuscripts of the sagas listed in this "Negative Results" group (however late or early) actually feature the formula, and, conversely, whether the extant manuscripts of the twenty-one sagas that do make use of the *blár* clothing formula all have it, and if not, what proportion of them do not. At the same time, the very lack of clear patterns that would explain why the formula has not been used in the sagas listed above may itself be illuminating. It may be pointing to the possibility that, rather than being unfamiliar with it, the storytellers/writers/scribes did not use the device for whatever complex (or simple) combination of reasons that trigger particular narrational choices. Lacking further information, however, I must leave the "Negative Results" for now as the enigmatic *blár* or *svartr* hole of the *blár* clothing formulaic cloud, to be explored more thoroughly and its significance pondered in the future.

METONYMIC MIGRATION OF THE FORMULA

I have already remarked on some areas of metonymic slippage between *blár* and *svartr* and their semantic overlaps (both being shades of black). I will now pick up this thread and suggest that, beyond being the result of unwitting substitution, *svartr* may have occasionally been used deliberately in the context of the *blár* clothing formula. This involves situations that require special treatment, such as when vengeance is not of the obvious kind, or when the person desiring revenge is a character whose lowly social status and/or personal characteristics do not merit *blár* clothing, in which case one of the main parameters of the formula is seriously compromised. Similar reasons underpinning variation according to the contexts of usage have already been mentioned above, but here these contexts have in addition inaugurated a change in the very wording of the formula, its most recognizable part: the colour of the clothing worn. Thus, while emanating from the "core" of the *blár* clothing formulaic cloud, the group discussed below and featuring *svartr* clothing can be seen as a small migrating lump, still adjacent to the main bulk, but perhaps at the point of tearing away.

The two aforementioned descriptions of Valla-Ljótr (in *Bolla þáttr* and *Valla-Ljóts saga*, see VI a, above), while clearly delineating the difference between the two black colour adjectives[34] and their symbolism, also point to the *necessity* of distinguishing them precisely because this difference might not always be very obvious. In fact, ironically, *Valla-Ljóts saga* violates this distinction itself only three chapters later when the "svartklæddir" Hrólfr the Snout and his men kill Valla-Ljótr's kinsman in revenge for Hrólfr's slain brother, Halli (ÍF IX, ch. 5, 247; CSI IV, 139). Thus in this example we find *svartr* performing the role of *blár*, as in the earlier discussed scene from *Fóstbrœðra saga* (ch. 23, see I a) in which Þormóðr wears the brown-black side of his reversible cloak on the outside, thus possibly creating a makeshift *blár* cloak in order to avenge his foster-brother.

The scene from *Fóstbrœðra saga* might in turn give us a clue as to which side of his reversible cloak Víga-Skúta wore on the outside when he ambushed his father-in-law, Víga-Glúmr (*Víga-Glúms saga*, ÍF IX, ch. 16, 52; CSI II, 290, and *Reykdœla saga ok Víga-Skútu*, ÍF X, ch. 26, 233; CSI IV, 297). *Víga-Glúms* and *Reykdœla saga* do not tell us which, perhaps presuming that their audience would know. There is potentially one further message here to be decoded beyond the immediate words used to describe the scene, namely that Víga-Skúta's ignoble surprise attack on the unarmed

34 In fact, in ch. 2 of *Valla-Ljóts saga*, the hero is said to wear a brown tunic ("brúnan kyrtil"), not brown-black ("svartan") when in good mood. However, a little later (in ch. 8), he is spotted by Guðmundr the Powerful dressed in a brown-black tunic ("í svǫrtum kyrtli"). That this is probably meant to be the same tunic as the one previously mentioned as "brúnan" testifies to the fact that Ljótr also carries his "good mood" double-bladed axe and not some other weapon.

Víga-Glúmr does not merit the honour of being conducted in *blár*, and that his double-sided cloak befits his double-faced dealings (i.e., the very source of conflict between the two men is that Skúta married Glúmr's daughter but then sent her back). Wearing *blár* is ideally supposed to make the intention of the avenger clear to the offender, so that he might defend himself and that the combat is fair – not that all avengers act so chivalrously in the sagas (consider, for instance, the manner in which Gísli slays Þorgrímr goði). Even if Glúmr's conduct is not always presented as beyond reproach in *Víga-Glúms saga*, when he wears *blár* (ch. 8, see I a), it is in full view of his enemy and before he launches the attack. The absence of *blár* on Skúta invokes this scene with Glúmr with the utmost economy,[35] and so one manner of attack is pitted against the other, adding further weight to the more overt contrasts the saga makes between the two men.

A particularly interesting example in which *svartr* possibly takes on the traditional semantic undertones of *blár* clothing occurs in *Eyrbyggja saga* (chs. 13–14, 23; CSI V, 140–141), when, after a successful venture in Norway, the teenage Snorri goði disembarks from the ship riding a black mare and wrapped "í svartri kápu." (Note the parallelism of this wording with the most recognizable form of the formula: *í blári kápu*.) Fooled by this modest attire, Snorri's uncle-cum-stepfather Bǫrkr concludes that Snorri had squandered all the money he had. This will prove crucial later at the Þing, when Snorri demands that they divide property, following the ill-feeling that has developed between the two kinsmen supposedly as a result of Bǫrkr's striking Snorri's mother after she attempted to kill her brother's slayer. Certain that Snorri has no ready cash, Bǫrkr sets the value of their jointly owned farm very low in hope to buy his nephew out cheaply, but the whole thing backfires since he earlier agreed that Snorri should decide which of them is going to buy the other out. Snorri then gives his uncle the money he had had in his foster-father's keeping all along, and effectively tricks him out of property. The trap that Snorri laid so carefully for his uncle suggests that the ill-feeling was in fact blossoming for a long time, and the ploy was meant to avenge more than a slap. The clothing Snorri wears thus proves instrumental in what is by no means an ordinary revenge. That it does not end in a killing does not say anything about the severity of the

35 We can at least claim this for *Víga-Glúms saga*, as, unlike *Reykdœla saga ok Víga-Skútu*, it features the use of *blár*.

revenge: traditionally, Snorri's battle arena involves strategic manoeuvring and diplomacy more than the usual heroics, and so tricking and socially ruining his opponent is quite on a par with a killing. In fact, when later on Snorri is featured "í blári kápu" upon a failed attack on his sister's lover (ch. 47, see I c, above), the reader is left wondering whether Snorri is not much better off conducting his affairs in the less glamorous but far more effective "svartri kápu." This invocation of Snorri as depicted across the saga corpus may feel illegitimate as an explanation for something he does as a mere youth, before he grows to became *the* Snorri goði of the *Íslendingasǫgur*, but the laws of time that are broken here are only those of our preconceptions about linearity of the saga texts and the rigid notion of chronology we imposed on them. Traditional distributed texts obey no such simple temporal laws, and each narrated node causes all others to which it is connected in the web of traditional meanings to reverberate, imbuing it with further significance. Thus, both the past and future (of the character, but of storytelling too) are constantly brought to bear on the present moment of narration.

In *Fljótsdœla saga* (ÍF XI, ch. 13, 249; CSI IV, 402) a lowly character, Nollar, sets off "í svǫrtum kufli" to incite Bersi the Dueller to take action against his foster-son Helgi Droplaugarson. Nollarr purports to act in the interest of Bersi's honour (Helgi is paying attentions to the woman Bersi himself likes), but in fact wishes to avenge the killing of his brother Þorgrímr Dung-Beetle. This is something that, being a lowly servant and a coward to boot, Nollarr can only accomplish by manipulating those with more power and less cunning. While wearing a brown-black cloak is a simple means of hiding (to be sure, Nollarr does not want his mission advertised), it is hard on this occasion to see it as nothing more than that. Not only does Nollarr have revenge in mind when he visits Bersi, but his plan ultimately succeeds, even if he does not get exactly what he wants. True, Bersi does not kill his foster-son, but he marries the girl Helgi loves, after which the young man is said never to have loved again.

Examples such as these invite questions as to why some other characters in the sagas wear brown-black; for instance, Grettir the Strong famously takes to wearing "svartan kufl" after being pronounced an outlaw (*Grettis saga*, ÍF VII, ch. 47, 148–49; CSI II, 120, 121), and the old Ófeigr has a black cloak on ("kápu svarta / í svartri ermakápu,"[36] *Bandamanna saga*, ÍF VII, ch. 5, 318; CSI V, 291) when, in a sly move worthy of Snorri goði, he sets up a trap into which, one by one, fall the greedy chieftains bent on financially ruining his son. Perhaps a cape is sometimes only a cape, and therefore an obviously useful means of concealment, but could it be that Grettir's "svartan kufl" is also a subtle hint that outlawry has morally deprived him from wearing *blár*, the colour of legitimate heroes and avengers? At the same time, Grettir is a fine trickster too, quite on a par with both old Ófeigr and Snorri goði.[37] Is the colour of his cloak supposed to carry this connotation too? However tempting it may be to draw such parallels, we should be weary, especially when the sagas examined do not feature *blár* at all (as indeed is the case with both *Grettis saga* and *Bandamanna saga*), and hence the familiarity with the formula cannot be demonstrated. This, of course, does not mean that the writers of these sagas and their audiences were *actually* not familiar with the convention, but simply that we cannot know this for sure or use these instances as any sort of evidence.

On the other hand, the fact that such instances constitute "no evidence" does not render them worthless. Their value is precisely in the questions they continue to provoke, in refusing to submit to our yearning for wholeness that would cut out neat little patterns (formulaic paper clouds, for instance) out of the complex traditional texts we study, better to hold them, better to see them, and then proceed to treat them as though they were there, round and whole all along, safe from our intervention, free from our desire for answers that is to yield satisfactory nuggets of interpretation, the rounded and cohesive stories of our own. Although the saga tradition ended (it died, as living things do) – never a closed system to begin with – its remnants with their messy, unsorted fringes testify to its evolutionary temporality, to its incessant budding and ceaseless transformative potential,

36 In the two versions of the saga featured in ÍF VII, Ófeigr is said to have had a brown-black cloak with one sleeve missing: "kápu svarta ok ein ermr á" (Konungsbók, Gl. Kgl. Sml. 2845, 4to) and to be in brown-black sleeved cloak: "í svartri ermakápu" (Möðruvallabók, AM 132 fol.), respectively. To iterate the point made earlier, it would be of great interest to compare how the formula varies in the manuscripts of the same saga, as well as across the saga corpus.

37 In fact, Snorri highly commends Grettir (ch. 68) for the wisdom he has shown in sparing the life of his unworthy son after his attempt to gain quick renown by killing the famous outlaw fails and he finds himself at Grettir's mercy instead.

which in turn is nothing in itself and is identifiable as a potential only by virtue of there being someone (me, us, readers) to remark upon it.

CONCLUDING REMARKS

A close, systematic study of the use of formulaic devices across the saga corpus seems to be a method that also has something to offer in terms of the more conventional view of saga dating (i.e. suggesting which sagas were written down for the first time earlier and which later, and around what date). It could potentially help tip the scale in favour of a later dating if there is enough of other kinds of evidence (such as linguistic, historical, palaeographic, etc.) to support the claim. While the regular usage is likely to be found in both "early" and "late" sagas, radical departures, misapplications, parody, and metatextual use seem more likely to be late developments. They also tend to be signs of an advanced literary culture, although, as discussed above, they need not be wholly dependent on writing. In fact, a cursory consideration of the results of this study (even if it is only of one formula) seems to generally support current divisions. So, for example, "early" sagas such as *Gísla saga*, *Laxdœla*, and *Víga-Glúms saga* feature some of the prime examples of the core usage of the formula, while "late" sagas, such as *Vatnsdœla*, *Flóamanna*, and *Víglundar saga* introduce quite radical departures.

As usually happens, however, a more thorough examination of the results reveals a much more complex picture. For instance, one of the most consistently conservative usages of the formula is to be found not in an "early" but rather a "late" saga, *Hrafnkels saga* (see I a, 3 and 4). On the other hand, while the aforementioned catalogue in *Laxdœla saga* (I a, 7) constitutes one of the most beautiful examples of a straightforward application of the *blár* clothing formula, it in the same breath represents one of the most radical departures – one that becomes obvious only when the reader starts wondering why the main protagonists are the only ones in the avenging party *not* dressed in *blár*. In making a distinction of Valla-Ljótr's moods according to the shade of black he wears, *Laxdœla*'s pendant *Bolla þáttr* reveals a keen metatextual awareness of the device, and the *blár* fringes of Guðrún's shawl smeared with her husband's blood seem suggestive of the ill fate that Bolli's killer will meet through the likewise "fringy" but effective machinations of their proud wearer. Thus, according to the way the formula functions in these texts, an "old" saga such as *Laxdœla* can easily strike one as "younger" than the "young" *Hrafnkels saga*.

An entirely new level of complexity comes into play when we consider that what at first glance may read as a creative departure or misapplication (and is thus likely to be a later development in the evolution of the formula) may in fact be an exploitation of an earlier layer of meaning, or even its rediscovery (as in I d, 1; II a, 4, etc.). Thus, while we can and should date the saga manuscripts, I hope the detailed study of the *blár* clothing formula has made apparent the sense in which we cannot date the sagas. This is because the reading of any saga text demands passage through the traditional idiomatic structures that point to its evolutionary temporality, to the multitude of that saga's possible past states (some of which could have easily become its future states too) and the multitude of directions it could have taken, or was about to take, or has taken anew, making both the past and future always present, and thus forever eluding the bonds of measurable, datable time.

Bibliography

Primary sources

Austfirðinga sǫgur 1950. Edited by Jón Jóhannesson (Íslenzk fornrit XI). Reykjavík: Hið íslenska fornritafélag.

Borfirðinga sǫgur 1938. Edited by Sigurður Nordal and Guðni Jónsson (Íslenzk fornrit III). Reykjavík: Hið íslenska fornritafélag.

Brennu-Njáls saga 1954. Edited by Einar Ól. Sveinsson (Íslenzk fornrit XII). Reykjavík: Hið íslenska fornritafélag.

The Complete Sagas of Icelanders (vols. I–V) 1997. Edited by Viðar Hreinsson. Reykjavík: Leifur Eiríksson Publishing.

Egils saga Skalla-Grímssonar 1933. Edited by Sigurður Nordal (Íslenzk fornrit II). Reykjavík: Hið íslenska fornritafélag.

Egils saga Skallagrímssonar: Bind I A-Redaktionen 2001. Edited by Bjarni Einarsson (Editiones Arnamagnæanæ 19). Copenhagen: C. A. Reitzels Forlag.

Egils saga Skallagrímssonar: Bind III *C-Redaktionen* 2006. Edited by Michael Chesnut (Editiones Arnamagnæanæ 21). Copenhagen: C. A. Reitzels Forlag.

Eyfirðinga sǫgur 1956. Edited by Jónas Kristjansson (Íslenzk fornrit IX). Reykjavík: Hið íslenska fornritafélag.

Eyrbyggja saga 1935. Edited by Einar Ól. Sveinsson and Matthías Þórðarson (Íslenzk fornrit IV). Reykjavík: Hið íslenska fornritafélag.

Fornaldarsǫgur Norðurlanda at: http://www.snerpa.is/net/forn/forn.htm.

Grettis saga Ásmundarsonar 1936. Edited by Guðni Jónsson (Íslenzk fornrit VII). Reykjavík: Hið íslenska fornritafélag.

Harðar saga 1991. Edited by Þórhallur Vilmundarson and Bjarni Vilhjálmsson (Íslenzk fornrit XIII). Reykjavík: Hið íslenska fornritafélag.

Heimskringla at: http://www.snerpa.is/net/snorri/heimskri.htm.

Íslendigasǫgur at: http://www.snerpa.is/net/isl/isl.htm.

Íslendingaþættir at: http://www.snerpa.is/net/isl/isl-th.htm.

Kjalnesinga saga 1954. Edited by Jóhannes Halldórsson (Íslenzk fornrit XIV). Reykjavík: Hið íslenska fornritafélag.

Laxdœla saga 1934. Edited by Einar Ól. Sveinnson (Íslenzk fornrit V). Reykjavík: Hið íslenska fornritafélag.

Ljósvetninga saga 1940. Edited by Björn Sigfússon (Íslenzk fornrit X). Reykjavík: Hið íslenska fornritafélag.

Vatnsdœla saga 1939. Edited by Einar Ól. Sveinsson (Íslenzk fornrit VIII). Reykjavík: Hið íslenska fornritafélag.

Vestfirðinga sǫgur 1943. Edited by Guðni Jónsson and Björn K. Þórólfsson (Íslenzk fornrit VI). Reykjavík: Hið íslenska fornritafélag.

Secondary sources

Andersson, Theodore M. 2002. "The Long Prose Form in Medieval Iceland." *Journal of English and Germanic Philology* 101, no. 3: 380–411.

——— 2006. *The Growth of the Medieval Icelandic Saga*. Ithaca and London: Cornell University Press.

Clover, Carol J. 1986. "The Long Prose Form." *Arkiv för nordisk filologi* 101: 10–39.

Delić, Lidija 2006. *Život epske pesme: "Ženidba Vukašinova" u krugu varijanata*. Beograd: Zavod za udžbenike.

Derrida, Jacques 1974. *Of Grammatology*. Translated by Gayatri Chakravorty

Spivak. Baltimore and London: Johns Hopkins University Press.

——1978. *Writing and Difference*. Translated by Alan Bass. London: Routledge & Kegan Paul.

Driscoll, Matthew J. 2010. "The Words on the Page: Thoughts on Philology, Old and New." In Judy Quinn and Emily Lethbridge (eds.), *Creating the Medieval Saga: Versions, Variability, and Editorial Interpretations of Old Norse Saga Literature*. Odense: University Press of Southern Denmark, pp. 87–104.

Einar Ól. Sveinsson 1953. *Studies in the Manuscript Tradition of Njáls saga*. Reykjavík: H. F. Leifur.

——1958. *Dating the Icelandic Sagas: An Essay in Method*. London: Viking Society for Northern Research.

Foley, John Miles 1991. *Immanent Art: From Structure to Meaning in Traditional Oral Epic*. Bloomington and Indianapolis: Indiana University Press.

—— 2002. *How to Read an Oral Poem*. Urbana and Chicago: University of Illinois Press.

—— 2005. "Fieldwork on Homer." In Mark C. Amodio (ed.), *New Directions in Oral Theory: Essays on Ancient and Medieval Literatures*. Tempe, AR: Arizona Centre for Medieval Renaissance, pp. 15–41.

Gell, Alfred 1998. *Art and Agency: An Anthropological Theory of Art*. Oxford: Clarendon Press.

Gísli Sigurðsson 2004. *The Medieval Icelandic Saga and Oral Tradition: A Discourse on Method*. Cambridge, Mass.: Harvard University Press.

——2012. "Poet, Singer of Tales, Storyteller, and Author." In Slavica Ranković et al., *Modes of Authorship in the Middle Ages*. Toronto: Pontifical Institute of Medieval Studies, pp. 227–35.

Honko, Lauri 2000. "Thick Corpus and Organic Variation: An Inrtoduction." In Lauri Honko (ed.), *Thick Corpus, Organic Variation and Textuality in Oral Tradition*. Helsinki: Finnish Literature Society, pp. 3–28.

Karadžić, Vuk Stefanović 1969. "Preface." In Vuk Stefanović Karadžić (ed.), *Narodne srpske pripovjetke*. Belgrade: Prosveta, 1969 [Vienna, 1821], pp. 1–60.

Kellogg, Robert 1979. "Varieties of Tradition in Medieval Narrative." In Hans Bekker-Nielsen et al. (eds.), *Medieval Narrative: A Symposium*. Odense: Odense University Press, pp. 120–29.

Kleut, Marija 2005. "'Mali Radojica', u krugu varijanata i tema o šamanu."

In Zoja Karanović (ed.), *Žanrovi srpske književnosti – poreklo i poetika oblika* 2, Novi Sad: Orpheus, pp. 7–19.

Lord, Albert B. 2000 [1960]. *The Singer of Tales*. Cambridge, Mass.: Harvard University Press.

Maretić, Tomo 1966. *Naša narodna epika*. Belgrade: Nolit.

Medenica, Radosav 1965. *"Banović Strahinja" u krugu varijanata i tema o nevernoj ženi*, Belgrade: Srpska akademija nauka i umetnosti.

Ong, Walter J. 1982. *Orality and Literacy: The Technologizing of the Word*. London and New York: Methuen.

Ranković, Miloš. "Developing Homunculicide Resistance: A Turn on Žižek's 'Plea'." Unpublished paper. Available online at: http://milos-and-slavica.net/papers/developing-homunculicide-resistance.pdf.

Ranković, Slavica 2006. *The Distributed Author and the Poetics of Complexity: A Comparative Study of the Sagas of Icelanders and Serbian Epic Poetry*. Available online at: http://ethese.nottingham.ac.uk/2098/.

—— 2007. "Who Is Speaking in Traditional Texts? On the *Distributed Author* of the Sagas of Icelanders and Serbian Epic Poetry." *New Literary History* 38, no. 2: 293–307.

—— 2010. "Communal Memory of the Distributed Author: Applicability of the Connectionist Model of Memory to the Study of Traditional Narratives." In Lucie Doležalová (ed.), *The Making of Memory in the Middle Ages*. Leiden and Boston: Brill, pp. 9–26.

Ranković, Slavica, and Miloš Ranković 2012. "The Talent of the Distributed Author." In Slavica Ranković et al., *Tradition and the Individual Talent: Modes of Authorship in the Middle Ages*. Toronto: Pontifical Institute of Medieval Studies, pp. 52–75.

Spearing, Anthony C. 2001. "Narrative Voice: The Case of Chaucer's *Man of Law's Tale*." *New Literary History* 32, no. 3: 715–46.

Taylor, Andrew 2005. "Review of Mark C. Amodio. 2004: *Writing the Oral Tradition: Oral Poetics and Literate Culture in Medieval England*." Notre Dame, IN, Bryn Mawr Classical Review, available at: http://bmcr.brynmawr.edu/2005/2005-08-05.html.

Vésteinn Ólason 1998. *Dialogues with the Viking Age: Narration and Representation in the Sagas of Icelanders*, Reykjavík: Heimskringla.

Wolf, Kirsten 2006. "The Color Blue in Old Norse-Icelandic Literature." *Scripta Islandica* 57: 55–78.

SKALDIC CITATIONS AND SETTLEMENT STORIES AS PARAMETRES FOR SAGA DATING

Guðrún Nordal

The sagas of Icelanders, which are around forty in number, differ in length, subject matter, literary sensitivity, and thematic emphasis, as well as in their use of stylistic devices, but they have three distinct features in common: the time frame of their narrative (long though it is, the settlement period to the establishment of the Icelandic church, around 870–1050), the main places of action (Iceland, Scandinavia, Greenland, and the British Isles), and the period in which they were written (the thirteenth and fourteenth centuries). The last point is problematic indeed. A precise dating of individual sagas within the two centuries in question is nearly impossible to achieve, particularly in those cases where no early manuscript exists to provide a *terminus ante quem*.

The process of dating is *de facto* another way of describing the evolution or the growth of a *genre*, as is apparent from the history of saga scholarship over the last hundred years or so, and we can question whether such an evolutionary idea is applicable to literary creations over a two-hundred year period. Scholars have sought to explain the making of the sagas of Icelanders from different viewpoints: the saga authors' sense of realism;[1] the sagas' interaction with other datable genres such as the kings' sagas and

1 Nordal 1952.

fornaldarsögur;[2] the extent to which the sagas are anchored in their time of writing and their thematic agreement with the contemporary sagas;[3] the alternative and changing ways in which social, moral, and political questions are treated in the sagas;[4] the sagas' origins in oral storytelling[5] and the date of the earliest manuscript,[6] to name but a few examples.

The dating of the sagas of Icelanders is not an idle pursuit. A date, however vague or loosely argued, places a saga in a historical context, and therefore has repercussions for our conclusions about its social relevance and cultural significance at a given time, ultimately influencing the way a saga is presented in a modern edition and interpreted by the scholar and the general reader. In his extended essay *The Dating of the Icelandic Sagas*, Einar Ól. Sveinsson enumerated different criteria for the dating of individual sagas; the date of the oldest manuscript of each saga (though some are only preserved in late copies of medieval manuscripts) was to him the most tangible criterion. Other valuable datable signs are references to specific legal codes and social practices, allusions to historical persons and known events, and linguistic evidence.[7]

Two of Einar Ól. Sveinsson's other categories may appear to be more subjective at first glance, even though they too have as much relevance to a specific historical context as references to named persons: that is artistry, "the skill displayed in the sagas" and literary relations between the sagas and texts such as *Landnámabók* (The Book of Settlements) (Einar Ól. Sveinsson 1958: 115).[8] In this article I will discuss two criteria of such a subjective nature, and consider whether the use of skaldic verse and the way the settlement is depicted in the sagas of Icelanders can be used as guidelines for establishing the time of writing. I will conclude by discussing the subtle differences between two sagas written in the same period, and consider the lessons that can be drawn from this attempt to date the sagas.

2 Andersson 2006; see also Vésteinn Ólason 2005, on the so-called fourteenth-century sagas.

3 Tulinius 2004. See also Heller 1976.

4 Byock 1982.

5 Gísli Sigurðsson 2002; Danielsson 2002.

6 Örnólfur Thorsson 1992.

7 Einar Ól. Sveinsson 1958.

8 Gísli Sigurðsson discusses the implication of intertextuality or *rittengsl* as it is termed, in Icelandic; see Gísli Sigurðsson 2002.

One of the most widely studied and practised literary forms of the medieval period was skaldic verse. The reception of skaldic verse in different types of texts, various saga genres, and poetic treatises reflects changing attitudes to the importance and significance of skaldic verse in the thirteenth and fourteenth centuries, that is, in the two centuries that also fostered the writing of the sagas of Icelanders. The challenge is to date the texts by using their skaldic variability. The transmission and rewriting of *Snorra Edda* in this period, that well-known textbook of skaldic poetics, reveals how the study of skaldic poetry developed over time.[9] Snorri Sturluson judged skaldic verse according to a historical yardstick when writing his *Edda* and *Heimskringla* in the first half of the thirteenth century. Stanzas attributed to known court poets, and therefore considered to be part of the respected skaldic canon, were interlaced into his royal chronicle in *Heimskringla*. Similarily, he relied to a large degree on the corpus of verse by known court poets in his explication of the skaldic art in his *Edda*. His nephew Óláfr Þórðarson, however, was not restricted by the historical skaldic canon in his choice of examples in the *Third Grammatical Treatise*, written no later than 1259, and his selection of examples is governed rather by aesthetic preferences than by the authenticity of the poetry. Moreover, we see that Snorri's original deference to the skaldic canon in *Skáldskaparmál* is undermined when particular versions of the work are placed directly in the context of Óláfr's work with the so-called A and B manuscripts of *Snorra Edda* from the fourteenth century. Consequently, it is possible to detect a subtle change from a historical perspective to an aesthetic one in the skaldic treatises produced throughout this period.

It is tempting to conjecture that references to skaldic verse in the different saga genres of the thirteenth and fourteenth centuries would be indicative of the time of writing, just as the application of verse in the skaldic treatises changed over time in the same period; that is, that we would expect a more relaxed attitude to the authenticity of the verse in the kings' sagas after Snorri's time and in the fourteenth century, a characteristic that could then be used as a basis for a later dating. This is true to a certain extent, but we must be careful to take into account the different historical perspectives inherent in the different saga genres, which also govern the way skaldic verse

9 See my discussion of the versions of *Snorra Edda* in my book *Tools of Literacy: The Role of Skaldic Verse in the Textual Culture of the Twelfth and Thirteenth Centuries* (2001).

is presented in the narrative just as much as the authenticity of the verse. There are, however, striking examples in the kings' sagas corpus. Snorri's strict historical rule is apparently relaxed in the great, amalgamated kings' saga compilations of the fourteenth century.[10] The author of *Óláfs saga Tryggvasonar in mesta* does not hesitate to refer to verse by poets who lived long after the events took place as source material for his narrative, thereby breaking the rule set out in the Prologue to *Heimskringla* that the poets had to be contemporary witnesses to the event. This distinction is not, however, as readily visible in the sagas of Icelanders. The verses are very rarely used as source material in the sagas of Icelanders, and when they do occur it is a striking authorial signature. We find verse integrated in the narrative in the earliest datable sagas of Icelanders – *Egils saga*, preserved in a mid-thirteenth-century fragment – where the saga character speaks in verse that cannot have been composed at the time of the saga.

In an essay on the use of verse in the sagas of Icelanders,[11] I approached the question of the role of verse in the sagas from the point of view of the number of stanzas in the narrative and the identity of the poets. If we take seriously the change in the appreciation of the skaldic canon that took place as the thirteenth century gave way to the fourteenth century, we would expect that consistent references to the respected court poets of the canon – as they are identified in *Skáldatal*, *Snorra Edda,* and thirteenth-century kings' sagas such as *Heimskringla* – would be indicative of the cultural milieu of the sagas authors in that period.

Six groups emerge when the corpus of the sagas of Icelanders is analyzed from the point of view of verse, which throws into relief the saga authors' different emphases and appreciation of skaldic verse. These groups are:

1. The sagas of the court poets (the skalds' sagas): *Bjarnar saga Hítdœlakappa*, *Egils saga*, *Fóstbrœðra saga*, *Gunnlaugs saga ormstungu*, *Hallfreðar saga* and *Kormáks saga*. The poets in the skalds' sagas are acknowledged and respected poets in the skaldic canon and their verse is cited in *Snorra Edda* and/or the kings' sagas (Fidjestøl 1985: 319–35; Nordal 2001: 78–79). The choice of stanzas highlights the generic borderline between the verse

10 These are also used as source material in the Latin chronicles by Theodoricus and Saxo, as is stated in their prologues, but no attempts are made to translate the verses into Latin.

11 Published in Margaret Clunies Ross's festschrift from 2007.

in the sagas of Icelanders and the kings' sagas, as there is very little overlap between the genres in the transmission of the poetry. *Egils saga* is preserved in a fragment from the middle of the thirteenth century. *Kormáks saga*, *Egils saga*, *Fóstbrœðra saga* (also in Hauksbók, c. 1300), and *Hallfreðar saga* are preserved in Möðruvallabók, c. 1330–70, the two last mentioned are also incorporated in the two great sagas of Óláfr from the fourteenth century. *Bjarnar saga* is preserved in a fragment from around 1300 and *Gunnlaugs saga* in a manuscript from the first half of the fourteenth century. The last two are most loosely connected to the the skaldic canon. Bjǫrn Hítdœlakappi is not a noted court poet in the canon, but his rival, Þórðr Kolbeinsson, is known for his poetry in *Snorra Edda* and the kings' sagas. The two rivals in *Gunnlaugs saga ormstungu*, Hrafn Ǫnundarson and Gunnlaugr ormstunga Illugason, are also unknown in the skaldic canon; Gunnlaugr is only added to the list of poets in *Skáldatal* in the Codex Upsaliensis's version of the *Edda* as the poet of King Athelred.

2. Sagas where the main protagonist is a poet: *Gísla saga Súrssonar*, *Grettis saga*, *Harðar saga ok Hólmverja*, *Víga-Glúms saga*, *Hávarðar saga*, *Víglundar saga*, and *Þórðar saga hreðu*. It is of note that Víga-Glúmr is among the acknowledged poets of the canon in *Snorra Edda*, cited four times in *Skáldskaparmál* in the Codex Regius manuscript, whereas Grettir Ásmundarson and Hávarðr are cited only once (Nordal 2001: 78–79). The authors of the poetic treatises never refer to Gísli Súrsson's verse, nor to the poetry by Hǫrðr, Víglundr and Þórðr hreða. None of the poets in this group, however, is cited in the kings' saga corpus, and none of their manuscripts predate the years from around 1330–70, or Möðruvallabók (where *Víga-Glúms saga* is preserved). Their earliest manuscripts span the period to the middle of the fifteenth century.

3. Sagas with a strong royal or courtly emphasis: *Laxdœla saga, Vatnsdœla saga* and *Finnboga saga ramma*. Theodore Andersson pointed out how *Laxdœla saga* and *Vatnsdœla saga* share a common interest in the Norwegian royal background and how, through their portrayal of strong and unassailable chieftains in the region, "[the sagas betray] the same taste for style and grandeur" (Andersson 2006: 155). Notwithstanding these thematic similarities, the two sagas are very different in their narrative style, and it is, therefore, misleading to categorize them together. Andersson does not note

their mutual disinterest in skaldic verse, but this is a significant feature. Skaldic verse did not fit into the new courtly framework that was emerging in Norway from the late thirteenth century onwards; the last known court poets listed in the two *Skáldatal* versions are from this period (Nordal 2001: 127–30). *Laxdœla saga* is preserved in a fragment from the late thirteenth century and *Finnboga saga* is contained in Môðruvallabók. The earliest manuscript of *Vatnsdœla saga*, however, is from around 1390.

4. Sagas dated to the fourteenth century, displaying a distinct learned interest in the past: *Bandamanna saga*, *Kjalnesinga saga*, *Flóamanna saga*, *Hœnsa-Þóris saga*, *Króka-Refs saga*, and *Bárðar saga Snæfellsáss*, and the two Vinland sagas, *Eiríks saga rauða* and *Grœnlendinga saga*. These sagas are not concerned primarily with the classic feud pattern, nor are they interested in unveiling moral or legal dilemmas in a close-knit Icelandic farming community (*Hœnsa-Þóris saga* is clearly an exception and should perhaps be categorized separately along with *Bandamanna saga* and *Hrafnkels saga*, as Andersson does).[12] Even though the narrative in these sagas opens in the traditional setting of the Icelandic countryside, a large part of the narrative of some of these sagas is played out outside Iceland's farming community, to a large degree abroad, such as in Norway, Greenland (*Króka-Refs saga*, *Flóamanna saga*, *Eiríks saga*, and *Grœnlendinga saga*), Vinland (*Grœnlendinga saga*, *Eiríks saga*), or in a quasi-human setting with giants in the mountains (*Kjalnesinga saga* and *Bárðar saga*). The manuscripts are relatively late (with the exception of *Eiríks saga* in Hauksbók, which is on the borderline of the sagas of Icelanders genre), featuring in the fragments of the great *Íslendingasögur* manuscripts of the late fourteenth and early fifteenth centuries, Vatnshyrna and Pseudo-Vatnshyrna, written in the north of Iceland (Stefán Karlsson 1970; McKinnell 1970). *Kjalnesinga saga* and *Flóamanna saga* have been associated with Haukr Erlendsson, the noted lawman and the author of one of the versions of *Landnámabók*, who lived most of his professional life in Norway (see Helgi Guðmundsson 1967: 77–83; Perkins 1978: 28–44).

5. Sagas relating events in the Eastfjords and the north-east of Iceland: *Fljótsdœla saga*, *Gunnar saga Keldugnúpsfífls*, *Hrafnkels saga*, *Vápnfirðin-*

12 Andersson 2006.

ga saga, *Þorsteins saga hvíta*, *Þorsteins saga Síðu-Hallssonar,* and *Ǫlkofra saga* in the Eastfjords; *Ljósvetninga saga*, *Valla-Ljóts saga,* and *Reykdœla saga* (the only stanza in the saga is also cited in *Víga-Glúms saga*) in the north-east of Iceland. The unique character of this region in medieval literary culture is not limited to the sagas of Icelanders. The same geographical distinctiveness is borne out by the known origin of poets in the thirteenth and fourteenth centuries, in the period when the sagas were committed to writing (Nordal 2001: 133), as well as in the poetry cited in the *Third Grammatical Treatise* (though Óláfr Þórðarson's choice of examples may be determined by his own regional knowledge (Sigurðsson 2002: 118–20)). The reason for the exclusion of skaldic poetry in these sagas is possibly regionally determined, rather than aesthetically conditioned. *Droplaugarsona saga*, the only saga of the Eastfjords to contain verse (6 stanzas), and *Ǫlkofra saga* are preserved in Möðruvallabók (from around 1330–70), but all the other sagas are preserved in manuscripts from around 1400 or later.

6. Sagas where verse is an integral part of the narrative although there is no principal poet: *Njáls saga, Heiðarvíga saga, Eyrbyggja saga,* and *Svarfdœla saga. Svarfdœla saga* is clearly the odd saga out in this list, yet it has narrative themes in common with *Njáls saga* (the depiction of Yngvildr fagrkinn) and *Eyrbyggja saga* (the description of the ghost Klaufi). All four sagas cite verse by known poets of the canon. In *Njáls saga, Heiðarvíga saga,* and *Eyrbyggja saga,* such verses are used to authenticate sections in parts of the narratives, and in *Svarfdœla saga,* two stanzas are attributed to the well-known poet Þorleifr jarlsskáld. A *þáttr* about Þorleifr is preserved in Flateyjarbók. Þorleifr jarlsskáld falls within the literary radar of Óláfr Þórðarson and the author of the *Fourth Grammatical Treatise*, being cited once in each text. The earliest manuscripts of these sagas are dated to the thirteenth century, such as the oldest fragments of *Eyrbyggja saga* and *Njáls saga. Svarfdœla saga,* however, is only in a manuscript from the fifteenth century.

The division of the sagas of Icelanders into these six groups according to the role of skaldic poetry in each saga does not take into consideration the dating of the sagas, nor the authenticity of the verse, yet interesting patterns emerge when these criteria are brought to bear. The canonized poets of

Skáldatal and *Snorra Edda* are found in groups 1, 2 and 6, while other poets or speakers of verse are less known, though there are some exceptions.[13] The oldest manuscripts of the sagas are linked to those groups, the skalds' sagas, *Laxdœla saga*, *Eyrbyggja,* and *Njáls saga*.

Skaldic verse that can securely be attributed to tenth- and eleventh-century poets remained the most distinctly oral legacy in the written sagas of the thirteenth and fourteenth centuries; perhaps the only authentic voices in the text. Some of the skalds' sagas contain poetry which can be authenticated, as Kari Gade has shown,[14] and stanzas in some of the others, such as in *Njáls saga* and *Eyrbyggja saga,* can be attributed to well-known poets of the canon. The dating of the verse of the sagas of Icelanders is fraught with difficulties; we can perhaps date verse by two poets with some certainty to the tenth century: the verses by Egill Skallagrímsson and Kormákr. The other court poets of the sagas of Icelanders, such as Hallfreðr, Bjǫrn Hítdœlakappi, and Þormóðr, are from the eleventh century. Finnur Jónsson was of the opinion that the poetry of Gísli Súrsson and poetry in *Eyrbyggja saga* had an early date; but scholarly opinion has been modified since then. The poetry of Gísli Súrsson has been dated to the twelfth century and the *Máhlíðingavísur* by Þórarinn Máhlíðingr to the eleventh century, to take only two examples. Finnur Jónsson also identified the verse by Glúmr in *Víga-Glúms saga* and Þorleifr jarlsskáld in *Svarfdœla* as having been composed in the tenth century. The latter of these two belongs to the skaldic canon, and these stanzas may have been regarded by thirteenth-century writers to be early, even though the actual dating remains insecure. Some of these poets belong to the respected canon in the learned tradition of the poetic treatises, even though the stanzas in the kings' sagas and *Snorra Edda* is not drawn from the same poetic corpus as the verse in the sagas of Icelanders.We must be cautioned, however, that the division of the sagas into different categories is always problematic, particularly when employing posthumous assessments of them.

Three groups of the sagas are rich in verse (1, 2, 6), but sagas in the other three groups (3, 4, 5) show little interest in skaldic poetry or omit such poetic references altogether. It is striking that these sagas have differ-

13 For example, the poetry of Grettir Ásmundarson and Víga-Glúmr is cited in *Snorra Edda*.

14 Gade 2001.

ent thematic or geographical emphases from the sagas that are more preoccupied with verse: these are the fourteenth-century sagas with learned interests, the sagas depicting events in the east and north-east of Iceland, and finally sagas that are particularly preoccupied with the royal court and therefore following the narrative model of other genres, such as courtly romance and heroic legend.

~

If we can agree that skaldic verse is one of the defining, aesthetic, elements behind the writing of the sagas of Icelanders, at least those sagas which make extensive use of verse, *Landnámabók* is certainly the other literary backbone for the writing of the sagas of Icelanders. The relationship between the sagas and the *Landnáma* versions is a complex one, and some modern scholars would say that the comparison between the stories of the settlement in *Landnámabók* and in the sagas of Icelanders is a futile undertaking. I beg to disagree. Extensive analysis of the relationship between the sagas and *Landnámabók* was undertaken by scholars such as Björn M. Ólsen and Jón Jóhannesson, and even though their insistence on direct borrowings does not hold in many cases – as Gísli Sigurðsson has demonstrated effectively – they throw into relief the same cultural milieu in which these stories flourished and suggest therefore a common audience.

Memories about the pagan past in Iceland and the settlement period were most likely preserved in oral memories from the ninth and tenth centuries to the period in which the sagas of Icelanders were written. Only seventeen out of the total of around forty sagas of Icelanders start before or at the time of settlement, and only one of these seventeen sagas refers to skaldic verse; this is the case with *Grettis saga* when Ǫnundr criticizes the cold climate in Iceland. Here the saga writer may be using the poetic evidence to introduce a different point of view in the narrative. The early stages of the writing of *Landnámabók* reveal social, cultural, or economic needs at the beginning of the twelfth century to establish an official account of the settlement. The motivation behind the construction of *Landnámabók* is contested, but the early settlements of Iceland may have been set down in writing in order to secure land claims by ruling families at the time of writing.[15] However, the

15 See Sveinbjörn Rafnsson 2001.

reason why these stories were preserved in a number of sagas of Icelanders in the thirteenth and fourteenth centuries is another matter.

The three known medieval versions of *Landnámabók*, Sturlubók, Melabók and Hauksbók, are all attributed to Icelandic lawmen in the post-Commonwealth period; men who had a special relationship with Norway. Only Hauksbók is preserved in its original manuscript: Melabók in a fragment of a late fourteenth-century manuscript and otherwise in seventeenth-century paper copies, and Sturlubók only in a seventeenth-century copy of a manuscript from around 1400.

The inclusion of the stories of the migration to and settlement of Iceland in a saga clearly affects its beginning and determines through which door the reader or listener enters the house of the narrative, to use a metaphor from Geoffrey of Vinsauf's *Poetria nova*. Unusually for a fictitious medieval genre, the sagas of Icelanders do not contain literary prologues that place the narrative in a context with other medieval genres at the very outset, nor is there any discussion of the writers' attitudes to the factual or fictive quality or the moral message of the narrative. For this reason, the beginning of each saga can be viewed as a prologue, in many cases foreshadowing the main narrative, in some cases comparing or contrasting the forefather or foremother to the main character in the saga.[16] It is illuminating to focus on the seventeen sagas that open at the time of settlement of Iceland, and thus reflect the author's, or the audience's, emphasis on the migration period and their interest in the neighbouring countries in the Viking period.[17]

Iceland had become part of the Norwegian kingdom (from 1262–64) at a time when most of the sagas of Icelanders had been written, with perhaps the exception of *Egils saga*, the skalds' sagas, and possibly *Laxdœla saga* and *Eyrbyggja saga*. Some of these sagas may reflect an interest by members of the Icelandic aristocratic elite to argue for the close ties between Iceland and Norway, the old homeland for many of the settlers, now the seat of the king. Although each saga treats the topic of the settlement differently, it is clear that the sagas which begin their story in Iceland and omit the migration story altogether place less importance on these ties. Moreover,

16 Hume 1973.

17 These sagas are, in alphabetical order: *Bárðar saga Snæfellsáss, Egils saga, Eyrbyggja saga, Flóamanna saga, Gísla saga Súrssonar, Grettis saga, Harðar saga, Hrafnkels saga, Kjalnesinga saga, Kormáks saga, Laxdœla saga, Reykdœla saga, Svarfdœla saga, Vatnsdœla saga, Víga-Glúms saga, Þórðar saga hreðu, Þorskfirðinga saga.*

the twenty-two sagas that begin their narrative after the settlement have less interest in the theme. Four patterns in the sagas' depiction of the settlement emerge:

1. Sagas containing a complex migration story and detailed elucidation of the migrating family's relationship with the king. This theme is rehearsed in sagas such as *Laxdœla saga*, *Vatnsdœla saga*, *Eyrbyggja saga*, and the sagas of the court poets, such as *Egils saga* and *Kormáks saga*. Some of these sagas are preserved in old manuscript fragments from the thirteenth century, and are probably among the oldest written sagas of Icelanders.

2. The emphasis on the history of a fighter-poet's family, where the family's life in Norway is played out in detail, such as in *Grettis saga* and *Gísla saga Súrssonar*. Other sagas in this group are *Harðar saga ok Hólmverja* (with no migration story), *Víga-Glúms saga*, *Víglundar saga*, and *Þórðar saga hreðu*. The portrayals of the saga hero seem to be modelled on the sagas of the court poets, but in fact these sagas focus on very different themes from the skalds' sagas. All of them deal with personal loss – the loss of land or the loss of freedom, as in the outlaw sagas – and some end on a tragic note. There is a strong tendency in all of these sagas to deepen the portrayal of the hero by linking him to the family's past in Norway. *Víga-Glúms saga* is not a typical settlement saga, but the family's "fylgja" in Norway settles in Iceland, so it can be argued that it depicts the settlement of the family.

3. Learned interest in the settlement and the mythic past of Iceland is attested in sagas such as *Bárðar saga Snæfellsáss*, *Flóamanna saga*, *Kjalnesinga saga* (which is not a migration story, beginning rather at the time of the settlement), and *Þorskfirðinga saga*. Some of the settlement stories are even drawn from external written sources such as in the case of *Flóamanna saga*. In this group there is an apparent interest in travels to Greenland.

4. In some sagas we find a silent reference to the settlement, where there is no migration story and little importance is placed on the settlement. Among those are sagas such as *Hrafnkels saga* and *Reykdœla saga*.

The correlation between this grouping and the earlier grouping of the sagas of Icelanders with reference to use of skaldic verse is arresting. Memories about the pagan past in Iceland and the settlement period were most likely preserved in oral memory from the ninth and tenth centuries to the period in which the sagas of Icelanders were written.

Only one of these seventeen sagas, *Grettis saga,* refers to skaldic verse about the settlement itself. Writers describing the settlement and the migration to Iceland from the British Isles and Norway do not pretend to substantiate their account of the early pagan settlements there, in the manner of the royal chroniclers. The account of the settlement in Iceland in the sagas of Icelanders, or for the most part in *Landnámabók*, is notably not anchored in datable verses. There is an interesting gap in the citation of skaldic verse in the context of events in Iceland in the earliest period depicted by the sagas; the earliest datable stanzas being from the tenth century. What is also noteworthy is that there are almost no verses cited in the sagas to substantiate the narration of events in the ninth century, that is, in the settlement period itself. It is striking that only one of the seventeen sagas describing the settlement period refers to skaldic verse – the, as mentioned above, fourteenth-century saga *Grettis saga*, when Ǫnundr criticizes the cold climate in Iceland. The writer here may be using the poetic evidence to introduce a different point of view in the narrative rather than using verse to substantiate the account of the settlement. However, exceptions exist and the stanzas, which seem old and possibly pagan, are cited only in *Landnámabók*. The earliest verse in the canon expounded by the learned scholars of poetics in the early thirteenth century is indeed the verse composed by Norwegian poets before c. 1000, cited in the context of descriptions of the early kings of Norway, from Haraldr hárfagri onwards, such as Þjóðólfr í Hvin and Þorbjǫrn Hornklofi.

The shifting focus on the migration to Iceland and the settlement in the sagas of Icelanders reveals the ambiguity in the sagas' deliberation and reconfiguration of the Viking past. The many Christian writers of the sagas regarded the pagan past in a markedly different way, and some went as far as to disregard the settlers' ties to their old homelands. The sagas of the Eastfjords reveal a significant indifference to the memories of the settlement. Only two sagas out of ten begin at the time of settlement (*Reykdœla saga* and *Hrafnkels saga*), but with no accompanying genealogy that linked the families with the "old" Viking world. The stories of the settlement seem to be predominantly associated with events and characters in the west and north-west of Iceland; the area where an interest in skaldic poetry and the writing about pagan myth was also most clearly attested, as in work such as *Snorra Edda*, *The Third Grammatical Treatise*, and *Heimskringla*. This geographic distinction within the genre can be no coincidence, and throws into relief the importance of keeping in mind the subtle differences between various sagas of Icelanders in their depiction of the Viking past.

Even though we can date sagas to the same period, it does not mean that we can draw up the recipe for the writing of a saga at a particular point in time, as my concluding remarks will demonstrate. *Laxdœla saga* is one of the most courtly or aristocratic sagas of all the sagas of Icelanders. The saga belongs to the same cultural milieu as that of *Eyrbyggja saga* and some of the skalds' sagas from the west of Iceland, yet the author develops his subject matter and characters in a strikingly different way. The author of *Eyrbyggja saga* builds a "royal" portrayal of the main character, Snorri goði Þorgrímsson, by authenticating the account with formal skaldic verse[18] and punctuating the main events in his life with verse citations, but the author of *Laxdœla saga* deliberately avoids such references to skaldic verse in the narrative. Both sagas are preoccupied with Norwegian pre-history, and describe the flight of independently minded Norwegian chieftains to Iceland via the British Isles, because of the tyranny of Haraldr hárfagri. The central characters are friends, Snorri goði and Guðrún Ósvífrsdóttir, and each plays a part in the other's saga. Both sagas are written in the second half of the thirteenth century but draw on opposite cultural reference points: *Eyrbyggja saga* is rooted in indigenous traditions, referring to local folklore, the power of the supernatural in the narrative and supposedly authenticated skaldic verse, whereas *Laxdœla saga*, while also drawing on local storytelling, is indebted to the mannerisms or literary techniques of courtly romances and heroic legends.

Even though the author of *Laxdœla saga* is clearly familiar with skaldic verse, he chooses to omit most of it. He notes in passing two poems by respected poets of the canon, *Húsdrápa* by Úlfr Uggason – who is mentioned in *Snorra Edda* – and a praise poem of Gellir Þorkelsson by Arnórr jarlsskáld, one of the most respected court poets of the kings' sagas. These references give away the author's background and his familiarity with the skaldic canon, but show at the same time that poetry had lost its allure for the audience of this particular saga.

18 See my discussion in Nordal 2007.

The difference between these two sagas, written at the same time and possibly in the same cultural milieu, describing even the same sort of people from two perspectives, must be explained in terms of the different goals of the authors in their depiction of their main characters. Snorri goði Þorgrímsson is depicted as an Icelandic aristocrat, his actions pre-empting his aristocratic descendants of the Sturlungar family in the thirteenth century, who most probably had a hand in shaping the saga in the mould of a king's saga, even underpinning the saga with a reference to a brief synposis of his life.[19] The saga of Guðrún Ósvífrsdóttir is no less strikingly "royal" in its character descriptions and visual traits.[20] The aristocratic patterns are not, however, drawn from the indigenous traditions of royal historiography, rather from courtly romance and the heroic legends of Sigurðr, Guðrún, and Brynhildr. The references to skaldic verse in the two sagas are most poignant in this respect, and bring home the significance of paying due notice to a saga's social and cultural context.

It is not surprising that *Laxdœla saga* has been the one saga in the corpus to be attributed to a woman, and similarly no one has doubted that a man wrote *Eyrbyggja saga*.[21] Yet rather than identifying the author as a woman, and thereby attributing an anonymous saga to a named author, I agree with those who have stressed that the audience of *Laxdœla* was made up of individuals who had been impressed by royal grandeur at the court and acquainted with the courtly romances translated at the Norwegian court in the middle of the century, finding them more entertaining than the sagas of the power struggles between the kings of Norway. The relationship between Norway and Iceland in the thirteenth century was not only played out by men. Many women joined their husbands or fathers on their trips to Norway, and even went alone with their children, staying there for long periods, some at the royal court if the testimony of *Sturlunga saga* is to be trusted.[22] Women were important as patrons of verse and prose in the thir-

19 This life of Snorri goði is only preserved in a late fourteenth-century manuscript (Melabók) and it has by some scholars been attributed to Ari fróði Þorgilsson.

20 Ármann Jakobsson 1998; Andersson 2006.

21 Kress 1980.

22 To take a few examples, Arnórr Tumason takes his two children, Arnbjǫrg and Kolbeinn ungi, with him to Norway. Arnórr dies in Norway, and the children later return. Solveig Sæmundsdóttir, who claimed kinship with the Norwegian king through her grandfather Jón Loftsson, takes her son Jón with to Norway after the death of her husband Sturla Sighvatsson. She stays in Norway for three years.

teenth century, as we know from other countries, such as in the troubadour tradition, and their literary preferences would have guided the writing of sagas as much as that of men. We would expect the same to have happened in Iceland. It is tempting to link the writing of *Laxdœla saga* and *Eyrbyggja saga* to a certain cultural milieu; Helgi Þorláksson has suggested that the Sturlungs wrote *Eyrbyggja*, and built the portrayal of Snorri goði on their kinsman Snorri Sturluson.[23] In the same way, it is tempting to propose that a certain group of women inspired and even patronized the writing of the saga of Auðr djúpúðga and Guðrún Ósvífrsdóttir.

Íslendinga saga tells the story of the proud Jóreiðr Hallsdóttir who as a young widow lived with her daughter Helga Þórðardóttir in Sælingsdalstunga, where Guðrún Ósvífrsdóttir had lived as a widow many centuries earlier with her young children. Jóreiðr resisted persistent marriage proposals from Ingimundr Jónsson, a grandson of Hvamm-Sturla, because "hún vildi eigi ráða fé undan dóttur sinni" (she did not want to make plans to take money from her daughter). Her statement implies that she was of the opinion that her only daughter, Helga Þórðardóttir, would not get a prominent husband unless she could secure her a handsome dowry, and this was indeed what happened when Helga married Sturla Þórðarson, the well-known saga writer. Jóreiðr's objections to her own marriage were not respected and Ingimundr abducted her from her farm to persuade her to marry him. He took her to his cousin Sturla Sighvatsson at Sauðafell, but Jóreiðr would not be bullied and showed her resistance by going on a hunger strike until Ingimundr had to take her back.

Like Guðrún Ósvífrsdóttir, Jóreiðr witnessed violence at close quarters in Sælingsdalstunga, when she was visited by a violent group of men in the escalating conflict between Þórðr kakali and Kolbeinn ungi in the year 1244. The attackers were bent on killing her son-in-law, Sturla Þórðarson, who had fled the farm, but when their visit was to no avail, they turned their weapons against the workers at the farm. Helga had given birth only four weeks earlier to her son Snorri, and sought sanctuary in the church.

Helga's husband gained perhaps the greatest recognition of all Icelanders at the Norwegian court when he was commissioned by King Magnús to write the sagas of King Hákon and then of himself in the 1260s. Sturla went

23 Helgi Þorláksson 1992.

to Norway alone, but when he had secured his position at the court, he sent for his wife Helga and their sons to join him – and it is noted in *Sturlu þáttr*: “var hún tekin í hina mestu sæmd af drottningu” (she was greatly honoured by the queen).

Dating a saga accurately gives us an opportunity to ponder the respective audience, and in the case of *Laxdœla saga* I can think of no other person in late thirteenth-century Iceland more likely to have been the patron of *Laxdœla saga* than Helga Þórðardóttir, her daughter Ingibjǫrg Sturludóttir or other women in their company. They were both born and bred in Sælingsdalr, and knew the oral stories of powerful women in their district, and had the opportunity, denied so dramatically to Guðrún Ósvífrsdóttir, to travel and be inspired by the wider world.

Bibliography

Andersson, Theodore M. 2006. *The Growth of Medieval Icelandic Sagas (1180–1280)*. Cornell: Cornell University Press.

Ármann Jakobsson 1998. “Konungasagan Laxdæla.” *Skírnir* 172 (1997): 357–83.

Benediktsson, Jakob 1968. “Formáli. Íslendingabók. Landnámabók” (Íslenzk fornrit 1). Reykjavík. Hið íslenzka fornritafélag.

Byock, Jesse L. 1982. *Feud in the Icelandic Saga*. New York, Berkeley, and London: University of California Press.

Danielsson, Tommy 2002. *Hrafnkels saga eller fallet med den undflyende traditionen*. Hedemora: Gidlunds forlag.

Einar Ól. Sveinsson 1958. *Dating the Icelandic Sagas: An Essay in Method*. London: Viking Society for Northern Research.

Fidjestøl, Bjarne 1985. “On a New Edition of Scaldic Poetry.” *The Sixth International Saga Conference 28.7.–2.8.1985. Workshop Papers,* Copenhagen: pp. 319–35.

Gade, Kari Ellen 2001. “The Dating and Attributions of Verses in the Skald Sagas.” In Russell G. Poole (ed.), *Skaldsagas. Text, Vocation, and Desire in the Icelandic Sagas of Poets*. Berlin and New York: Walter de Gruyter, pp. 50–74.

Gísli Sigurðsson 2002. *Túlkun Íslendingasagna í ljósi munnlegrar hefðar: Til-*

gáta um aðferð. Reykjavík: Stofnun Árna Magnússonar.

Helgi Guðmundsson 1967. *Um Kjalnesinga sögu: Nokkrar athuganir* (Studia Islandica 26). Reykjavík: Menningarsjóður.

Helgi Þorláksson 1992. "Snorri goði and Snorri Sturluson." *Skírnir* 1966: 295–320.

Heller, Rolf 1976. *Die Laxdæla saga. Die literarische Schöpfung eines Isländers des 13. Jahrhunderts.* (Abhandlungen der sächsischen Akademie der Wissenschaften zu Leipzig. Philologisch-historisch Klasse, 65.1). Berlin: Akademie Verlag.

Hume, Kathryn 1973. "Beginnings and Endings in the Icelandic Family Sagas." *Modern Language Review* 68: 593–606.

Kress, Helga 1980. "Mjǫk mun þér samstaft þykkja. Um sagnahefð og kvenlega reynslu í Laxdæla sögu." In Valborg Bentsdottir et al., *Konur skrifa til heiðurs Önnu Sigurðardóttur*. Reykjavík: Sögufélag, pp. 97–109.

McKinnell, John 1970. "The Reconstruction of Pseudo-Vatnshyrna." *Opuscula* 4 (Bibliotheca Arnamagnæana 30). Copenhagen: Munksgaard, pp. 304–38.

Nordal, Guðrún 2001. *Tools of Literacy: The Role of Skaldic Verse in the Textual Culture of the 13th and 14th Centuries*. Toronto and London. University of Toronto Press.

—— 2005. "Attraction of Opposites: Skaldic Verse in Njáls Saga." In Pernille Hermann (ed.), *Literacy in Scandinavia from Middle Ages to Early Modern Time* (Viking Collection 16). Odense: University Press of Southern Denmark, pp. 211–36.

—— 2007. "The Art of Poetry and the Sagas of Icelanders." In Judy Quinn, Kate Heslop, and Tarrin Wills (eds.), *Learning and Understanding in the Old Norse World: Essays in Honour of Margaret Clunies Ross*. Turnhout: Brepols, pp. 219–37.

—— 2008. "The Sagas of Icelanders." In Stefan Brink and Neil Pryce (eds.), *The Viking World*. London and New York: Routledge.

Nordal, Sigurður 1952. "Sagalitteraturen." In *Nordisk kultur VIII B, Litteraturhistorie Norge og Island*. Copenhagen: A. Bonniers, pp. 180–273.

Perkins, Richard 1978. *Flóamanna saga, Gaulverjabær and Haukr Erlendsson* (Studia Islandica 36). Reykjavík: Menningarsjóður.

Stefán Karlsson 1970. "Um Vatnshyrnu." *Opuscula* 4 (Bibliotheca Arnamagnæana 30). Copenhagen: Munksgaard, pp. 279–303.

Sveinbjörn Rafnsson 2001. *Sögugerð Landnámabókar. Um íslenska sagna-*

ritun á 12. og 13. öld (Ritsafn Sagnfræðistofnunar 35). Reykjavík: Sagnfræðistofnun Háskóla Íslands.

Tulinius, H. Torfi 2004. *Skáldið í skriftinni*. Reykjavík: Hið íslenska bókmenntafélag.

Vésteinn Ólason 2007. "The Fantastic Element in Fourteenth Century Íslendingasögur. A Survey." *Gripla* 18: 7–22.

Örnólfur Thorsson 1992. "'Leitin að landinu fagra'. Hugleiðing um rannsóknir á íslenskum fornbókmenntum." *Skáldskaparmál* 1: 28–53.

CONTRIBUTORS

Theodore M. Andersson, Professor emeritus of Germanic Studies at Indiana University.

Jürg Glauser, Professor of Scandinavian Studies at the University of Basel and the University of Zurich.

Emily Lethbridge, PhD in Old Norse-Icelandic Literature from the University of Cambridge. At present she holds a research fellowship at the Centre for Medieval Studies, University of Iceland.

Jonna Louis-Jensen, Professor emerita of Icelandic Language and Literature at the University of Copenhagen, former director of the Arnamagnæan Institute, same place.

Else Mundal, Professor emerita of Old Norse Philology at the Centre for Medieval Studies, University of Bergen.

Guðrún Nordal, Professor of Icelandic and director at the Árni Magnússon Institute for Icelandic Studies at the University of Iceland.

Slavica Ranković, PhD in English Literature and Slavonic Studies from the University of Nottingham. At present she is a researcher at the Centre for Medieval Studies, University of Bergen.

Torfi H. Tulinius, Professor of Medieval Icelandic Studies at the University of Iceland.

INDEX